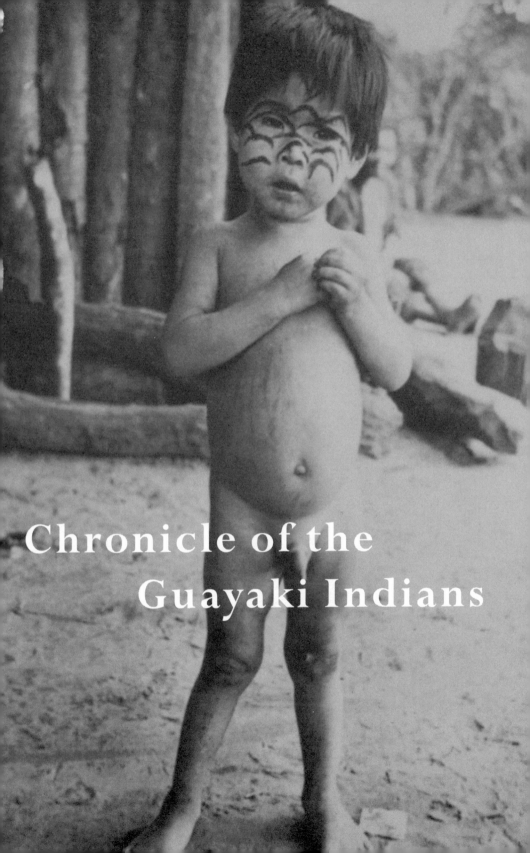

Chronicle of the
Guayaki Indians

Translation & Foreword by Paul Auster

Pierre Clastres

Chronicle of the Guayaki Indians

ZONE BOOKS • NEW YORK

2000

The publisher would like to thank the French Ministry of
Culture for its assistance with this translation.

Translation © 1998 Paul Auster
Translator's Note © 1998 Paul Auster
ZONE BOOKS
611 Broadway, Suite 608
New York, NY 10012

First Paperback Edition

Originally published in France as *Chronique des indiens Guayaki*
© 1972 Librairie Plon.

Drawings by Jean-Marc Chavy.
Photographs by Pierre Clastres.

Printed in the United States of America.

Distributed by The MIT Press,
Cambridge, Massachusetts, and London, England

Library of Congress Cataloging-in-Publication Data

Clastres, Pierre, 1934–1977
     [Chronique des Indiens Guayaki. English]
     Chronicle of the Guayaki Indians / Pierre Clastres; trans-
lated by Paul Auster.
          p.   cm.
     ISBN 0-942299-78-7 (paper)
     1. Guayaki Indians. I. Title.
F2679.2.G9C5513 1998
989.2'00498382—dc21
                                        97-20623
                                          CIP

Contents

Jyvukugi, "chief" of the Atchei Gatu.

Translator's Note

This is one of the saddest stories I know. If not for a minor miracle that occurred twenty years after the fact, I doubt that I would have been able to summon the courage to tell it.

It begins in 1972. I was living in Paris at the time, and because of my friendship with the poet Jacques Dupin (whose work I had translated), I was a faithful reader of *L'Éphémère*, a literary magazine financed by the Galerie Maeght. Jacques was a member of the editorial board — along with Yves Bonnefoy, André du Bouchet, Michel Leiris, and, until his death in 1970, Paul Celan. The magazine came out four times a year, and with a group like that responsible for its contents, the work published in *L'Éphémère* was always of the highest quality.

The twentieth and final issue appeared in the spring, and among the usual contributions from well-known poets and writers, there was an essay by an anthropologist named Pierre Clastres entitled "De l'Un sans le multiple" [Of the one without the many]. Just seven pages long, it made an immediate and lasting impression on me. Not only was the piece intelligent, provocative, and tightly argued, it was beautifully written. Clastres's prose seemed to combine a poet's temperament with a philosopher's depth of mind, and I was moved by its directness and humanity, its utter lack of pretension. On the strength of those seven pages, I realized that I had discovered a writer whose work I would be following for a long time to come.

When I asked Jacques who this person was, he explained that Clastres had studied with Claude Lévi-Strauss, was still under forty, and was considered to be the most promising member of the new generation of anthropologists in France. He had done his fieldwork in the jungles of South America, living among the most primitive Stone Age tribes in Paraguay and Venezuela, and a book about those experiences was about to be published. When *Chronique des indiens Guayaki* appeared a short time later, I went out and bought myself a copy.

It is, I believe, nearly impossible not to love this book. The care and patience with which it is written, the incisiveness of its observations, its humor, its intellectual rigor, its compassion — all these qualities reinforce one another to make it an important, memorable work. The *Chronicle* is not some dry academic study of "life among the savages," not some report from an alien world in which the reporter neglects to take his own presence into account. It is the true story of a man's experiences, and it asks nothing but the most essential questions: how is information communicated to an anthropologist, what kinds of transactions take place between one culture and another, under what circumstances might secrets be kept? In delineating this unknown civilization for us, Clastres writes with the cunning of a good novelist. His attention to detail is scrupulous and exacting; his ability to synthesize his thoughts into bold, coherent statements is often breathtaking. He is that rare scholar who does not hesitate to write in the first person, and the result is not just a portrait of the people he is studying, but a portrait of himself.

I moved back to New York in the summer of 1974, and for several years after that I tried to earn my living as a translator. It was a difficult struggle, and most of the time I was barely able to keep my head above water. Because I had to take whatever I could get, I often found myself accepting assignments to work on books that had little or no value. I wanted to translate good books, to be involved in projects that felt worthy, that would do more than just put bread on the table. *Chronicle of the Guayaki Indians* was at the top of my list, and again and again I proposed it to the various American publishers I worked for. After countless rejections, I finally found someone who was interested. I can't remember exactly when this was. Late 1975 or early 1976, I think, but I could be off by half a year or so. In any case, the publishing company was new, just getting off the ground, and all the preliminary indications looked good. Excellent editors, contracts for a number of outstanding books, a willingness to take risks. Not long before that, Clastres and I had begun exchanging letters, and when I wrote to tell him the news, he was just as thrilled as I was.

Translating the *Chronicle* was a thoroughly enjoyable experience for me, and after my labors were done, my attachment to the book was just as ardent as ever. I turned in the manuscript to the publisher, the translation was approved, and then, just when everything seemed to have been brought to a successful conclusion, the troubles started.

It seems that the publishing company was not as solvent as the world had been led to believe. Even worse, the publisher himself was a good deal less honest in his handling of money than he should have been. I know this for a fact because the money that was supposed to pay for my translation had been covered by a grant to the company by the CNRS (the French National Scientific Research Center), but when I asked for my money, the publisher hemmed and hawed and promised that I would have it in due course. The only explanation was that he had already spent the funds on something else.

I was desperately poor in those days, and waiting to be paid simply wasn't an option for me. It was the difference between eating and not eating, between paying the rent and not paying the rent. I called the publisher every day for the next several weeks, but he kept putting me off, kept coming up with different excuses. At last, unable to hold out any longer, I went to the office in person and demanded that he pay me on the spot. He started in with another excuse, but this time I held my ground and declared that I wouldn't leave until he had written out a check to me for the full amount. I don't think I went so far as to threaten him, but I might have. I was boiling with anger, and I can remember thinking that if all else failed, I was prepared to punch him in the face. It never came to that, but what I did do was back him into a corner, and at that moment I could see that he was beginning to grow scared. He finally understood that I meant business. And right then and there, he opened the drawer of his desk, pulled out his checkbook, and gave me my money.

In retrospect, I consider this to be one of my lowest moments, a dismal chapter in my career as a human being, and I am not at all proud of how I acted. But I was broke, and I had done the work, and I deserved to be paid. To prove how hard up I was during those years, I will mention just one appalling fact. I never made a copy of the manuscript. I couldn't afford to xerox the translation, and since I assumed it was in safe hands, the only copy in the world was the original typescript sitting in the publisher's office. This fact, this stupid oversight, this poverty-stricken way of doing business would come back to haunt me. It was entirely my fault, and it turned a small misfortune into a full-blown disaster.

For the time being, however, we seemed to be back on track. Once the unpleasantness about my fee was settled, the publisher behaved as if he had every intention of bringing out the book. The manuscript was sent to a typesetter, I corrected the proofs and returned them to the publisher — again neglecting to make a copy. It hardly seemed important, after all, since production was well under way by now. The book had been announced in the catalogue, and publication was set for the winter of 1977–78.

Then, just months before *Chronicle of the Guayaki Indians* was supposed to appear, news came that Pierre Clastres had been killed in a car accident. According to the story I was told, he had been driving somewhere in France when he lost control of the wheel and skidded over the edge of a mountain. We had never met. Given that he was only forty-three when he died, I had assumed there would be ample opportunities for that in the future. We had written a number of letters to each other, had become friends through our correspondence, and were looking forward to the time when we would at last be able to sit down together and talk. The strangeness and unpredictability of the world prevented that conversation from taking place. Even now, all these years later, I still feel it as a great loss.

Nineteen seventy-eight came and went, and *Chronicle of the Guayaki Indians* did not appear. Another year slipped by, and then another year, and still there was no book.

By 1981, the publishing company was on its last legs. The editor I had originally worked with was long gone, and it was difficult for me to find out any information. That year, or perhaps the year after that, or perhaps even the year after that (it all blurs in my mind now), the company finally went under. Someone called to tell me that the rights to the book had been sold to another publisher. I called that publisher, and they told me, yes, they were planning to bring out the book. Another year went by, and nothing happened. I called again, and the person I had talked to the previous year no longer worked for the company. I talked to someone else, and that person told me that the company had no plans to publish *Chronicle of the Guayaki Indians*. I asked for the manuscript back, but no one could find it. No one had even heard of it. For all intents and purposes, it was as if the translation had never existed.

For the next dozen years, that was where the matter stood. Pierre Clastres was dead, my translation had disappeared, and the entire project had collapsed into a black hole of oblivion. This past summer (1996), I finished writing a book entitled *Hand to Mouth*, an autobiographical essay about money. I was planning to include this story in the narrative (because of my failure to make a copy of the manuscript, because of the scene with the publisher in his office), but when the moment came to tell it, I lost heart and couldn't bring myself to put the words down on paper. It was all too sad, I felt, and I couldn't see any purpose in recounting such a bleak, miserable saga.

Then, two or three months after I finished my book, something extraordinary happened. About a year before, I had accepted an invitation to go to San Francisco to appear in the City Arts and Lectures Series at the Herbst Theatre. The event was scheduled for October 1996, and when the moment came, I climbed onto a plane and flew to San Francisco as promised. After my business onstage was finished, I was supposed to sit in the lobby and sign copies of my books. The Herbst is a large theater with many seats, and the line in the lobby was therefore quite long. Among all those people waiting for the dubious privilege of having me write my name in one of my novels, there was someone I recognized — a young man I had met once before, the friend of a friend. This young man happens to be a passionate collector of books, a bloodhound for first editions and rare, out-of-the-way items, the kind of bibliographic detective who will think nothing of spending an afternoon in a dusty cellar sifting through boxes of discarded books in the hope of finding one small treasure. He smiled, shook my hand, and then thrust a set of bound galleys at me. It had a red paper cover, and until that moment, I had never seen a copy of it before. "What's this?" he said. "I never heard of it." And there it was, suddenly sitting in my hands: the uncorrected proofs of my long-lost translation. In the big scheme of things, this probably wasn't such an astonishing event. For me, however, in my own little scheme of things, it was overwhelming. My hands started to tremble as I held the book. I was so stunned, so confused, that I was scarcely able to speak.

The proofs had been found in a remainder bin at a secondhand bookstore, and the young man had paid five dollars for them. As I look at them now, I note with a certain grim fascination that the pub date announced on the cover is April 1981. For a translation completed in 1976 or 1977, it was, truly, an agonizingly slow ordeal.

If Pierre Clastres were alive today, the discovery of this lost book would be a perfect happy ending. But he isn't alive, and the brief surge of joy and incredulity I experienced in the atrium of the Herbst Theatre has by now dissipated into a deep, mournful ache. How rotten that the world should pull such tricks on us. How rotten that a person with so much to offer the world should die so young.

Here, then, is my translation of Pierre Clastres's book, *Chronicle of the Guayaki Indians*. No matter that the world described in it has long since vanished, that the tiny group of people the author lived with in 1963 and 1964 has disappeared from the face of the earth. No matter that the author has vanished as well. The book he wrote is still with us, and the fact that you are holding that book in your hands now, dear reader, is nothing less than a victory, a small triumph against the crushing odds of fate. At least there is that to be thankful for. At least there is consolation in the thought that Pierre Clastres's book has survived.

Paul Auster
February 20, 1997

13

Pichugi and her baby.

CHAPTER ONE

Birth

"Beeru! Ejo! Kromi waave!" whispered a voice, at first distant and confused, then painfully close to me. The words were strange, and yet I understood them. It was the middle of the night. How difficult it was to tear myself from the comfort of sleeping beside a warm fire. Insistent, the voice repeated the words: *"Beeru! Ejo! Pichugi memby waave! Nde ro ina mecha vwa!* White man! Come! Pichugi's child is born! It was you who asked to watch!" Suddenly everything became clear. I knew what was going on, and I felt angry and discouraged. What was the good of asking them several days in advance to call me at the first signs of labor if they let me sleep while the event was taking place? For a child's coming into the world was an increasingly rare occurrence in the tribe, and I had been very eager to see Pichugi give birth.

It was her brother, Karekyrumbygi, Big Coati, who was leaning over me. The fire played on his broad, quiet face; his massive features showed no emotion. He was not wearing his labret (lip ornament), and a thin stream of glittering saliva flowed through the hole in his lower lip. Seeing that I was no longer asleep, he stood up without another word and vanished into the darkness. I followed at his heels, hoping that the baby had only just been born and that I would find something to satisfy my curiosity as an anthropologist: for it was quite possible that I would not have another chance to see a child born among the Guayaki.

There was no telling what I might have missed — what gestures made during the event, what unusual words of welcome addressed to the new arrival, what rites of greeting for a baby Indian might have been irretrievably lost to me. No matter how precise my questions were, no matter how accurate or faithful an account I received from an informant, neither could replace direct observation. For it is often in the innocence of a half-completed gesture or an unconsciously spoken word that the fleeting singularity of meaning is hidden, the light in which everything takes shape. That was why I had been waiting with as much impatience as the Indians for the birth of Pichugi's child. I was determined not to let the slightest detail escape me: for this was something that could not be reduced to a simple biological process. It had a very definite social dimension.

Every birth is experienced dramatically by the group as a whole. It is not simply the addition of an individual to one family, but a cause of imbalance between the world of men and the universe of invisible forces; it subverts an order that ritual must attempt to reestablish.

A short distance away from the hut in which Pichugi and her family lived, a fire was burning; its heat and brightness barely tempered the cold of the June night. It was winter. A screen of large trees protected the small camp from the south wind; everything was quiet, and over the faint and steady rustling of wind-shaken leaves, the only sound came from the dry crackling of family fires. Several Indians were there, crouching around the woman. Pichugi was sitting on a bed of ferns and palm leaves, her thighs open. With her two hands she was holding onto a stake solidly fixed in the ground before her. By pulling on it, she was able to work in harmony with the muscular movements of her

16

pelvis and thus ease the "fall" of the child (*waa*, to be born, also means to fall). Reassured, I realized that I had been unfair to Kare-kyrumbygi. In fact, he had warned me in time: a bundle suddenly appeared, I stole a glance and saw traces of blood on it, and then, suddenly, a passionate wailing came from it. The child had "fallen." The mother, who was panting slightly, had not uttered the slightest moan. I was not sure whether this was because she was stoical or simply not very sensitive to pain. In any case, the Indians are reputed to give birth very easily, and I had the proof of it before my eyes: the *kromi* was there, howling, and everything had taken place in just a few minutes. It was a boy. The four or five Atchei who surrounded Pichugi did not say a word; nothing could be read on their attentive faces, and not even a smile came to their lips. If I had been less experienced, I might have interpreted this as an example of the brutal insensitivity of savages before what in our societies evokes powerful and joyful emotion that is immediately expressed. *When a child is born, the family gathers round....* In reality, the attitude of the Indians was no less ritualistic than ours; far from denoting indifference, which they would find scandalous if they detected it in anyone, their silence was actually deliberate, intentional, and the *discretion* they displayed on this occasion was their way of showing concern for the infant: from now on they had to look after this helpless member of the group, they were responsible for keeping him in good health. From now on they would have to protect him from those-who-cannot-be-seen, the nocturnal forest dwellers who were already lying in wait for the young prey and who needed nothing more than a signal, a noise, a word to locate and kill him. If these enemies learned that Pichugi's baby had been born that night, it would be all up with him; he would be smothered to death by *Krei*, the deadly ghost: thus, while a woman is giving birth, one must *not talk or laugh* — the birth of a child must be kept separate from any human noise.

Preparations for childbirth.

Purification ritual after Pichugi has given birth.

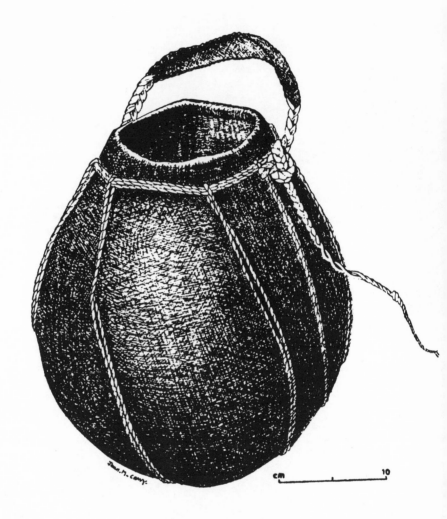

Daity, container for transporting liquids.

So I knew that the Guayaki were happy, especially since their preference for boys had been gratified. Not that they had less affection for girls: girls were coddled with as much tenderness as their brothers. But the nature of life in this tribe was such that the arrival of a future hunter was welcomed with more satisfaction than that of a girl.

Among those who formed a sort of protective circle around Pichugi, two people would play a particularly decisive role. The *kromi chapira* (the young child with bloodshot eyes) had just let out his first cry. He was still lying on the ground. A man got down on his knees, holding a long splinter of bamboo in his hand; this was the Guayaki knife, and it was much sharper and more dangerous than one would think. With several precise and rapid movements, he cut and tied the umbilical cord: the separation from the mother was complete. On the ground nearby was a large *daity* — an egg-shaped container woven from fine strips of bamboo and covered on the outside with a layer of wild bee's wax, which made it waterproof. It was filled with cold water. The man cupped a little water in the hollow of his hand and began to bathe the child. Pouring the water over all parts of the small body, he firmly and gently washed away the fluids that covered it, and the cleaning was soon finished. A young woman then crouched down, took the child in the crook of her left arm, and pressed him against her breast. This was to warm the baby after his cold bath in the chilly night. With her right hand, she began the *piy*, a massage of the limbs and trunk, her fingers softly kneading the baby's flesh. This woman is sometimes called *tapave* — she who has taken into her arms — but more often *upiaregi* — she who has lifted up. Why do the Indians prefer to name her after this apparently insignificant action of lifting the child from the ground rather than the action of taking him into her arms and rubbing him to make him warm? The choice is not arbitrary;

it is governed by a subtle logic. First of all, the verb *upi*, to lift, is the opposite of the verb that means to be born: *waa*, to fall. To be born is to fall, and to cancel this "fall" the child must be lifted, *upi*. The function of the *upiaregi* is not simply to provide warmth and comfort; in Indian thought it consists, above all, of completing and closing the process of birth, which is begun by a fall. To be born in the sense of falling is, so to speak, not yet to be born, and the act of lifting assures the infant access to, ascension to, human existence.

This ritual of birth is undoubtedly an illustration of the myth of the origin of the Guayaki, which is essentially the myth of the *Atchei Jamo pyve*, the Guayaki's first ancestors. What does the myth tell us? "The first ancestors of the Guayaki lived in the huge and terrible earth. The first ancestors of the Guayaki came out of the huge and terrible earth, they all left it. To come out, to leave the earth, the first ancestors of the Guayaki scratched with their nails, like armadillos." To transform themselves into humans, into inhabitants of the world, the original Atchei had to leave their underground dwelling. To reach the outside they *rose up* the length of a vertical tunnel they had dug with their nails, like armadillos, who hollow out their burrows deep under the soil. The progress, clearly indicated in the myth, from animality to humanity, therefore involves abandoning the prehuman dwelling, the burrow, and overcoming the obstacle which separates the inferior animal world (the lower) from the human world of the surface (the higher): the act of "birth" of the first Guayaki was an *ascension* that separated them from the earth. In the same way, the birth of a child takes place not at the moment of the *waa*, the fall that renews the old union of man and earth, but at the moment of the *upi*, which breaks this bond: here is the individual's true beginning. The woman raises the infant, tearing him away from the earth on which he was left lying — and this is a silent metaphor

24

for that other bond which the man broke several moments earlier with his knife. The woman frees the child from the earth, the man liberates him from his mother. Text and image, the myth of origin and the ritual of birth express and illustrate one another, and every time a child is born, the Guayaki unconsciously repeat the first episode in Guayaki history in a gesture which must be read in the same way that one listens to a spoken word.

The fact that the sequence of events in the myth determines the organization of the various phases of the ritual (or, inversely, that the pattern of the ritual furnishes the story with its syntax) is even more evident in the correspondence between one moment in the ritual and one sequence in the myth. Once the umbilical cord has been cut and tied, the infant is bathed, so that his first movement toward human existence consists of contact with water, whose presence here, while obviously necessary, is also probably dependent on the ritual order. In deciphering the meaning of the bath as a ritual act and not only as something performed in the interest of hygiene, it is helpful to conceive of it as the operation that precedes and prepares for the *upi*: in this way, the joining of child and water is preliminary to the separating of child and earth.

Though it is somewhat obscure, there is a reference in the myth to water — in leaving the earth, the mythological Atchei had to pass through water: "The path of the first ancestors of the Guayaki for leaving and going out upon the huge earth was through a lovely water." The myth also seems to justify the reference to water because of the state in which the first men found themselves at the bottom of their hole: "The first ancestors of the Guayaki had very stinking armpits and bitter skin, very red skin" — which is as much as to say that they were dirty and, like a newborn child, they needed a bath. The mirror play between myth and ritual is confirmed even more decisively by the fact that for

25

the Guayaki a camp in which a woman has just given birth is called *ine*, stinking. The secret order of things is thus uncovered little by little, the history and the ceremony share the same logic, the same mode of thought imposes the law of its unconscious forms on the succession of words and gestures, and once again the old forest is witness to the faithful celebration of their juncture.

The Indians were still silent. Words would have been useless, for each person there knew what he had to do. The woman continued to hold the child, who was now warm. Once again the *jware*, the man who had given the bath a moment ago, intervened. He began massaging the baby's head vigorously. The widely spread palm of his right hand pressed forcefully on the skull, as though it were material to be molded. This is exactly what the *jware* was trying to do: he was hoping to give the head the rounded form the Indians consider to be the most beautiful, but, as might be expected, the massage had no real result. This "deformation" was the *jware*'s responsibility, but others could also work on it – it was proof of affection for the baby and the desire to participate directly in the ritual – and even the mother during the next three or four days would submit the child's head to the same treatment. The man stopped and gave up his place to another Indian. The wind played on the fire and sometimes opened a slash of light in the darkness. Indifferent to the cold, the Guayaki gave their attention exclusively to the *kromi*: they were committed to welcoming him, and the slightest deviation from the seriousness of their work could have been fatal. The glances, the movements of the hands and naked bodies around the new Atchei, circumscribed a space filled with the devotion, even devoutness, which marks the relationship of adults to children among the Indians.

The birth had gone very well; the delivery of the afterbirth had followed quickly upon the baby's coming into the world. A man gathered up the pile of ferns on which the placenta had slipped out, put the bundle together, and went off to bury it at some distance from the camp — for the sake of cleanliness, naturally, but also, and even more importantly, from a basic prudence: the dangers contained in the matter that had issued from a woman's entrails had to be kept at a distance. Of course, the mere burying of the afterbirth was not enough to neutralize it, and more had to be done to exorcise the demons it had attracted.

This was the object of the second phase of the ritual, which would occupy a good part of the next day's activities: the safety of the adults had to be watched over once the safety of the child had been ensured.

For tonight, everything seemed to be over. The *upiaregi* gave the baby to his mother, who placed him in the wide carrying cloth she had strapped around herself. From now on, this would be the infant's home, day and night; he would leave it only when he began to walk. In the meantime, he would live in complete symbiosis with his mother, who would be quick to anticipate his cries by giving him her breast at the first sign of a grunt or grimace. It is rare to hear a child crying among the Indians; he is not actually given enough time to cry, for as soon as he opens his mouth to wail, the breast with its milk is stuffed inside, cutting short any display of bad humor. This is a doubly effective system, since it allows the adults to rest and keeps the child in some sense permanently replete.

Pichugi studied her baby, and the infinite tenderness of her smile made one forget the destitution of the tribe for a moment. She stood up and went back to her hut with the child in her arms, not needing any help; she did not seem very worn out. Her two husbands, Chachugi and the old Tokangi, were not there, but she would have company because an Indian and his family were going to spend the night with her. Making no more noise than before, the Indians separated, and each went back to his *tapy*. "*Opa*,"

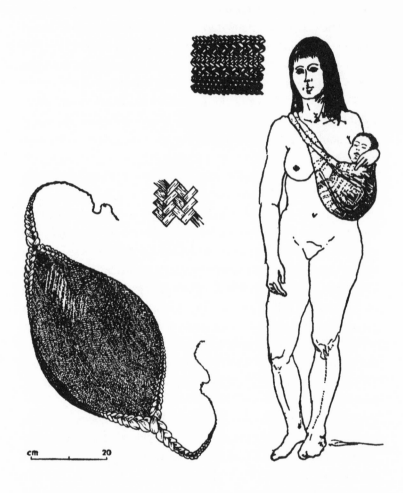

Strap for carrying a baby.

murmured Karekyrumbygi, "it is finished." Several minutes later, everyone in the camp was asleep. The wind and the forest continued their endless dialogue, the fires crackled in the night, and there was a new member of the tribe.

There was nothing tropical about the gray dawn. The sun had barely reached the horizon of the low sky, and my body, still frozen with the night's cold, waited in anguish for the warmth of day. The camp consisted of eighteen huts — or rudimentary shelters — which formed a rough circle around a cleared space. On all sides was the thick, dark wall of vegetation, the tangle of creepers, branches, and parasite plants extending like a roof over our heads. A little farther off, a small clearing broke the continuous stretch of forest. At this time of year, the grass that covered it was more yellow than green; but this morning, it was white with frost that would not disappear until the sun was at its height. A few naked children were already running around. "Are you cold?" "*Duy pute.* Very cold," they answered, shivering and smiling. They did not complain: like their parents, they put up with it. The Indians had been awake and about for some time. Usually the men did not even wait for daybreak to go off hunting, but today they felt *kyrymba ia*, without courage; numb with cold, their muscles would not be able to pull back the bow, and the hunters preferred to doze for a little while around the fire. In addition, some of them would have to be present for the *kymata tyro*, which had been made necessary by the birth of Pichugi's baby. Sitting on her heels, she nursed the baby. "He eats well," she said, "he will be *bretete*, a great hunter!" Kajapukugi — Big Wildcat — was getting ready to leave without his bow and arrows, armed only with his metal machete. "Where are you going?"

"*Kaari kymata eru vwa.* Into the forest to bring back *kymati.*" The word *kymati* refers to a kind of creeper called *timbo*, whose

29

toxic effects on fish are known to a great number of South American tribes and used by them in a special fishing technique. This creeper contains a substance that literally asphyxiates all the fish when it spreads through the water. But the Guayaki do not use *timbo* for fishing, only for rituals. This, then, was what Kajapu-kugi had gone off to find.

I questioned Pichugi's husbands, her principal husband, Chachugi (the *chachu* is the great wild pig) and her secondary husband, Tokangi (the toucan). Neither one of them had spent the night in the hut they all shared. Chachugi had slept at his brother's. He was the *apaete*, the real father of the newborn child: not in the sense of biological paternity, but according to the institution of polygamous marriage. At the moment of birth, both husbands of the woman are the fathers of the child, but unequally, so to speak, since the *japetyva*, or secondary husband, has a status and privileges that are clearly inferior to those of the *imete*, or principal husband. That is why Tokangi — even if, in spite of his age, he had been able to obtain Pichugi's favors — would only be an *apa vai*, a sort of half father to the child. Without question they would show affection and respect for each other, but Pichugi's son would nevertheless know that of his two fathers Chachugi was the Father. I joined Chachugi in the hut. He was stringing his huge bow, which was about eight feet high. He then tested the points of his long wooden arrows with his finger, sharpening the dull ones with the pierced shell of a big snail, a creature that is quite common in the forest. "*Nde bareka o?* Are you going hunting?"

"*Go.* Yes." He was not very talkative.

"Why didn't you sleep in your *tapy?*" "*Pané vwa.* Because of *pané*," he answered laconically, without lifting his eyes from his work.

The idea of *pané* occupies a central place in Guayaki thought. The Indians had already referred to it often in connection with both serious and "futile" situations in their daily life, and I would later learn from a thousand other instances not to underestimate what for them was almost an obsession and what, from a certain point of view, directed and regulated a great part of their actions and outlook on life. I should not have been surprised by the brevity of Chachugi's response, since the rules of conduct imposed on him as the husband of a woman who had just given birth were so self-evident to him. What is *pané*? This apparently harmless little word is actually highly charged and designates the worst thing that can happen to an Indian: bad luck with hunting. The scope of this kind of failure for a hunter can be understood when one considers that the entire economic life of the tribe depends on hunting and gathering, especially hunting. To come back empty-handed from the forest means that one has nothing to give and thus, in the end, that one will get nothing in return, for the balance of food production is too precarious to support the dead weight of a *pané* individual very long. The men therefore must kill animals to feed the tribe. For a Guayaki there is no possible alternative to the role the group has given him: by definition and on principle, his vocation is to be a hunter. As the mainstay of the community and the concern of each man's individual honor, hunting or not hunting determines the very limits of the society. So a hunter's main and constant concern, his obsession, we might say, is scrupulously to avoid any circumstances that might make him *pané*. Chachugi was in precisely this situation, for a husband is directly implicated when his wife gives birth. First of all, he must not be present — that is why Chachugi left the hut. If he so much as saw his wife in labor, the penalty for this visual contact would quickly descend on him — he would become *pané*. But he had taken precautions. Out of fear that he might accidentally catch a glimpse of Pichugi, he had resolutely turned his back on the place where she was; and until the celebration of the ritual was completely over, he would not go back to her. Perhaps because of this, because of the dangerous situation he was in, he was not very eager to talk about these things. And I did not want to insist. Indians are not information machines, and it would be a great mistake to think that they are always ready to answer questions. They answer if they want to, if they are in a good mood, if they have the time. Usually, most of them would rather sleep than talk with an ethnologist, and in any case the best information I received was often what the Indians volunteered spontaneously. Be that as it may, Chachugi had finished checking his arrows and was about to leave — he even seemed in a great hurry.

Of all the hunters present, he was the only one to go off into the forest that day. It was not, however, a good day for hunting: it was cold and the animals would be taking cover in their holes, in the hollows of trees, and in the depths of the foliage. Yet Chachugi had not prepared his weapons for nothing; his behavior was not at all unreasonable, and if anyone had a chance of encountering and killing some game, it was he. It was even probable that, if I had asked him, he would have answered that he was *certain* he would come back with something. Not that he considered himself a better hunter than the others — such an idea does not exist in Guayaki psychology. Of course, each Indian would say with conviction: "*Cho ro bretete.* I am a great hunter." But he would never say, "I am the best hunter of all," and would be even less likely to say, "I am better than this man or that man." Although each Guayaki hunter feels that he is really excellent, none would dream of comparing himself to the others, and each would admit with good grace that perfection is a quality that can be shared by everyone equally. Chachugi's certainty, therefore, did not stem from arrogance, which he would have been incapable of, but from sure knowledge: "*Ure kwaty.* We know." That was always the Indians' comment when I did not understand their explanations or when something seemed too obvious to them: "We know; that's the way it is..." When what they were saying became dogmatic in this way, I knew that I was on the path of some particularly interesting piece of information and that it would be wise to pay attention.

Where did Chachugi's knowledge come from? From the fact that for the Indians the world around them is not a purely neutral space but the living extension of the human world: what happens in the one always affects the other. When a woman gives birth, the situation of the group is profoundly changed; but the disorder also affects nature, and the very life of the forest is given a fresh impetus.

Since the previous night, since the birth of the baby, Chachugi had been *bayja* — he who attracts living creatures — the center around which the inhabitants of the forest converged. In the wake of his silent progress through the jungle, there emanated from him what our words are almost incapable of describing — a power that surrounded him but was not under his control, a power that with every step he took spread the signs of his presence. When a man is *bayja*, animals come in great numbers: Chachugi knew this, and that was the source of his certainty. If there was ever a time when a hunter could use his talents at his leisure, that time had come for Chachugi: he was going hunting because he knew he would find animals, he was *bayja* because his wife had just given birth (*bayja* only affects men and can only be caused by women). This was why he had taken such care to stay away all night and not look at his wife: he would have been mad to risk *pané* on such a day, when his chances of bringing back game were for the moment so much greater.

But that was not all. Chachugi was not going off to hunt just to take advantage of an exceptional opportunity, an easy way to increase his food "production." Actually, it was not the desire for

33

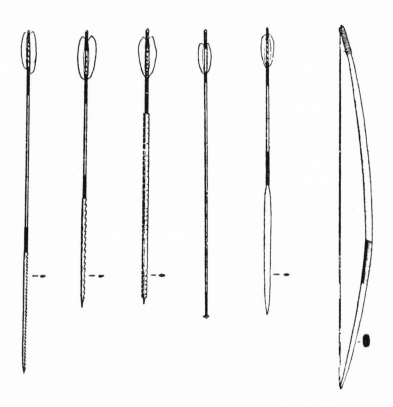

Types of arrows used by Guayaki hunters.

food that made him go out and brave the cold; even if he had had abundant stores of meat in his hut, he would still have gone. Very simply, there was no way he could *not* go into the forest, for he was completely involved in the situation of Pichugi's giving birth and was not free to choose. He was obliged to go hunting not in order to bring back meat so much as to *save his own life*: a terrible threat weighed on him; being *bayja* had brought him face-to-face with a deadly risk, and in order to escape it he absolutely had to kill some animals. What was this threat? The power of attraction that he now possessed, and which the Guayaki seemed to think of in some sense as the man's invisible double, was driving in his direction the very creatures he had to shoot with his arrows — the wild animals.

Apparently, then, everything was for the best: it would be all the easier for the hunter to fulfill his mission because the animals would be running toward him — the terms of the problem and the means for solving it went hand in hand. In fact, because of the hidden presence of the double who accompanied him, the man benefited from the "complicity" of the animals, who would practically jump into the path of his arrows. In reality, things were not so simple, and the strange call the animals responded to only helped a little — for all the animals would respond, without discrimination.

The Guayaki divide animals into two main classes: there are the animals normally hunted by the Indians (monkeys, armadillos, wild pigs, roe bucks, etc.), and then there are the jaguars. Jaguars are the first to discover that there is a man in a state of *bayja* in the woods, and the Indians say, "*Ache bayja bu baipu tara iko.* When a Guayaki is *bayja*, jaguars come in great numbers."

As Chachugi walked swiftly along the path, therefore, he was being watched by a thousand eyes. The entire forest was silently stirring with hidden life, and the hunter knew that even if he

35

could not see them or hear them, the jaguars were close by, spying on him from the dark thickets or squatting on the low branches of trees. They would be lying in wait for the man, biding their time for the right moment to attack him and tear him apart, drawn by the *ete-ri-va*, the strange power that accompanied Chachugi that day. They were the threat that weighed on him, and he could overcome it only by killing one or more animals. In other words, if the man did not fulfill his role as a hunter by snatching away from the forest some of the game it had so amply provided that day, he himself would become the prey of that other hunter, the jaguar.

This, then, was no ordinary hunt. The jaguar was usually Chachugi's rival, since both were after the same animals. But for now, the man was both hunter and hunted, for he himself was the animal the jaguar would be trying to tear apart. In order to win back and hold onto his threatened humanity, in order not to regress to animality by becoming the jaguar's prey, he had to prove himself as a hunter, as a killer of animals. To remain a man, he had to be a hunter. Chachugi had two alternatives: to die like an animal or kill like a hunter. This is the effect of *bayja*: it provides the man it infects with the means to reaffirm his humanity by giving him the power to attract animals, but at the same time it increases his danger because of the many jaguars who will approach him. To be *bayja* therefore means to live in ambiguity, to be both hunter and hunted, to exist somewhere between nature and culture. This is perhaps the deeper meaning of *bayja* underlying the conscious explanation given by the Guayaki: the danger threatening Chachugi was only a concrete manifestation of the unsteadiness of his ontological situation; the price of life was to run the risk of death.

This helps to explain why Chachugi took such care not to be with his wife or let his eyes rest on her. For just as the hunting expedition he undertook that day had a cosmological dimension and even a sacred dimension — steeped as it was in ritual — so the

36

ill fortune that would befall the man if he gave in to his curiosity would have consequences far more terrible than the normal "technical" *pané*. He would find himself irrevocably defenseless in this confrontation with the jaguars just when he was most in need of good luck. This time, to be *pané* was not simply to return to camp empty-handed; it meant that he would fall under the fangs and claws of wild beasts. And if he did not return in a few hours, we would know what funeral oration to deliver: "*Baipu ro upa.* The jaguar devoured him completely."

Of course, I had no idea what Chachugi was thinking. (It would have been very naive of me to imagine I could penetrate the inner world of a savage.) But I do know that, careful not to give in to the misleading calls of the forest and brave as usual, he walked briskly into a world that was dangerously alive.

In reality, he was walking ahead of himself, in quest of his own self, his own substance. Not that he was already lost to himself, but as we have seen, this was the risk he ran. The important thing was not so much to avoid dying (the Indians are not afraid of that) as to force the earth he was walking on, the animals who lived on it, the men who inhabited it, and the forces that controlled it to recognize him. The possibility of dying in the jungle was a lyrical expression of a deeper questioning of his being: he was in effect being put to death, even though symbolically, and this shook him to the core of his existence. Everything was happening as if the world had shut Chachugi out, as if it wanted to deny him the place he had held in it until now. He was therefore committed to reimposing his own existence on the world, to reaffirming by his acts as a hunter his right to live on the earth.

Yet what was the source of the brutal subversion that was affecting Chachugi's fate this way; what sudden power — insuperable in that it was forcing the man to follow the path it had chosen — was trying to annihilate him by bringing him face-to-face

with death? (The real state of the world had ceased to be perti-
nent: Chachugi was sure that jaguars would come in great numbers; they were thus really present in the forest.) To ask such a
question implies that we are not satisfied with the conscious
explanations given by the Indians and that we want to descend to
a deeper meaning, the realm of their unconscious attitudes.

Very explicitly, the Guayaki believed that Chachugi's situation
was related to the fact that he was *bayja*, and this was because his
wife had just given birth. As a consequence, when a woman gives
birth she puts the life of her husband (or husbands) in danger. But
men are not threatened by *bayja* only in cases of childbirth: the
threat is also present during a daughter's first menstrual period
and when a woman has aborted (either accidentally or deliberately). It seems, then, that the dangerous force of *bayja* is let
loose only when a woman's femininity erupts in both her own
body and the social life of the group. Sociologically, an abortion
or a woman's first period has the same effect as a birth on the life
of the tribe, and these events are always integrated in the traditional way: through ritual, a raw, immediate event is socialized
and transformed into a mediated symbolic system; or, to put it
another way, in and through the space of the ritual the natural
order becomes the cultural order. Should we then link *bayja* to
the woman as woman — that is, to what is impure in her (according to the Indians, at least), something which threatens to con-
taminate the men, who take great care to avoid it, as I observed
on a thousand occasions?

The differences in the way the ritual is carried out are sufficient to answer this question: although each of the three situations
mentioned earlier requires the same ceremony of purification
(at that very moment being prepared by the men who had helped
Pichugi the night before), only in the case of a birth must the
husband go off hunting. Of course, the first menstruation, an

abortion, and a birth all have certain things in common and pose identical problems to the men of the tribe (since all three situations produce *bayja*, with all its dangers) and impose the same ritual obligations on them: all this makes up an integrated whole, a system that could no doubt be covered by one general explanation. But the birth was clearly too special to be confused with the other situations. The group attached greater meaning to it; it held a "surplus" of signification, an excess, so that the surplus or excess ritual of Chachugi's hunt was only appropriate. The *bayja*, whose danger he was trying to overcome by hunting, was not the ordinary *bayja*, which could be expelled by purification with a *timbo* creeper.

The difference in the ritual response clearly stems from a difference that exists at the level of the problem *bayja* poses for the men: What is it about a birth that forces the woman's husband to go off hunting, when in other situations this is not necessary? The difference, quite simply, is the child. Although the woman's relation to the man is all that determines the purifying ritual that follows the first menstruation and an abortion, it is only part of what determines it in the case of a birth, since now there is an additional bond, a bond uniting the man to the newborn child and making the husband of a woman into the father of a child. From the child's presence emanates an aura of much greater danger; anguish enters the father's soul, and he goes off to fight in the dark thickets. The symbolic weight of the woman, who is felt as a threat by the men, tends to obliterate the existence of the child: one forgets him because he is too present. Birth therefore demands a more complex ritual than the rituals concerned with other aspects of female biology. For the man it has two parts: the purifying bath liberates him from the *bayja* that originated in his wife, and the ritual hunt can be interpreted as having to do with the child.

39

Why does a baby's coming into the world put its father in such a dramatic position? The father has to go out and compete with great numbers of jaguars for the game that will save him from their attacks. Therefore, at the very moment when the child enters the world, which everyone wants to make welcoming, peaceful, and friendly for him, this same world becomes hostile to the father; it becomes charged with aggressiveness and tries to annihilate him by throwing unusually large numbers of jaguars on his trail.

Mysterious and mocking, the rule of this division becomes codified in a dry law: the joining of the world and the child signifies the separation of the world and the father. Indian thought, as expressed in their actions, seems to say that the father and the child cannot live together on the earth. The jaguars, bearers of death and messengers of the child, delegated to restoring the order of the world, fulfill a destiny unconsciously thought out by the Indians as a form of parricide: *the birth of the child is the death of the father*. The father, whose existence has been challenged, can survive only by killing an animal; this vanquisher's act imposes him on the jaguars — that is to say, on the child himself, whose power they incarnate. By its very nature, a birth is a provocation to social disorder and, beyond that, to cosmic disorder: the birth of a new being can come to pass only through the negation of another human being, and the order destroyed by a birth can only be reestablished through a compensatory death. Even if the father escapes the jaguar by killing an animal, symbolically he has already been sentenced to death by the birth of his child. In the end, the ritual actions of the Indians lead to the discovery — repeated again and again — that men are not eternal, that one must resign oneself to finitude, and that one cannot be himself and someone else at the same time. Here there is a curious meeting ground between savage thought — which is unconscious of itself in that it is expressed only through action — and the logos of Western thought most powerfully in command of itself: the Indian and the philosopher share a way of thinking because, in the end, the obstacle to their efforts lies in the sheer impossibility of thinking of life without thinking of death.

The fact that fear of the jaguar — not as a beast of the forest but as an agent of invisible powers — is central to the Indians' thought was confirmed by information I had acquired several weeks earlier. While I was away, a woman gave birth. The next day, her husband went off hunting, but he came back that night empty-handed: "*pané*," he commented soberly. Perhaps he had not been scrupulous enough about observing the restriction against looking. In any case, the situation was becoming increasingly dangerous, and he could only hope for purification through *timbo* to keep the danger at bay: "What are you going to do?" "*Ai mita tatape jono baipu ia vwa. Throw beeswax in the fire so there will not be any jaguars.*" There is only one other situation in which the ritual burning of wax takes place: during an *eclipse*, when the blue jaguar, the celestial jaguar, tries to devour the moon or the sun. Then the smoke from the burned wax rises up to him and forces him to retreat; the threatened star is saved, and the end of the world is once again put off.

The sun, which was almost overhead now, had melted the frost. The air was warmer, and the Indians had emerged from the torpor brought on by the cold night. A group of women was coming back from the forest; bowing under the weight of their large baskets made of woven palms, they strained their necks in an effort to hold up the load that hung from their foreheads by a large band. They were bringing back fifty or sixty pounds of oranges, which they immediately distributed to all the members of the tribe. The oranges were not passed from hand to hand but thrown

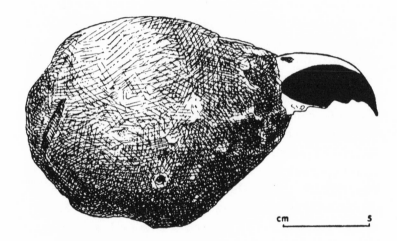

cm _____ 5

Ball of *ganchi* wax used as glue, pressed around a toucan's beak.

on the ground in front of each person. Since the ground sloped, the fruit rolled and bounced all over. These oranges were not native; they had nothing to do with the *apepu*, the wild "orange" that was abundant in the forest but was much too acidic for the Guayaki's taste. These oranges had been brought into Paraguay by the Jesuit missionaries in the seventeenth century during the famous Guarani conquests. The Jesuits had long since disappeared, but the orange trees had remained, had even proliferated — no doubt because the animals and birds had carried the orange seeds deep into the jungle, so that a traveler would occasionally round a bend in the path and be delighted to discover a peaceful orange grove in the heart of the forest. When the fruit was ripe, the wild pigs, birds, monkeys, ... and Guayaki would gather there and feast.

Kajapukugi had also returned; he had not had to go far away, because *timbo* could be found everywhere. He had brought back a thick bundle of creepers and stripped them of their bark. With short blows of his machete, he sliced off thin shavings, which fell in curls and little by little formed an impressive pile. He worked without stopping because the purification would begin as soon as Chachugi returned, and since everyone who had been involved in the birth would have to undergo the ritual, a considerable quantity of *timbo* would be needed. The *kymata tyro* (*timbo* cleansing), or purification by creeper, takes place so often among the Guayaki that it seems to serve as an almost universal panacea. Rather than using it only at certain crucial times in the life of an individual or of the group, they resort to the ritual bath every time they need to protect someone (usually a man) from a possible danger — this was the case at the moment — or stop a process that has already begun and threatens to become more serious. A man might be sick, for example, because he has disobeyed a food taboo. His health and even his life are in danger, and to drive away the "spirit" of the illness that is in him they make him under-go *kymata tyro*. But whether preventative or therapeutic, the *timbo* is always used as part of a ritual, and its purely symbolic effective-ness arises from its distinctly "supernaturalistic" etiology.

So Kajapukugi was preparing the *timbo*, which would allow them to exorcize the *bayja*, drive it away from the men who might be its victims and the women who run the risk of transmitting it to other men. The jaguars are not the only danger brought by the *bayja*.

Less immediately present than the lords of the forest, but just as dangerous, is a fearful monster who rules the sky, sometimes visible but more often hidden — the *memboruchu*, the Great Ser-pent, the rainbow. The rainbow's bands of color are actually two giant serpents, one inside the other. When the rainbow stretches the curve of its body across the sky after a storm, the Indians greet it with furious shouts: it has to be driven away, frightened by the noise. It is usually so dangerous that it is better not to point at it. But its true malevolence is unleashed against men who are victims of *bayja*. It tries to swallow them alive, and as long as they are not purified by *timbo*, the *memboruchu* lies in wait above, ready to swoop down on them, to attack them in the streams and clearings.

The Great Serpent is frightening because he announces the presence of death, but what is worse, when he stretches across the sky, the Indians know that the jaguars want to tear them to pieces: this is why it is urgent that men who are victims of *bayja* undergo the purification ritual.

It was early afternoon. Chachugi emerged from the forest. He had avoided *pané*, since two large *kraja*, howler monkeys, were hanging from his left shoulder. No one said anything; he gave the two animals to the other Indians. He did not keep either of them because he was not allowed to eat his own game, and since his

44

wife had just given birth she was subject to various food prohibitions, one of which concerned *kraja* meat. If she disobeyed the taboo, she would get a headache and her eyes would become bloodshot. A pregnant woman has to obey the same interdictions concerning the meat of the howler monkey, but for different reasons. If she does not, her future baby will be a victim of *kyrypy opo*, an expression that remained obscure to me: translated literally, it means *anus jump* and perhaps refers to a congenital abnormality.

In any case, it is similar to the insults the children shout at each other (Red ass! Monkey's ass!) and certainly refers to the peculiar anatomy of this monkey.

Meanwhile, Kajapukugi had carried his supply of *timbo* to the place where Pichugi had given birth. He had also taken up a large container (*daity*) full of water. Clutching handfuls of the tangled shavings, he soaked them in the water and carefully squeezed them to get all the sap out. The liquid quickly turned white, and he did this over and over again until he felt that a sufficiently rich mixture had been obtained. Now everything was ready, the ceremony could begin, the "impure" Guayaki were there — Pichugi's two husbands and all those who had directly participated in the birth. The purification began with Pichugi. Standing, the woman leaned with her two hands on a stick planted in the ground. Helped by another Indian (it is always the men who perform the purification), Kajapukugi took a handful of shavings that had not yet been used, plunged them into the water, and began to rub Pichugi's back vigorously. The two men applied themselves scrupulously to this act of cleansing, and not one part of her body, not one intimate fold, not one cranny of her face was spared their zeal. The white foam that the *timbo* exuded was just as effective as soap. As each part of Pichugi was purified, it was rinsed with the same water. The purifiers worked silently, busily indifferent to my presence.

45

Then, from a nearby hut, came the strident sound of a *chenga ruvara*, the women's ritual song. This "song" is really a lamentation: leaning forward, the woman hides her face in the palms of her hands and lets long sobs burst out through her fingers; after this she produces a singsong that is hardly modulated, at once plaintive and shrill. The words, sometimes extremely prolonged and sometimes broken up or contracted, are comprehensible only to the Guayaki. This ranting goes on for a minute or two, and then the sobs begin again, and so forth and so on. The *chenga ruvara* rarely lasts more than ten minutes. It is known as the *tearful greeting*. In many tribes, a stranger encountered for the first time or a member of the group who has been absent for a long time is greeted by tears of welcome. The Guayaki use the *chenga ruvara* this way too, but for them it also accompanies all the special events in their life, for example, the purification ritual. What is more, the *chenga ruvara* is never performed by only one woman. The woman who had just begun singing — she was the wife of one of the two Guayaki chiefs — sang and wept alone for several moments; this was a signal, because all at once, every woman present followed suit and on all sides a great wailing arose from under the trees — an anguishing sound to someone not prepared for it. When the last outburst had died away, the heads lifted again and the hands fell to reveal not tortured masks, but peaceful faces from which the tears had vanished. A few feet away, the indifferent children played without bothering to look at what the adults were doing. Nor had this concert interrupted the work of the purifiers. Pichugi had been replaced by another woman, who was being bathed with the same care, and one by one all the "patients," women first, then men, passed under the diligent hands of the two men who were officiating. Now no one remained but them. With what was left of the water and the creeper shavings, they purified each other without slacking off for a moment: one of

46

them even went so far as to pick out some forgotten mucus from the nose of the other with a merciless finger.

At one point in the ceremony, I saw Pichugi's oldest daughter, who was about ten years old, perform a series of rapid movements that at first seemed strange. A fire was burning under her parents' shelter; she took a smoldering stick from it, plunged it into the container of purifying water, which extinguished it, and then took it back to the hut and returned it to its place in the fire with the other sticks. In answer to the questions I asked in my astonishment, the Indians said that it was to prevent "*y pira mombo, y pira wachu ubwy mombo*: to prevent the red water from falling, to prevent the thick red water from rising up and falling." The expression *red water*, or *thick red water*, in Guayaki mythology refers to the Universal Flood that long ago wiped out almost all of the first men.* The purpose of the girl's action (at the request of an adult, naturally) was to ensure that such a cataclysm was not repeated. This simple act and the concise commentary with which the Guayaki explained it to me summed up in a condensed form — such is the tortuousness of the savage mind that it hides its mysteries in the most innocuous guises — the whole of their cosmological thought and their philosophy about the destiny of the world.

What we have to do, then, is in some sense unravel this "text," which is so concentrated that it is reduced to a single gesture; we must allow it to speak by analyzing and freeing the rich cluster of meanings bound into one act by the nimble hand of an obedient little girl. That the Guayaki mind entrusts to this silent message — an elusive realm where a world of meaning secretly vibrates — the responsibility for determining the meaning of the world limits how far an anthropologist can go: we cannot know everything, there is always something irreducible, something that refuses to

---

* See the complete text of the myth at the end of the chapter.

be domesticated, and the Indians are still aware enough of their thoughts to be able to seal up what they want to keep enigmatic.

But what was the meaning of this act, which I so easily might have missed if I had been distracted for a moment? First of all, there is a paradox here: although water and fire have always been conceived of as diametrical opposites, here they seem unexpectedly united, since the negation of fire — the extinguished stick — permits the negation of water, thereby avoiding the Universal Flood. Let us pursue the explanation of this and see how "the thick red water" might be unleashed. Women are almost always the potential cause. If a woman should be imprudent enough to touch water while she is menstruating, the earth will inevitably be afflicted with a catastrophe and be submerged in water. But even the men risk unleashing it. The purifiers of a girl who has just reached marriageable age or a man who has murdered another Atchei must not come in contact with water or they will risk bringing on a flood, as long as the evil power they carry in them has not been neutralized by the ritual bath.

But this was not the case at the moment; no one was about to commit the sacrilegious act of touching water: the danger came from elsewhere. Of course, there must be some connection between the possibility of a flood and Pichugi's labor — especially the birth of her child, whose new presence in the world, as we have seen, had already brought about a disorder capable of setting the sky, the earth, and men in turmoil. On the other hand, what does this have to do with the stick that was dipped in the water and put back in the fire? The explicit reference to the Universal Flood — in other words, to one moment in the Guayaki "cataclysmology" — compels us to take a closer look at the meaning of this flaming stick.

Although Atchei mythology does not contain any direct allusion to a burning of the earth (which is the complement of the other devastation, the flood), it does describe a time when the world was not in darkness; this was the period of eternal day, when the sun, permanently fixed at the zenith, burned everything. Here we see the equivalent of the burning of the world. Since we know, then, that the destruction of the earth by fire is present in Guayaki cosmological thought, and taking into consideration the atmosphere of cosmic disorder brought about by the recent birth, we can say that this extinguished stick takes on a greater, almost sacred meaning from the context in which it appears and that it is there in some sense to fill the empty place designated by "the thick red water." The fire that consumes this piece of wood takes on the metonymic form of the universal fire, and the extinction of the burning stick in the purifying water becomes an act by which to conjure that other fire, which is secretly smoldering, and destroy its threat.

So there will be no universal fire. Now the problem can be formulated as follows: in order to prevent the flood, the heavenly fire must be prevented. Does this mean there is a causal relationship uniting two separate terms (fire and water)? If there was, it would have been very difficult, even impossible, for me to discover this link, because the Indians said nothing more about it. But sticking to what we can find out about the unconscious thought of the natives, we are forced to consider fire and water as a structurally linked couple, as something that must be seen as a system if it is to be understood. We must assume, then, that the universal fire and the universal flood are two parts of a whole. They are the two forces that wiped out the first men, they are the two faces of the Indian apocalypse, they are the system of death. On the other hand, since one does not exist without the other — not at the same time, of course, but over an endless lapse of time — the danger posed by one is naturally increased by the danger its complementary opposite poses, especially if the circumstances are such that the disorder involves the whole cosmos. In short, a birth brings with it fire as well as flood. It follows that, if the appearance of one necessarily causes the other to appear, then the disappearance of the second will cause the first to disappear, so that to ward off the danger of a widespread fire by extinguishing its symbolic image could certainly prevent a universal flood.

Now we must ask why Indian ritual resorts to killing fire in order to kill water. In the first place, it is easier to imagine suppressing fire with water than the opposite. Nevertheless, this is really a problem of chronological antecedents: in Guayaki mythology (like that of many other tribes), the burning of the earth took place *before* the flood. In the act of extinguishing the burning stick — of averting the danger of fire — in order to ward off the danger of flood, we can see the repetition in ritual of the myth's temporal order in which fire appears before water.

One last detail calls for an explanation: could an adult have done what the little girl did, or could that task only have been carried out by a child? Taking note of the fact that she dipped the burning stick not in just any water, but in the purifying mixture of creeper bark, we must remember that since the previous night the atmosphere surrounding the life of the tribe, and the life of the universe itself, had been heavy with the impurity that produces disorder. This was why the Indians used lustral water: to dissolve this impurity and eliminate the disorder; and since, like all other adults, they believed in the purity of childhood, they entrusted the hand of an innocent child, still untouched by the contamination which would inevitably burden her once she reached maturity, with the task of saving them. What, finally, do the Indian words say, and what do their gestures describe? What we hear in their language is the familiar sound of the most humble and painful truths. The birth of a child carries within it the seeds of mortality; it throws into question the existence of others: we are haunted by the inevitable and cruel fact that men are not gods and that every stage of life brings us closer to death.

Now the ritual was over, and the evil forces had been controlled. The life of the tribe, which had been briefly disrupted, resumed its peaceful course and its everyday rhythm. Yet it would be a mistake to think that the Guayaki's attitude toward the birth of Pichugi's little boy was completely negative and that the only thing such an event meant to them was that they had been exposed to certain dangers. The discreet but obvious joy they showed in the presence of the baby was enough to prove that this was not so. But what was even more important was that the addition of a new member to the group greatly strengthened its cohesion and solidarity: this was the essential way in which the tribe benefited from it. And how did this work? A birth created definite bonds between the child and certain adults, and it was also the occasion for forming alliances among families, which strengthened the community feeling of the group in which the baby had been born.

Of the various people who take part in a birth, two play the most important roles, and it is with them that the child maintains the most affectionate relations, from that moment until their death. As might be imagined, these two people are the woman who lifts the baby from the ground — the *upiaregi* — after the umbilical cord has been cut by the *jware* and the *jware* himself: in some sense, they are the equivalents of the godmother and godfather in our society. Their "godchild" is known by a special term — *chave* — and their position is similar to that of the child's father and mother. The *jware* cannot have sexual relations with his *chave* daughter, and the *upiaregi* cannot have sexual relations with her *chave* son. This prohibition is rarely disobeyed (though it does happen now and again), and relations between the child and those who presided over his birth are marked not by tension because of the prohibition but by kindness, affection, and gentleness. Throughout his childhood, the *chave* is given little presents by his godparents, most often food. Later, when the boy has become a hunter, he in turn will present them with game that he has killed. But what is most important is that the *upiaregi* and the *jware* will assume a vital role at one other point in the life of their *chave*: when the girl menstruates for the first time, and when the boy is felt to be worthy of being considered an adult, when he is about fifteen years old. The critical moment of the initiation rite, which the girls and boys confront with a feeling of anguish, becomes easier to face because of the kindly presence of their godparents, who helped them come into the world.

The *chave* is deeply affected by the death of the *upiaregi* and especially, it seems, by the death of the *jware*. The crying that greets their death may be part of a ritual, but it is no less sincere for all that; the very visible tears attest to it. And for several days funeral chants can be heard, each "verse" punctuated by a few notes played on the panpipes, sadly lamenting the irreversible departure of the godfather: "My *jware* has not come back, he will not come back, my *jware* is no longer alive, and as for me I cry and cry..."

The ritual of birth also establishes a close friendship between the godparents and the parents of the child. And, since the first are not necessarily close relatives of the second, a birth is also an occasion for establishing new relations among several families that had previously been "strangers." These bonds are immediately sanctioned by certain linguistic usages. From now on, the godparents and parents will call one another by the terms required by the new context that has brought them together, or made them "artificial" relatives: *cha vaichy*, the child's mother will say to the *upiaregi*; *cho kaveru*, the mother and father will say when addressing the *jware*; and they will call the children of the

52

upiaregi and the jware, kave. In this way, family groups are formed (except when the godfather and godmother are already close relatives of the child's father and mother, which happens fairly often) who feel more strongly committed to helping one another and working together. They move around the forest together, exchange food, assist one another in case of illness or during certain ritual acts, and so on.

A birth, then, is not simply the private affair of one family but becomes socially useful to the group because of the chance it affords to enrich the life of the society as a whole. If the circumstances demand it or encourage it, such an event can even provide an opportunity to establish truly *political* relations by joining two self-contained units. The birth of Pichugi's son is a perfect illustration of this unifying function. The event was politically exploited to benefit everyone in the following manner.

The Indians I found myself among actually came from two different groups; they belonged to two small tribes that until recently had had no contact with one another, did not know one another, and even considered one another to be enemies, although both belonged to the Guayaki "nation" (later I will tell how they came together). For the moment it will be enough to say that, although the two groups had for some time decided to coexist peacefully, on many occasions in their daily life they showed a certain reserve, even a marked coldness, toward one another. They were no longer enemies, naturally, but in spite of a recent "mixed" marriage, they still considered one another *Iroiangi*, Strangers. Such a situation could not go on for very long without becoming somewhat absurd. The Indians understood this very well. They therefore resolved — at least those who had first come to the camp and who played the role of hosts — to indicate to the others that they were prepared to do away once and for all with the "dispute" that still divided them. Pichugi's preg-

53

nancy, or rather the name she would choose to give the child she was carrying, provided them with the opportunity to do this.

All the Guayaki are named for animals (or almost all: as a matter of fact, Pichugi is an exception, since the *pichu* is a kind of larva). A person's name is made up of the name of an animal along with the suffix *gi*, which indicates that this is the name of a human being. Most of the species that inhabit the forest are represented in the list of Guayaki names. The most notable exceptions are a certain number of birds who play a particularly important part in the mythology of the Indians, who call them "the domestic animals of Thunder." Also, none of the Guayaki is named after the agouti — probably because this word refers not only to the small rodent but also the penis. To call oneself Tavwagi would certainly be ridiculous. A few days earlier, a jolly and high-spirited woman pointed out how well proportioned her husband's virile member was. He was present and seemed more embarrassed than flattered. Turning toward him, I said: "Then your name should be Tavwapukugi, Large Penis." This provoked general hilarity, to the great confusion of the husband, who had not been prepared for this kind of joking. But his wife was delighted. The names are not differentiated by sex — men and women can have the same names: this makes conversation rather confusing, since one must constantly identify the sex of the person one is talking about.

How is a name chosen? It is chosen before the child is born, and the mother is responsible for choosing it. During the last months of her pregnancy, she chooses the meat of one particular animal among the various kinds of game that are brought to her to eat and decides that this will be the *bykwa*, the "nature" of her future baby, who will consequently be named after this animal. For example, several weeks earlier, Pichugi had eaten the meat of a *kande*, a species of small wild pig, and had decided that this was the "nature" of the child she was carrying; the name of the baby born last night was therefore Kandegi.

What criteria does the woman use in making her choice? Is she guided by a preference for one meat over another, a preference that may be rather irrational, like the "cravings" of pregnant women in our society? This is quite possible, judging from the answers several Indians gave to my questions. But perhaps it is really a function – individual and unconscious – of a social intention: by choosing a certain animal, that is to say by eliminating other possible species, other possible names, the woman is establishing social relations between herself, her husband, and her child, on the one hand, and the hunter who gave her the meat she chose – the *chikwagi* – on the other hand. For if the hunter and the child inevitably feel affection and friendship for one another (how could the child forget what he owes the hunter, who was responsible for his name, his personal identity?), this special relationship between two individuals extends to include the social world of the adults around it. As in the case of the *jware* and the *upiaregi*, it goes without saying that the bonds between the relatives of the child to be born and the *chikwagi* extend beyond the moment of name giving and are invested with an organizing function in the group as such. This was certainly the case with Pichugi. For the future name of her child, she had chosen the pig that had been given to her as a gift by a hunter from the other tribe: of course, it was a gift of meat, but it was also a faintly disguised peace offering between the two groups that until then had been rivals. By proposing himself in this way as the *chikwagi* of one of the "Strangers'" children, the man clearly and tactfully indicated that he and his companions wished to form permanent and friendly relations with the others. And what better occasion was there than the birth of a child, for whom he could become a "father"! In reciprocation – since all the Guayaki share a certain political wisdom — the courted group responded favorably to this gesture: among all the possible *chikwagi*, Pichugi decided to choose the representative from the Strangers, who would cease to be strangers and instead become allies from that moment on. Such is the deeply rooted and realistic diplomacy of the savages in their forest .... Having provided the "nature" and the name of the child, Kajapukugi would in some sense become his "creator," and the recognition of this role and its meaning, which was political, would seal a social pact between the two tribes.

To put this agreement into practice without wasting a moment, Kajapukugi and his family had chosen to spend the previous night in Pichugi's hut, which her two husbands had temporarily abandoned. There was no question, of course, of leaving the mother and her child alone: the invisible being coveted the young life of the baby, and it had to be protected for several more days. To keep watch against the people of the night, against spirits and phantoms, Pichugi's group had chosen a man from the other tribe, a man who had been a Stranger; they were all now *irondy*, people who were "used to being companions." A meal prepared by the wife of the "guard" was eaten together by Pichugi, her children, and Kajapukugi's family after the purification was over. It was, of course, a solemn meal, since it was sanctioning both a birth and an alliance — each of which by its very nature was enough to bring joy to the hearts of the Indians — but it was not a banquet, since there was no meat: the food consisted only of a sort of cereal extracted from the marrow of a *pindo* palm that had been cooked in water. As a matter of fact, the meals which follow the celebration of a ritual almost never include game. But though this meal consisted only of vegetables, it was enriched by the fact that its purpose was to nourish not so much the individual participants as the social life of the group as a whole.

56

The Indians are always anxious to use each event in an individual's life as a way of restoring tribal unity, as a way of reawakening in all the members of the tribe the certainty that they formed a community. There is an opposition here between rich food, consisting of meat and eaten by the family, and poor food, consisting of vegetables and eaten by the society. This opposition is an expression of a system of personal ethics and a philosophy of society which states that man's destiny is interwoven with the collectivity and that each person must renounce the solitude of self and sacrifice private joy.

The daylight disappeared, and with it the serious, somewhat tense atmosphere that had marked this day entirely devoted to the ritual activities which had begun at dawn. The rules had been respected, the necessary words had been uttered by the proper lips, and no gesture had been forgotten. Having done what they had to do, the Indians could now feel at ease and give themselves up to sleeping through a night that would be just as cold as the one before. They had resumed their everyday life; the logs crackled in the huge fires of the camp as they slept.

Several hours later, in the middle of the night, I was awoken by a familiar noise: a man was singing. Kneeling and sitting back on his heels, Chachubutawachugi — Big Peccary with the Thick Beard — was singing so forcefully that he seemed to be defying the darkness. Now and then, he absentmindedly poked the fire; the light from the flames played over his completely naked body. He would inhale the air deeply and slowly let it out with an "eh-eh-eh-eh...," which went on until his lungs were empty. He would take another breath and another series of "eh-eh-eh-eh..." would follow, and so on. The chant was hardly modulated at all, but you could definitely hear a subtle play of the glottis, which produced agreeable and exact changes of pitch. At rare intervals the chant was followed by a few words that were more or less incomprehensible. Since the night before, Chachubutawachugi had played a prominent role: he had been the child's *jware* and during the afternoon had been one of the two purifiers. Now he was all alone, singing. His song was truly a challenge — a triumphant challenge to the creatures of the night, to Krei especially, whose job it was to strangle newborn babies, but who could not approach now because the ritual had placed the baby beyond his grasp. The song raised a protective barrier around the child; the noise of the voice frightened the phantoms and drove them back into the darkness. Twenty-four hours ago, when Pichugi was giving birth, it had been exactly the opposite: a wall of silence, broken only by a few whispers, assured little Kandegi a peaceful coming into the world. It had been necessary to avoid making any noise that might alert Krei. Now that the Atchei had done everything they had once learned from an ancient wisdom, they could return to the normal order of things, they could once again fill the night with a victory song; it was even proper to provoke and threaten Krei: the world of the living was now inaccessible to his menace.

Without a break, hour after hour, the night resounded with Chachubutawachugi's voice crying out to heaven and earth: mortals are not guilty; they have once again won the right to exist in the eyes of the gods.

The Myth of the Universal Flood

When the red water, the thick red water, began to rise, count-less Atchei were swept away. The red water, the great red water swept away many Atchei. A man and his wife climbed to the top of a palm tree, to the top of an old palm tree they climbed. See-ing from above that the water was not disappearing, they began to cry. And the water continued to rise. The flood rose so high that it knocked down the tree and the two Atchei had to climb to the top of another old and solid palm tree. This one was not knocked down. Grasping the fruits of the palm tree, they threw them down: *ploof*! The water still had not disappeared. Later, they began to throw down more fruit: *poom*! They had hit a rock. Then they could go down. The water had carried away all the Atchei, and they had been transformed into *capivara*. Transformed into *capivara*, the souls of these Atchei now lived in the water.

The *betagi* Kajapukugi.

Two Peace Treaties

1953. The coatis did not seem any more excited than usual that day. With stupid obstinacy that made the children laugh, they persistently gnawed with their long canines on the bushes or the poles of the shelters they were tied to. But this was nothing to worry about, because they were always trying to get free. It was a waste of time: the short rope that was carelessly tied around the animals' necks kept them fastened right up against the poles and was too short to allow them any movement at all. They could just manage to reach the bark of the wood, and then they would tear it off furiously with their teeth. No one paid any attention to this, except occasionally the children when they wanted to amuse themselves for a moment. Of course, any unusual agitation among the coatis, even their sharp cries, would put all the Indians on their guard. This was the way the *bita* — domestic animals — warned them of the presence of unknown and probably undesirable visitors near the camp, especially at night: some snake who had absentmindedly wandered by, or a *baipu*, an insolent jaguar who was prowling around the Atchei fires. When he came near, the coatis would go crazy with fear or anger, spitting in rage, their bodies twisted in a vain effort to break their ropes; they would half strangle themselves, and their uproar would immediately alert the people. Most often, nothing extraordinary would happen. Alerted that his presence had been discovered, the beast would head back to where he had come from, the coatis would gradually calm down, and everyone would go back to sleep.

For some time now, the Atchei had not been troubled by the *baipu*. They did not appear as frequently as they once had, and even the young people could recall a time when the hoarse growling of hunting jaguars was heard much more often. Things had changed in the forest, and the old people, surprised more by the freedom of their youth than by the bitterness of the last few years, told about the days when they could stand on the bank of a river or at the edge of a clearing waiting for thirsty bucks or wild pigs to pass fearlessly by. Now people no longer hunted in these places, and in many other places as well; the west had become dangerous, and the old beliefs, according to which the souls of the dead live near the setting sun, seemed to have been contradicted: death had abandoned its home and had come to strike down the Atchei. During the last few years, the Atchei had had to give way before the encroachments of death, and from time to time in their slow retreat through the forest toward the east, they had left behind the body of one of their companions.

The Atchei had always known that they had to stay away from the savannas, those large islands surrounded on all sides by the forest, and give a wide berth to those open spaces which the *Beeru* preferred and stayed close to. Nevertheless, a few bold hunters dared to approach the large dwellings of these terrible creatures. In silence, they would stop at the edge of the forest, crouching in the thick undergrowth or perching on the lower branches of a tree. Holding their arrows to their bows, they would watch them for hours, their hearts beating with fear but too spellbound to tremble. They were resigned to die but already calculating how long a story they would be able to tell that evening when they returned to the distant camp, already eager to hear the men's enthusiastic exclamations and the women's cries, but also expecting the *Beeru* to unleash their thunder at any minute. They watched them, ready to plunge straight into the forest more noisily than the tapirs, even though at the moment they were more still than the forest. They watched these powerful beings with their bizarre customs go about their daily life, so fatally powerful that they could not even be regarded as enemies (enemies were close and familiar, you knew what to do with the Machitara or the *Iroiangi*, you could foresee what their reactions would be and even, in the case of the *Iroiangi*, talk to them before piercing them with your triumphant arrows — but what could you do with the *Beeru?*). The *Beeru* were so numerous and so quick to nibble away at the old forest with their fires that they were as ridiculous as parrots and more discouraging than ants. The Atchei were spying on white men.

Bravery was needed to do this, and prudence as well; few hunters were willing to go very far away from the tribe's territory: they were really testing themselves when they played this dangerous game. The *Beeru*'s animals, their cows and horses, grazed peacefully without trying to wander away, while the Atchei watched their masters coming and going, sometimes on horseback competing in incredible races. The Indians were quite appreciative of the elegance of the horse and called it *bai-pura*, the beautiful animal. But they were even more moved by the very sweet taste of its meat. In fact, for a long time now, they had been in the habit of killing isolated horses and cows — which they called *Achi-pura*, beautiful horns — when the first glow of dawn gave the hunters enough light to aim their arrows at the animals, who were half asleep.

The cold season, from June to August, was particularly fruitful because this was when the animals left the grasslands to take shelter under the trees from the icy south wind. More wary than the cows, the horses often trotted away before the Atchei could come within range. But the "beautiful horns" were almost always choice hunting. Ridiculously easy targets because of their large size, they would low under the bite of the long arrow, which sometimes went right through them without breaking against the bones, and quickly fall to the ground, stumbling over roots and creepers. This was good, because the Indians almost never followed the wounded animals out of the forest. They did not waste any time waiting for the cow to die; they had to act quickly, before the *Beeru* arrived, and without hesitating they would take their bamboo knives and hastily cut enormous hunks out of the animal while it was still alive. Each man would throw all the meat he could carry onto his shoulder, and they would all disappear into the shadows of the forest, anxious to return safely to their wives and children, who were waiting for them with empty stomachs.

Because of the long periods they spent observing the *Beeru*, the Indians often became familiar with the habits of the animals and found out which places they preferred. The white men's laughter reached the Indians also, when they were not too far away: "The *Beeru* laugh very loudly," they would say to themselves, displeased. One of the white men's allies was a terrifying creature. The strength of his howling, his constant rage, and his eagerness as he followed the trail of the Atchei once he had caught their scent filled the Atchei with fear; men who were brave enough to confront the jaguar alone with their bow and arrow ran like women when in the distance they heard the barking of the *baigi*, which was their name for the dog: "he-who-is-the-animal," the epitome of natural violence.

The dogs and their masters were penetrating farther and farther into the forest. In the old days, the division had been quite distinct: the *Beeru* in the savanna and the Atchei in the woods.

But now the large fires which the white men lit at the end of winter were gradually eating away the Indian territory; roads were opening up, which the *Beeru* used for carrying out the tree trunks they had cut down, and little by little the forest was being taken over by them. This made the Atchei's life very complicated. Their ancient hunting grounds were constantly diminishing; when a *Beeru* built a house somewhere, he would immediately burn an area in which to plant his manioc and corn; his horses and cows would spread out all around, his dogs would bark, and his children would cry; the game would leave the once silent area, and the Indians would not be able to hunt there anymore. This was also why the jaguars had left. And the *Beeru* were doing the same thing all over. Encounters with them took place more and more often, in spite of the Atchei's prudence, and now there was almost always one woman in the tribe whose face was painted black and whose head was shaved in mourning for a father, a brother, or a son who had disappeared. What was most incomprehensible, most frightening of all, what filled their hearts with anguish and hatred was that the *Beeru* were pursuing them into the forest in order to steal their *kromi*, their children. No one knew why, no one knew what they did with them, but many boys and girls had already been carried off by the white men. The women cried and chanted sadly, and the men, who could not cry but who were upset by their wives' harsh sobs, beat themselves fiercely with their bows to drive out of their breasts the sadness that was weighing down their hearts and half killing them. When the men suffered too much, they became *yma chi ja*, violent forces — then they would start fighting, they would want to strike out at everyone. The children would run away, and the women would yell: "They want to shoot their arrows! Don't shoot! Do-on't sh-oot!" And they would bravely rush at the men, who were getting excited and clashing their arrows; the women would put their

65

bodies in the way of the men's arms as they were about to release the string of the bow. The men allowed themselves to be calmed fairly easily; they had only been half angry, and a good *piy*, a caressing massage over their whole bodies, would be enough to soothe them, although sometimes a woman would be sent rolling over the ground by an enraged punch to the head.

For all these reasons, the Atchei Gatu were forced to wander over an area which, though vast, was constantly being diminished by the advancing white men. Jyvukugi, the chief, was worried. He asked: "How can I lead the Atchei into good forestland if we keep coming upon the *Beeru*'s roads everywhere?" The small tribe had trouble staying alive. He had been in charge of it ever since the day he single-handedly attacked and plundered a small camp of Paraguayan woodcutters and returned to his tribe loaded down with axes and machetes, which he passed out to all the men. Because of his bravery and generosity, as well as the prestige he had acquired from this raid, one of his fathers, old Bywangi, who was himself the leader of the tribe, told the Atchei shortly before he died during a fight with white men: "This man will be your *Eruaregi*, he will be your leader when I die, he is *Kyrymba*, my son, he is brave."

After that, Jyvukugi's duty consisted of leading his people not only where there was an abundance of game but also, even more importantly, far away from the *Beeru*. By keeping the tribe constantly on the move, sleeping only a few nights in one camp — even at the risk of not following the rules strictly about holding initiation ceremonies for boys when their lips were pierced and for girls when their blood came down — for a long time Jyvukugi had managed to guarantee the tribe a life that was almost peaceful, troubled only occasionally by the death of an *irondy* struck down by the white men's thunder. Now it had become very difficult: there were too many white men, they were coming in every-

66

where at once, and, worst of all, they were taking the children. And yet how was one to confront them, with their *chuvi*, the thunder that killed from so far away? Arrows were worthless against them, and the hunters did not really rely on them, in spite of the old women with dried up vaginas, the very ancient *waimi*, who cried out to them in voices full of hate as they left at dawn to go hunting: "Go along the white men's road! Hide behind a fallen tree and wait for them! Shoot them with arrows and dig out their eyes! Then hang their bodies head downward!" They expected nothing but death from the white men. A short time before, several women accompanied by one man had approached a manioc plantation. The women were busy filling their baskets when the *chuvi* thundered. *Teeh*! shouted the man, who fell down, vomiting blood. The women ran off. The next day the group came to take away the body. They found their companion's head stuck on a pole and a cloud of flies swarming around the dried blood.

That day in 1953 the sun had not yet reached the top of the sky. All the Atchei Gatu were there together, except for a few families who had gone off hunting. The arrival of the *Beeru* was so sudden that the coatis did not even have time to react. The horrifying noise of the little red flames and the smoke that rose from them drove away the peace of the camp, and time stood still for the Atchei. For half a second, for an eternity, it was an island of silence and immobility. A hand that had been polishing an arrow remained motionless, holding the snail shell; a mouth gaped open, about to eat a snail; a woman smiled endlessly at her baby. The explosions crackled and the bitter smell of powder drove out the smell of roasting meat. Children began to cry and their mothers bowed their heads, clapping their hands over their ears. Hidden behind trees several dozen yards away from the camp, the

67

attackers fired their heavy military rifles. Leaves and branches broken off by the bullets fell around them. As they fired into the air, their leader coolly tried to estimate how many Guayaki there were. But his men were scared, because there was no telling what these creatures might do. They were the most savage creatures in the forest, and they had tails, according to people who knew. These legendary and certainly very ancient stories were often believed by so-called "cultivated" people, such as the Englishman George F. Masterman, whose *Seven Eventful Years in Paraguay* was published in Buenos Aires in 1870. This is what he says about these Indians, whose name he misspells: "They evidently belong to the lowest type in the human species; their small stature, their skin, which was nearly black, and their thin arms and legs re- minded me unpleasantly of monkeys; they seemed less intelligent than animals. They do not build huts, do not wear clothes, and do not know how to use fire; they live in the forests and eat fruits and roots.... They do not seem to have an articulate language.... The Guyracuis [*sic*]... have short tails and because of this are forced to carry a pointed stick so that they can dig a hole in the ground in order to sit down comfortably." What was clear was that the Indians were as happy as monkeys living in the trees and that, since God had abandoned them, they were not even bap- tized — "*Bichos del monte no más....* Just forest animals....." The fear and excitement of finding themselves in the heart of the for- est surrounding the camp of what was supposed to be one of the country's most savage tribes heated the half-breeds' blood; their nervous fingers lowered the barrels of the *chuvi*. Young Brejugi (River Ridge), full of hate and despair, seized his bow and arrows: "*Epyta* — Stop!" cried the attacker closest to him in Guarani. "Stop!" And his finger squeezed the trigger of the Mauser. The bullet struck Brejugi's chest, and the man and his arrow fell as the explosion sounded.

The men were pleased with their boss, Pichin Lopez, a professional Indian hunter and expert guide in these woods, which cover most of the east of Paraguay, though they are often broken by immense *campos* where sheep graze. The men were pleased because the catch had been good; the fact that the whole group had been taken without a fight filled them with enthusiasm and made them forget the long weary days of tracking the Guayaki. The profits would be substantial. There in front of them were forty heads — males, females, and children — dumb with terror and crowded together around the men, who were helpless, their hands tied behind their backs. Throughout the region of San Juan Nepomuceno, the Guayaki were highly valued, their average price being one cow or one good horse apiece, that is, four or five thousand guaranis (between thirty and forty dollars). This was an extraordinary profit for these poor men, who owned nothing but their horses, their machetes, and their heavy .38s. This was also the first time an entire pack had been captured. Usually only one or two children were taken. There was never any problem disposing of these forest products, because the demand for young Guayaki was much greater than the sporadic supply. The demand was even growing, and many families were eager to buy a young savage. In order to satisfy this demand, several *montaraces* — strong men who were used to the hard life of the forest — had gradually become specialists in this lucrative hunt, which was pure profit when it was successful. The problem was to locate the Indians.

This could take days or even weeks of patient tracking in the woods. The Guayaki were always on the move, they left few traces, and one could pass very close to a camp without realizing it. Yet this job was made easier by the fact that the area in which the Atchei Gatu tribes wandered had been greatly diminished by the encroachments of the settlers, who cut down a little more of

the forest every year. What was more, there was no way the Indians could escape now: to the north, a large paved road had
recently been built, joining the capital, Asunción, to Paraná and
definitively cutting the Indians' ancient territory in half; to the
west and the south, there was an uninterrupted line of Paraguayan settlements; and to the east (although the white men
were unaware of this), there was an enemy Guayaki tribe whom
the Atchei Gatu feared, even though they had heard nothing
about them for a very long time. They traveled in circles; their
refuge was surrounded.

Why were the Paraguayans so eager for Guayaki children?
Some of them were convinced that they were doing the savages a
great favor by raising them from the condition of animals to that
of human beings, by giving them a quick baptism. But most did
not bother to disguise what was in fact a very crude economic
motive: a Guayaki child would become the slave of the family
which bought it and would work for that family for nothing all
its life.

The Indians who were captured were not necessarily mal-
treated, as long as they did not try to escape. By running away,
they would not only deprive their master of their work, but,
more seriously, they would damage his prestige: he would no
longer be able to call himself a master once his slave was gone — a
situation to which he would not easily resign himself. Guayaki
girls seldom ran away, because they quickly became the mistresses of their owners and were destroyed by prostitution. But
once the boys entered adolescence and realized that they would
never be able to have sexual relations with a woman — since no
Paraguayan woman would agree to have sexual relations with one
of these half animals — they would become obsessed by the idea
of returning to the forest and the camps of their people; sooner
or later they would try to escape. They were always pursued,

sometimes in vain. One man lost his life trying to save his pride by recovering his slaves. This was in 1943. The man owned two young men who had been abducted by white men during an attack. One night, the two Guayaki escaped. Their master immediately went after them, borrowing three Indians owned by another man who lived in the region. A few days later, the small expedition overtook the two Indians, who had not had time to find the tribe. The man gave the runaways a severe whipping as punishment, and they all started back home. When evening came, they set up camp. The master was so firmly convinced of his power over the Indians and so scornful of them (would he be afraid that a dog or a cow would try to take revenge, after all?) that after he had eaten he lay down next to the fire and went to sleep wrapped up in his poncho, certain that things had returned to normal and that no precautions were necessary. He died because he could not for one instant believe that the Guayaki were capable of human feelings or that they might value their freedom. The chance was too good to miss. While he slept, the two Guayaki explained to the others that they did not want to return to the white men, that they were going to run away again, but that this time they had to kill the *Beeru*. Whispering passionately in the dark because they knew that the tribe was very close by, they tried to persuade their three fellow tribesmen to come with them. One of them agreed; the other two were resigned to going back to the Paraguayan world because they had lived there too long and were undoubtedly afraid they would not be able to get used to the old freedom of the forest. But they agreed to do nothing to stop the others. The conspirators then proceeded to kill the white man. It was a cruel death. Two Indians held him to the ground by pressing on his head and feet, while the third plunged the flaming end of a burning stick into his throat. He died quickly and silently. Once they had taken their revenge, they disappeared into the night carrying their victim's weapons and were never heard of again.

The other two reached the Paraguayans several days later and told what had happened. I heard the story from the son of the victim. Anxious to avenge his father, he had become a Guayaki hunter and took part in the 1953 attack.

The Paraguayans had another reason for being eager to own Guayaki children: in addition to wanting to save the souls of these pagans by putting their bodies to work for them, they were curious about one particular aspect of the Indians. There were numerous legends about them, and people's imaginations ran wild because there was no way of verifying these stories, since the Indians remained well hidden. While some people believed that they resembled monkeys because of their tails and because they lived in trees, other people believed they were superhuman in the sense that they were spirits of the forest with fearful powers and knowledge and on top of that had a most unexpected physical appearance, with blond hair, blue eyes, and white skin. This was the story, and as we shall see there was some truth to it.

What the Paraguayans found most exciting was the idea that the Guayaki had white skin. They were so sensitive to this that they wanted to own one of these white-skinned creatures. Although they were not aware of it, by feeling this way they were admitting that they themselves were dark skinned. A majority of Paraguayans, especially the country people, were descended from heavy interbreeding between Guarani Indians and Spaniards that began in the first half of the sixteenth century when the *Mburuvicha*, the Guarani chieftains, agreed to enter into an alliance with the earliest conquistadores against their common enemy, the warlike tribes of Chaco. The newly arrived white men were trying to reach the legendary Eldorado in the west, which the Indians said was the source of the gold, silver, and copper objects that went through a long series of exchanges before winding up on the Atlantic coast of Brazil. Domingo de Irala and the handful of soldiers under his command had arrived in the New World in the south and had traveled up the Río de la Plata as far as the site of Asunción, which was founded in 1536; they did not yet know that the Eldorado their gold lust was driving them toward was the kingdom of the Incas and that their own compatriots, Francisco Pizarro and his men, had just overthrown it, imprisoning and executing its last emperor, Atahualpa. Between them and the gold mines stretched the immense, hostile Chaco. In order to cross it, they had to organize powerful expeditions capable of fighting off attacks by the Mbaya or the Payagua, who had been crossing the river in small groups and endlessly tormenting the Guarani villages. This was why the Guarani were quick to see the offer of an alliance with the *Karai*, the white men — who had weapons and horses — as a prudent way to win a fast military victory over their hated enemies. And since the Indians felt that an alliance could only be guaranteed by the creation of family bonds, they made their Spanish associates into brothers-in-law and sons-in-law by giving them their sisters and daughters.

The Guarani plan failed because of the aggressive resistance of the Chaco Indians. They became the victims of their own plan in that they allowed their "brothers-in-law" to accumulate harems that contained dozens of women. The Spaniards, who were less inclined to respect family ties than the Guarani, exploited the Indians of the region so savagely that two or three decades after they had arrived there were almost no natives left where once there had been tens of thousands. On the other hand, there were now a number of half-breeds, the offspring of hidalgos and beautiful Indian women. This was the original core from which the present population of Paraguay developed over the succeeding generations. Their features and rather coppery skin clearly show

73

that there is Indian blood in their veins, although they might not want to admit it.

Evidently, this is a common trait among many half-breed peoples: they show the same scorn for their native cousins that the white men show for them. Of course, because of the origin of the Paraguayan population, there are so many degrees of racial mixture that at times it is difficult to speak of interracial relations. Yet a Paraguayan farmer feels he has nothing in common with an Indian, even a *manso*, or domesticated, Indian, and his attitude toward him alternates between amused condescension and hatred, even though the Indian might be only slightly poorer than the farmer. And he would be very surprised to learn that he and the Indian share the same ancestors — in fact, he would refuse to believe anything so absurd. He instinctively puts a high value on what he does not have: not material wealth, to which he attaches little importance, but white skin and light-colored eyes. This preoccupation is evident in the popular aesthetic's ideal woman, expressed bluntly in Guarani: the most desirable woman is *kyra, moroti ha haguepa* — fat, white, and with thick hair. This taste for white skin combined with the belief that the Guayaki were very fair made them seem desirable to the Paraguayans, though in a rather ambiguous way.

These were the conscious and unconscious elements that had formed the relationship between the Indians and the Paraguayans; their confused conception of one another makes it easier to understand how an armed group managed to capture the tribe of Atchei Gatu that day in 1953. This time, however, the Indian hunters did not receive any profit from their expedition. In some sense, it even made them look ridiculous. When they were near San Juan Nepomuceno, where they planned to sell them, they could not find any place large enough to hold the forty or so captives and apparently decided to leave them outside in a corral meant for cows. "The Guayaki are so used to the freedom of the forest that if they are shut up somewhere they are paralyzed and don't know how to get out," the men reasoned. By using such ingenious logic, the Paraguayans wound up treating the Indians like a herd of cows. Naturally, during the night Jyvukugi gave the signal for them to escape, and at dawn the enclosure was empty. At the time, this incident became rather notorious. The details of it came to the knowledge of highly placed people in Asunción, and they decided to put an end to these practices. A decree was passed protecting the natives, and for the first time in the history of the country it became a crime to kill an Indian. But the effectiveness of this decree was limited by an inability to enforce it, and in the following years the Atchei Gatu continued to be hunted almost as much as before.

In any case, for them this was only a temporary reprieve, and in August 1959 the Indians gave in. The forest had become more a prison than a shelter for them, they were coming into contact with the *Beeru* more and more often, their hunters were killing more and more cows and horses, and the retaliation of the white men was increasingly brutal. Jyvukugi could see no way out of the situation and decided to surrender. Eight or ten miles from San Juan Nepomuceno lived a farmer whose plantations adjoined the forest. He had once been an Indian hunter and had kept two adults he had captured on an expedition, one of whom was rather old. This crude and clever Paraguayan (who no doubt imagined that one day he would be able to get his hands on the treasure that the Atchei were guarding!) was never violent with his Indians; they were never overworked in his fields and were well fed. He managed to persuade them that, incredibly enough, he was a *Beeru* who was not *tawy*, brutal. He had even made some effort to learn their language. Because of this, the two Atchei felt no fear or distrust and gradually became convinced that Arroyo Moroti (White Stream, which was the name of the place) would be the salvation of the tribe, the island of peace where the only *Beeru* who would protect the Indians lived. One day they disappeared. The white man who had cleverly set himself up as a model of goodwill compared to the other white men, who were very violent, was not surprised to see the two Indians emerge from the woods one night several weeks later followed by the whole tribe: Jyvukugi, yielding under the pressure put on him by the two Indians — one of whom was his brother — and exhausted from his life of continuous, desperate flight, had given up everything and come to ask for help and protection in the white man's world. The nomads had reached their final stopping place.

Thanks to the efforts of Léon Cadogan, a modest and hard-working self-taught Paraguayan who has devoted a large part of his life to defending the Indians and who has done invaluable research into the Guarani religion, the news spread in ethnological circles: at last this enigmatic tribe, which had been in hiding for centuries, could be studied. Alfred Métraux, who took an interest in everything concerning the Indians, was excited by this possibility and offered me something which I could not fully appreciate at the time and which I now realize was an extraordinary opportunity: a chance to study the Guayaki. With the help of the Centre national de la recherche scientifique, I arrived in the forest with my colleague S. at the end of February 1963. Yet there had not been anything very dramatic about my preparations for this trip, which I hardly thought of as an "expedition."

The trip would not begin until I had spent several months becoming acquainted with the language and was in a position to penetrate the inner world of the Indians little by little, something I would not have been able to do by observation alone. When I arrived among the Guayaki, I was not totally unprepared. Cado-

76

gan had gone to Arroyo Moroti several times, and because of his thorough knowledge of the three dialects spoken by the last Guarani Indians in the east of Paraguay, he was able to understand Guayaki and learn to speak it fairly quickly, since it is closely related to Guarani. Cadogan made a number of tapes of the Indians speaking, transcribed and translated them, and sent them to the Musée de l'Homme in Paris, so that I had a chance to become familiar with an unknown Indian language before meeting the people who spoke it. In the four months before I left, I spent several hours a day listening to the tapes over and over again, growing accustomed to the strange phonetics and assimilating the vocabulary: I was able to carry out this work effortlessly in Paris, whereas it would have taken many more months and a great deal of patience if I had done it in Paraguay among the Indians. Almost immediately after arriving in the camp, I was able to understand and speak a few sentences — simple ones, it is true, but enough to establish some form of rudimentary communication, without which everything would have been discouraging and tiresome. "*Nde iko ma ko*," a Guayaki said to me a few hours after we arrived. Standing there before me, speaking to me, was a Stone Age man (a description that turned out to be more or less accurate). He was talking to me, and I understood him: "So you've arrived?" he asked politely, as he would have asked one of his own people. "*Cho iko ma.* Yes, I have arrived," I answered courteously, delighted and relieved at how easy this first contact with the Indians had been. That was the end of the conversation; it could not have continued much longer. My knowledge of the language was scanty and was actually more of a hindrance than a help to me during the first few days because the Guayaki, convinced by my first achievements that I spoke perfectly, the way they did, refused to believe that I often did not understand them and thought that in some sense, for incomprehensible reasons, I was tricking them.

Because of this, they showed a certain distrust of me, thinking I knew more than I was letting on. Fortunately, this misunderstanding was resolved, thanks mainly to the children, who were better able to appreciate the real extent of my linguistic skill than their parents were.

Our luggage was being taken by a heavy oxcart. After we left San Juan Nepomuceno, a village built in a checkerboard pattern on the ruins of an old Jesuit mission, we crossed vast *campos*. From time to time a man on horseback would appear riding along the red earth road, barefoot but wearing spurs on his heels: these horsemen were taciturn half-breeds with very Indian features who always carried a machete and often a Colt .38 in their belts. When you leave Asunción, you hardly ever hear Spanish spoken; few country people can speak it correctly. The countryside of Paraguay is Guarani territory; only recent immigrants and a few city snobs claim that this is not so. Every time our driver and guide met one of these horsemen, the two men would greet each other briefly: "*Mbaeixapa?*" "*Iporante ha nde?*" "How are things?" "Fine, and you?" Then there would be some quick questions: "*Ha ko gringo kova, mo'opa oho?*" "And these gringos, where are they going?" Our driver's answers were rather imprecise. He knew we were going to visit the terrible Guayaki, but why? Maybe we were Protestant missionaries, or maybe we wanted to get information from them about the treasures they knew of in the forest. In any case, we were very rich, and we certainly were not going to "study" the Indians: gringos were much too clever to waste their time on such nonsense! And the man would go on his way, his horse moving off at a rapid pace; under the down-turned brim of his straw hat, his eyes would be shining with surprise. Soon the *campos* were replaced by *capueras*—abandoned plantations that had been entirely overgrown by tall and unpleasant brambles, shrubs, and thick bushes, spoiling the land for cultivation. At this point, the countryman, like his Indian ancestor, cleared a path for us. The heat was so overwhelming that we could hardly admire the magnificent plumage of the toucans, who were easy to see because of their enormous beaks; but on the horizon, the dark mass of the forest drew closer, and at last we reached the shade of the large trees. It was distinctly cooler there, but now I was bitten and stung by hordes of relentless insects — a scourge much worse than the heat.

The oxen walked placidly on, indifferent to the shouts of the driver (*Hake, anamemby!* Get on, son of your mother the devil!). After several miles, we descended a gentle slope and reached a clearing: this was Arroyo Moroti.

There were no Guayaki in sight. Huts were hidden in the forest, but no one came out of them. Later, I understood that the Indians' impassivity was a form of courtesy: they pretended not to notice a newcomer so that he could make his arrival calm and discreet. A long time would go by, sometimes an hour, before someone would come and greet the stranger or the friend returning after a long absence. "Have you arrived?" he would ask. "Yes, I have arrived." Also, the Guayaki were with good reason mistrustful of white men and reluctant to be very familiar with them. Besides, something much more important and interesting to the Indians had taken place that day, and it somewhat overshadowed our arrival. As I said, Jyvukugi and his group had been there since August 1959. The Atchei Gatu — this was what they called themselves: the Good Guayaki — had lived a half-nomadic, half-sedentary life from then on. They continued to roam the woods, hunting and gathering food; sometimes they would only stay away for one day, and sometimes they would stay away for as long as a month, but in the end they always returned to the permanent camp at Arroyo Moroti that seemed destined to be their home. This was their haven, their refuge, the only one in a world that was completely hostile to them. Besides, their Paraguayan protector did not like them to go away for very long because he wanted to keep control of them. Naturally, these comings and goings gave the men less time to hunt, which meant that the tribe had less to eat. The Paraguayan had gained great prestige throughout the region for having succeeded in pacifying the Guayaki. But he also benefited directly from his new power. For one thing, he took advantage of the young girls in the tribe (he would have had to be a saint not to succumb to the temptation of those graceful bodies). But he was also the tribal chieftain now. The government of Paraguay had sanctioned the existing situation by giving him legal status, and, though his salary was modest, a large quantity of food — flour, fat, sugar, powdered milk — was sent to the Indians from Asunción through him. Undoubtedly the Atchei received part of it, but the rest was siphoned off by their white leader, who sold it to the country people. The size of these shipments was based on the size of the Indian population that was supposed to receive them, so the Paraguayan's business dealings would have been even more profitable if there had been more Indians. It so happened that for centuries another Guayaki tribe had been living a few miles away in the craggy hills of Yvytyrusu.

Although these Indians were no more fairly treated by the white men than their cousins, the Atchei, they had never been forced to give in. Their territory, the Cordillera, was a natural refuge and Paraguayans seldom ventured there. It was the Indians who occasionally launched an attack and then climbed quickly back up the wooded slopes where no one dared pursue them. It seemed likely that they would be able to go on living in freedom for a number of years, since the Paraguayans were not invading their hunting territory — it was too broken up to make good grazing land. But the relative calm in which they had been living up to now was not destined to last much longer, because the master of the Atchei Gatu was anxious to increase the source of his revenue and he had decided to take over this new tribe.

For anyone else, it would have been impossible; but with the help of Jyvukugi and his people, he would easily be able to do it. To find a group of nomads in the forest is almost out of the question for anyone but other nomads: for them it is child's play to follow trails that seem invisible. But Jyvukugi still had to be persuaded to attempt to contact the other tribe. The Atchei Gatu had shown very little enthusiasm for this project when it was suggested to them about two years after they settled in Arroyo Moroti. They knew that this tribe existed and that it lived to the east of their own territory, but they had never met any of the tribesmen. The two groups had tacitly agreed to avoid meeting, and they were both careful not to set foot on each other's hunting territory. If hunters came across tracks that did not belong to their own group, they knew that they had come too far and were stepping on ground that belonged to the *Iroiangi*, the Strangers. They would immediately turn around, afraid of coming upon a group of tribesmen reputed to be ferocious even though they were fellow Atchei. "If you meet the Strangers," an Indian would say in an excited voice, "then big arrows! Lots of arrows! The Strangers are terrible, and we're not brave, we're afraid. So we run, we run very far!" Each overestimated the belligerence of the other, and in this way the two tribes managed to coexist peacefully, keeping to their own territories for fear of the horrible reprisals they would incur if they crossed the border. And the horror they felt was expressed in a serious accusation: the other tribesmen were cannibals!

So Jyvukugi was rather reticent: the Atchei Gatu were afraid, convinced that the Strangers would riddle them with arrows as soon as they stepped on their territory and then devour them. Eventually their uneasiness was assuaged by the presence of the

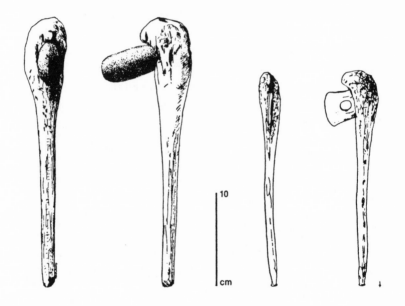

10

cm

Similarly constructed stone and metallic hatchets.

white chief with his guns, and at the beginning of 1962 a small group of Indians left to search for the *Iroiangi*. Of course, they were not about to reveal their own reason for wanting to make this expedition, which they saw as a good opportunity to take revenge on these enemies, whom they had never seen; they looked forward to the fine time they would have massacring the scorned and hated savages without much risk to themselves. Naturally, things did not turn out this way, since there was no profit for the Paraguayan in dead Indians. In a few days, the Atchei spotted the signs they were looking for: a tree trunk had a tiny notch in it a man's height off the ground – this was a signal to the women who were coming along behind; at another point, the branch of a shrub had been broken deliberately; and farther on, there was clear proof that they were on the right path – a felled palm tree had been stripped of its leaves, and the condition of its fiber showed that a stone hatchet had made a gash in it. They were nearing their goal, and the Indians were becoming nervous; they sensed the presence of the *Iroiangi*, and at any minute they expected to hear the whirring of bowstrings and the whistling of arrows: if the *Beeru* had not been armed with his thunder, they would have stopped their exploring then and there, prepared to tell their people that they had driven off the enemy.

One morning they heard the sound of hammering: it was not far away, but it was muffled by the thick vegetation. The Atchei recognized the evenly spaced blows as the familiar sound of a stone ax striking a tree trunk. "The *Iroiangi* are going after honey," they whispered. They silently approached the sound, and a few dozen yards away they saw a man in a tree trying to enlarge the entrance to a hole in which some bees had made their hive so that he could get at the honey. At the foot of the tree stood a young woman; she had set her basket of woven palm on the ground next to a *daity*, a watertight vessel for gathering honey, and was wait-

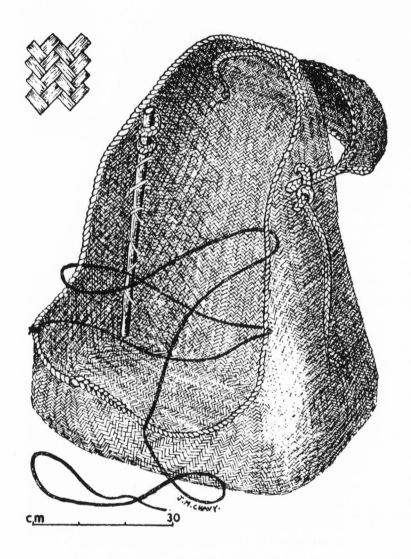

Naku, woman's basket.

ing for the man to finish. Neither of them had heard anything; the man went on with his work, and the woman watched him. The Indians easily overcame the woman, who was astounded to see unknown Atchei accompanied by a white man. The man was so startled that he let his heavy ax fall to the ground. Down below, three or four arrows were being pointed at him. "*Machi pira eme!* Don't shoot the arrows!" he managed to blurt out. "*Ejy modo! Ejy modo!* Get down! Get down from there!" the Atchei Gatu shouted. The honey gatherer did not understand: what were these *Iroiangi* doing here? They were certainly going to kill him. And what about the *Beeru*, why was he with the Atchei? He resigned himself to the fact that his life was finished and came down from the tree.

His name was Kandegi, Little Wild Pig, and the young woman was his daughter. Kandegi was already a *chyvaete*, an old man, and he had grandsons. He no longer hunted with a bow and arrow, but he could still roam around the forest, follow the flight of bees, and scale the trees in which they had made their hives. Early that morning he had left the group to go after some honey he had spotted earlier. And since he was a widower, and had been for a long time now, he asked his daughter to go with him to carry the honey in her *daity*, a job he could not do himself, since carrying was women's work. He expected to return to the camp before the sun reached the top of the sky, and then this incredible thing happened. Kandegi stood on the ground now but did not move away from the tree trunk. He put his arm around it. He was waiting for an arrow to hit him in the neck and break his skull or for the white man's *chuvi* to let loose its thunder. Instead, the Atchei threw themselves at him, snarling furiously, pounded him with their fists, and insulted him: "You *Iroiangi* are very stupid and bad! You are Atchei Vwagi, eater of Atchei, cannibals!" The man did not try to defend himself. The white man, who until then had not said anything, gave some orders. The men calmed down, bound Kandegi's arms behind him, pulled him and his daughter up off the ground, and the group started away. The Atchei Gatu knew that the *Iroiangi* would follow them as soon as they realized that two members of their tribe had disappeared. They therefore had to get away quickly; the *Iroiangi* would not dare track them beyond the limits of their territory. They made a forced march back the way they had come and a few days later arrived safe and sound and victorious at Arroyo Moroti.

Kandegi found himself both among enemy Atchei and in the world of the *Beeru*. And they were all hostile to him. As soon as the two *Iroiangi* appeared in the camp, the Atchei Gatu women hid themselves and the men muttered: "Let's kill them! They are very wicked!" An old man went up to Kandegi and punched him hard in the head. The old man was Paivagi, the oldest of the Atchei Gatu. For some time now, he had been irritated because his wife had abandoned him for more vigorous men, saying that he was no longer capable of making love. And yet he himself sometimes wanted to possess a *dare*, one of the beautiful young women in the tribe. He gave them grubs, hoping to win their favor: "*Meno vwa!* To make love!" But they insolently laughed in his face: "*Nde ro tu ja praruete! Meno kwa ia!* You're a feeble old man! You can't make love!" All this made him furious, and when he saw one of the *Iroiangi* whom his tribe had always hated so much, he took out his anger on him.

Later Paivagi and Kandegi became good friends; from time to time they would give each other small presents of food. Except for short-tempered Paivagi, who had not really hit him very hard, no one insulted Kandegi. His arms were untied. Dumb-founded, he looked at the white man's house and could not believe his eyes; he ran around it three times and shouted, which excited the women watching him from a distance. The *Beeru* had

meat brought to him and gave him other foods he was not familiar with, including something delicious and almost as good as
honey — candy. The first few days they spent at Arroyo Moroti
convinced Kandegi and his daughter that they were not going to
be killed; their fear vanished, and they were able to observe the
strange life of the Atchei and the *Beeru*. The white man was much
more friendly to them than the Atchei. If he wanted Kandegi's
cooperation in carrying out his plan, he not only had to win him
over, but also persuade him that it was in the best interests of his
tribe to join the other Guayaki at Arroyo Moroti, so he patiently
explained to the two captives that, thanks to him, the Atchei no
longer had anything to fear from the *Beeru*, that he was there to
prevent any violence from taking place, and that this camp was
the only spot in the forest where the Indians could be sure of
being safe. Kandegi found these arguments convincing: Had he
not passed his whole life in fear of white Indian killers? How
many of his companions had ended their lives with bullets in
them? How many *kromi*, children, had been taken away and never
seen again? Everything the *Beeru* said seemed to point to the
Atchei's nightmare being over for good.

After three weeks, the white man summoned Kandegi and his
daughter. To Kandegi he gave something that made him happier
than anything else could have: a metal ax and a machete, white
men's tools that the Atchei only got hold of from time to time,
often at the cost of their lives. To the young woman he gave a
tyru, a prettily colored dress that she immediately put in her basket. They were now free to rejoin their people; all they had to do
was to tell the tribe about what they had seen and show the presents they had been given. The white man also promised that
later he himself would go into the *Iroiangi*'s mountains to get
acquainted with them and take them more presents. They left, all
the more charmed by the outcome of their trip because when it

began they had thought they were going to die far away from their people. But thanks to the *Beeru Gatu Meete*, the good and generous white man, they were alive and on the way back to their *irondy*, their companions.

And what amazing stories they had to tell their follow tribesmen, who undoubtedly thought they had fallen prey to jaguars and vultures — the women with their heads shaved as a sign of mourning and the men fighting one another with their bows in order to cure themselves of their grief! Their return trip went very quickly. They were greeted by great *chenga ruvara*; the first evening home Kandegi sat by his fire and spent all night chanting the story of their adventures. The people were lying down and seemed to be asleep, but they were really listening to him with passionate attention. During the following days, whenever all the hunters were present in the camp, the men gathered in long meetings. No one doubted what Kandegi had said, because he was a *chyvaete* and for many years now he had been too old to talk like a child. Yet should they trust strange Atchei and this white man, who wanted them to go and live with him? But then there were the gifts to consider, the heavy, shining *jamo jy*, the metal ax: none of the men knew how to use it very well yet, but when it came to cutting down a tree or hollowing out a beehive, the old *itagy*, the stone axes, seemed ridiculous, only good for being used as pestles by the women. And the *Beeru* had promised to give metal axes to everyone!

Karewachugi, Large Coati, was hesitant. He had been the leader of the Atchei for a long time. With the help of his brother Kajawachugi, Large Wildcat, he had always been able to avoid conflicts between his people and enemy Atchei. He was the strongest man in the tribe, and with his enormous arms he could bend a bow until it broke; his fellow tribesmen were afraid of his blows when it came to fighting duels, and none of them thought

88

he was exaggerating when he chanted, "*Cho ro bretete*. I am a very great hunter." He was the first to find the *kaa gatu*, the good forest where there was plenty of game. But should he now go along with Kandegi and become *cheygi*, friend and ally of the white men? He could not forget that fifteen years ago a number of *Beeru*, all armed with their *chuvi*, had invaded the country of the Atchei, spreading death and terror among them for days, while explosions sounded on all sides. The tribe, which had killed a large number of horses and cows during the preceding months, had had to withdraw far away from its usual hunting grounds. Some of the Atchei, demoralized by this defeat, had completely abandoned the territory and gone far north, where other Guayaki lived: these Guayaki were reputed to be very mean, but no doubt less mean than the white men. So they left and were never seen again. Had the Atchei eaten them or received them as *pave*, as brothers? The rest had not been able to bring themselves to leave their familiar places and had established their *etoa*, their hunting area, in the Yvytyrusu.

From the hills where they lived, they watched the lights which the white men lit at night shining in the distance. Sometimes they even heard a heavy rumbling on the *Beeru*'s roads: this was one of their *bita*, a domestic animal that was monstrously big and made a loud roaring noise — *itapegi*, truck. The Atchei could see all this from their ridges, where they knew they would be left in relative peace: should they exchange this partial security, which they could count on, for a mere promise of complete security? Some of them wanted to accept the white man's offer right away, among them Pychapurangi, Twisted Foot; he had survived a rattlesnake bite but had been left crippled by it. From then on he had had difficulty following the others as they moved from place to place and had hobbled along behind them on his deformed stump. Others refused to believe in the *Beeru*'s good faith. The Atchei were divided. Finally, the majority — more drawn by the prospect of adventure, perhaps, than put off by the risks they would be running — decided in favor of joining the other tribe, and Karewachugi went along with them: now all they had to do was wait for the white man to come.

The expedition was organized in May 1962. It was larger than the group that had captured Kandegi and consisted of several Paraguayans and a dozen Guayaki men and women. The presence of the women was intended to show the *Iroiangi* that the group's intentions were peaceful: when Atchei went off to fight, only men took part. So it was a sign of peace to have women along. But the white men, knowing that they were going to be facing the whole tribe and not knowing if the mission they had entrusted to Kandegi had succeeded, preferred not to be caught unprepared; there had to be enough of them present to resist an ambush, if necessary. As it happened, there was no violence.

One morning, their camp was surrounded by the sound of whistling, sharp cries, and shouts, although no one saw any sign of an Indian. Two arrows shot out of the foliage, but they were aimed well over everyone's heads. The Atchei Gatu were beginning to be afraid when suddenly from behind the trees came about sixty *Iroiangi* — men, women, and children. Though the hunters were carrying bows and arrows, they had not painted black patterns on their faces and chests, as they did when they wanted to terrify an enemy during an attack; they had no hostile intentions. One of the men came forward and briefly reminded them of the promises Kandegi had transmitted. Using the Atchei Gatu as intermediaries, the white men confirmed this: a few metal tools were handed out, the women moaned their welcome to the Atchei and the *Beeru*, and the group set off. The *Iroiangi* were leaving their *etoa* for good, as the Atchei Gatu had done three years before.

There were a stubborn few, however — not more than about ten — who were not able to reconcile themselves to this decision; among them was Torangi, who hated and scorned the *Beeru*, and two children. The small band disappeared and the others thought they would never see them again. But on February 23, 1963, the very moment we arrived in Arroyo Moroti, they came out of the forest and walked into the camp. They had not been able to endure their nine months of solitude far away from their companions, whose traces they kept discovering — this tree had been chopped down by so-and-so, and these grubs had belonged to so-and-so. Sole masters of Yvytyrusu now, they were afraid to live there alone. What was more, one of the children, a little girl of eight or nine, was very sick, *mano ruwy*, almost on the point of dying: maybe the white men would be able to save her. They made up their minds, and at the very moment we reached the Atchei — an amazing coincidence that I chose to interpret as an omen — Torangi's group appeared in the camp.

The eight men and women had shaved their heads. A little cape made of wildcat skin covered the child's shoulders. Silently, clustered tightly together in a single mistrustful block, with the free forest behind them, they gazed at their new life. The furtive arrival of the Atchei's friends and relatives distracted their attention from us. Turning their backs on our cart, which was loaded with presents we had expected to hand out in an elaborate ceremony of exchanges, the Indians went off to tend to the newcomers. Actually, this meant that several hours later we were able to witness for the first time what certain sixteenth-century chroniclers, such as André Thevet and Jean de Léry, described in connection with the Tupinamba Indians of the Brazilian coast: the tearful greeting, the ritualized way of saying hello to strangers. Jakugi, an Atchei Gatu hunter, was not there at the moment. When he returned at the end of the afternoon, they told him the news.

Two *Iroiangi* women, one old and the other young, went to his hut. He stood up; the *waimi*, the old woman, stood facing him, her hands on his shoulders, while the young one stood behind him in the same position. He was caught between the two women, who pressed their bodies tightly against him and squeezed him in their arms. Then the *chenga ruvara* began, an empathic recitation of phrases that were hardly articulated and were broken by gloomy sobs in a sort of refrain to the strange weeping song. From time to time, Jakugi was given the *piy*, a massage of the chest and neck, which is a sign of respect. All this lasted ten minutes and was marked by an impressive dignity; it formed an island of grace and virtue in the midst of the other Indians, who were discreetly paying no attention. For a long time, I remained standing there, charmed by this exquisite courtesy; it was a welcome distraction from the heat and the mosquitoes. I had really arrived among Savages.

Grub harvest.

Jyvukugi, "chief" of the Atchei Gatu.

CHAPTER THREE

Looking Backward

They really were savages, especially the *Iroiangi*. They had only been in contact with the white man's world for a few months, and that contact had for the most part been limited to dealings with one Paraguayan. What made them seem like savages? It was not the strangeness of their appearance — their nudity, the length of their hair, their necklaces of teeth — nor the chanting of the men at night, for I was charmed by all this; it was just what I had come for. What made them seem like savages was the difficulty I had in getting through to them: my timid and undoubtedly naive efforts to bridge the enormous gap I felt to exist between us were met by the Atchei with total, discouraging indifference, which made it seem impossible for us ever to understand one another. For example, I offered a machete to a man sitting under his shelter of palm leaves sharpening an arrow. He hardly raised his eyes; he took it calmly without showing the least surprise, examined the blade, felt the edge, which was rather dull since the tool was brand-new, and then laid it down beside him and went on with his work. There were other Indians nearby; no one said a word. Disappointed, almost irritated, I went away, and only then did I hear some brief murmuring: no doubt they were commenting on the present. It would certainly have been presumptuous of me to expect a bow in exchange, the recitation of a myth, or status as a relative! Several times I tried out the little Guayaki I knew on the *Iroiangi*. I had noticed that, although their language was the same as that of the Atchei Gatu, they spoke it differently: their delivery seemed much faster, and their consonants tended to disappear in the flow of the vowels, so that I could not recognize even the words I knew — I therefore did not understand much of what they said.

But it also seemed to me that they were intentionally disagreeable. For example, I asked a young man a question that I knew was not indiscreet, since the Atchei Gatu had already answered it freely: "*Ava ro nde apa?* Who is your father?" He looked at me. He could not have been amazed by the absurdity of the question, and he must have understood me (I had been careful to articulate clearly and slowly). He simply looked at me with a slightly bored expression and did not answer. I wanted to be sure I had pronounced everything correctly. I ran off to look for an Atchei Gatu and asked him to repeat the question; he formulated it exactly the way I had a few minutes earlier, and yet the *Iroiangi* answered him. What could I do? Then I remembered what Alfred Métraux had said to me not long before: "For us to be able to study a primitive society, it must already be starting to disintegrate."

I was faced with a society that was still green, so to speak, at least in the case of the *Iroiangi*, even though circumstances had obliged the tribe to live in a "Western" area (but in some sense, wasn't their recent move to Arroyo Moroti more a result of a voluntary collective decision than a reaction to intolerable outside pressure?). Hardly touched, hardly contaminated by the breezes of our civilization — which were fatal for them — the Atchei could keep the freshness and tranquillity of their life in the forest intact: this freedom was temporary and doomed not to last much longer,

but it was quite sufficient for the moment; it had not been dam-
aged, and so the Atchei's culture would not insidiously and rapidly
decompose. The society of the Atchei *Iroiangi* was so healthy that
it could not enter into a dialogue with me, with another world.
And for this reason the Atchei accepted gifts that they had not
asked for and rejected my attempts at conversation because they
were strong enough not to need it: we would begin to talk only
when they became sick.

Old Paivagi died in June 1963; he certainly believed that he
had no more reason to remain in the world of the living. In any
case, he was the oldest of the Atchei Gatu, and because of his age
(he must have been over seventy) I was often eager to ask him
about the past. He was usually quite willing to engage in these
conversations but only for short periods, after which he would
grow tired and shut himself up in his thoughts again. One evening
when he was getting ready to go to sleep beside his fire, I went
and sat down next to him. Evidently he did not welcome my visit
at all, because he murmured softly and unanswerably: "*Cho ro
tuja praru. Nde ro mita kyri wyte.* I am a weak old man. You are
still a soft head, you are still a baby." He had said enough; I left
Paivagi to poke his fire and went back to my own, somewhat upset, as one always is when faced with the truth.

This was what made the Atchei savages: their savagery was
formed of silence; it was a distressing sign of their last freedom,
and I too wanted to deprive them of it. I had to bargain with death;
with patience and cunning, using a little bribery (offers of presents
and food, all sorts of friendly gestures, and gentle, even unctuous
language), I had to break through the Strangers' passive resistance, interfere with their freedom, and make them talk. It took
me about five months to do it, with the help of the Atchei Gatu.

They had been living at Arroyo Moroti for two and a half years.
This is enough time to break up an Indian tribe if it has been

in constant contact with white men. But the semi-isolation of this place, which Paraguayans rarely visited, actually left the Indians in seclusion; their daily habits were undoubtedly affected, but their culture had not altered very much yet. For example, they had had to learn to eat manioc every day and meat less often, which made them very sad. But since no one had made any effort to convert them to Christianity, their spiritual life had not been shaken and the world of their beliefs remained very much alive, protecting their society from the fatal doubt which would inevitably have followed any evangelization forced on them from the outside.

The Atchei Gatu were therefore still the Atchei, in spite of the fact that they were relatively accustomed to dealing with white men. But when the *Iroiangi* joined the camp, Jyvukugi's people became very conscious of having arrived two and a half years earlier and adopted a haughty attitude toward them, as though they were initiates dealing with neophytes, or even lords dealing with their subjects. A hierarchy was established right away between the two tribes; or rather, the Strangers accepted what the others wanted without arguing, because in the same way that the Paraguayan chief was the Atchei Gatu's only protection against the white man's world, Karewachugi and his people needed the protection of the other Indians. Without them, they might not be able to understand what they should do, and they would risk missing their chance to enter the world of the *Beeru*. They therefore depended on the goodwill of the Atchei Gatu, who were only too pleased by such a favorable arrangement.

The arrival of the *Iroiangi* had not filled them with joy — far from it. They had not fought it, because this was what the white man wanted, but as the unwilling hosts of these bothersome guests, they gave them only a surly welcome. The two groups had always lived in the forest without trying to get to know one

another, each was the potential enemy of the other, so there was
no reason to make a show of friendship when no one felt it. On
top of that, Jyvukugi knew very well that the Strangers were
going to benefit from the *Beeru*'s generosity and that the Atchei
Gatu's share would be proportionately smaller. But above all,
the difference in numbers was upsetting, and when the others
made their timid appearance, it seemed to the Atchei Gatu like
an invasion. Jyvukugi's group did not consist of more than thirty
people: fourteen men, seven women, and the children. There
were sixty Strangers, and a little later they were joined by the ten
I saw arrive. This was crushing: "*Tara pute ro Iroiangi!* An enormous number of them, the Strangers!" sighed the Atchei Gatu.
Wouldn't they take advantage of their numbers to carry off the
few wives whom the men were sharing? All their fears were justified, as was the scorn they felt for the *Iroiangi*: the Strangers were
given axes and machetes, and they did not even know how to use
them or how to sharpen the blades; these rustics had to be told
everything. The Atchei Gatu therefore decided to avoid any sort
of indiscriminate mingling with the newcomers, who agreed to
settle at some distance.

So there were really two clearly separated camps under the
trees at Arroyo Moroti, one on either side of the stream. And the
Strangers were made to feel who the real masters were. Superiority in numbers could never make up for their profound igno-
rance: "*Iroiangi kwa ia ete, ure kwa ty.* The Strangers do not know
anything, but we are accustomed to knowing things." The *Iroiangi*
were not easily offended. They did not dream of challenging the
preeminence of the Atchei Gatu, who had acquired considerable
knowledge from the white men. They humbly accepted their sub-
ordinate position, and because of this Jyvukugi, though he did
not try to diminish Karewachugi's prestige among his own people,
became the leader of all the Atchei. A skillful politician as well as

a brave hunter, he soon learned how to exploit the Strangers' shyness and awkwardness to the profit of his own group. To start with, he took a wife for his brother Pikygi, Little Fish, whose own wife had left him for another man. When the *Iroiangi* first came, Karewachugi had had two wives, one old and the other new; the latter was a young woman whose husband had been killed by the Paraguayans. Karewachugi had taken her to be his *japetyva*, his second wife. An arrangement was made whereby Karewachugi gave over his rights to Pikygi. He accepted the separation without too much sorrow, even though his young wife had given him a little girl; by his principal wife, he had two sons who were already married and the heads of families. But when a man has two wives, he has to hunt twice as much. Karewachugi also saw that he would win favor with Jyvukugi by giving up his rights. As for the young woman, she was delighted to have a new husband who was one of the Atchei Gatu — they were so rich and sure of themselves. The transaction had two good results: the Atchei Gatu gained one more woman, and the marriage transformed the two formerly hostile groups into allies. Through Pikygi and his wife, the people in the two tribes became brothers-in-law. What had been unthinkable when all the Atchei were living independently in the forest — their reconciliation into one single community where all were *irondy*, companions — came about once they had lost their freedom. From now on, they were *pave*, brothers, even though they had not wanted this at all.

So there was a good understanding between the two groups; a secret feeling of bitterness persisted, but it did not come out into the open very often. For example, both tribes avoided treating one another as *Iroiangi*, which would have been offensive behavior on the part of *va ja*, brothers-in-law. But among their own people, they did not pretend: they forgot they were *va ja* and spoke only of Strangers.

One day Kybwyragi revealed the true state of their relations to me. Looking vaguely at a group of *Iroiangi*, he said: "When they're all dead, we'll take their wives. That way, we'll have lots of women." The old women were less circumspect. One evening I was chatting in a low voice with Jygi, Frog, a rather old Atchei Gatu woman. The camp was quiet. Everyone was almost asleep. Suddenly a fart issued from a *tapy*, resonant in the silence around us. Laughing, I asked Jygi: "*Ava ro pyno?* Who farted?" No doubt thinking that I was accusing her, she cried out furiously at the top of her voice, so that everyone could hear: "The Strangers are great farters. *Ine pute*, they stink terribly! We Atchei Gatu never fart!" No one challenged this insult, which was extremely slanderous. The Guayaki are very discreet about their natural functions, except for belching, which they regard as a healthy indication of a satisfied appetite. Nothing else is allowed. Even the children go far away from the huts to relieve themselves, invisible and inaudible among the trees. Sometimes we would hear laughter at a distance: young women were going off to pee together. And if it happened that someone absentmindedly stayed too close to the camp, an old woman would be sure to cry out sharply: "*Wata reko! Kaari ro puchi!* Keep going! Go defecate in the forest if you have to!"

The little stream had a bed of very light sand — which was why the Guarani Indians had named it *Moroti*, White — and its water was used by both the Strangers and the Atchei Gatu for washing. Nevertheless, the Atchei refused to treat their brothers-in-law as equals, and Jyvukugi's hunters rarely went off hunting with Karewachugi's men. This bad-tempered attitude sometimes made them look ridiculous; even Jyvukugi, who was deliberate in his actions and his speech and more likely to paralyze the person he was speaking to with his heavy, ironic gaze than to make casual remarks, sometimes fell into these ways.

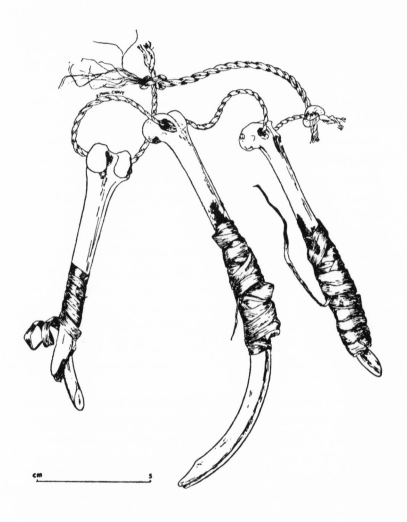

Prachi, primary tool for making arrows.

One day he was attentively watching an *Iroiangi* carve an arrow. After a moment, he called to him, wanting to examine the arrow. "*Mecha vwa.* Let me see," he said, without moving. The other hurried to bring it to him. It was a good arrow, with barbs all on one side, the way almost all Atchei arrows were made. Jyvukugi checked to see if it was straight and solid and carefully peered at the notches to see how regular and deep they were. Then he showed it to his wife, who was sitting next to him, and pronounced his judgment, overwhelmed with sadness and wearing a smile of pity on his lips: "*Vai pute!* Hopelessly ugly!" His bad faith was obvious, because that arrow was as good as any other. Then why did Jyvukugi, who was an expert, disparage it? Because the other man did not have a metal blade and had made it with the Guayaki's traditional chisel: the *prachi*, a long *capivara* canine tooth mounted on a monkey bone that served as a handle, the whole thing glued with beeswax and bound with creeper bark. As a result, the notches did not have the distinct and polished look that was so easy to achieve with a white man's knife but almost impossible with a *prachi*. Jyvukugi knew all this, but he wanted to base his domination on his people's technical superiority, and he made fun of the *Iroiangi*'s rustic arrows. Since he was not able to compete with the *Beeru*, he took it out on people who were poorer than he was: in the white man's world, there was no such thing as equality, and Jyvukugi had quickly learned that.

But the fact that he protected the interests of his tribe above all else did not mean that he neglected the interests of the Strangers. Just as the Strangers felt that he, even more than Karewachugi, was their true leader, he felt almost the same responsibility for them as for his own people, so that when the white man distributed any food, medicine, or tools, he saw that all the Atchei were given their rightful share. In the same way,

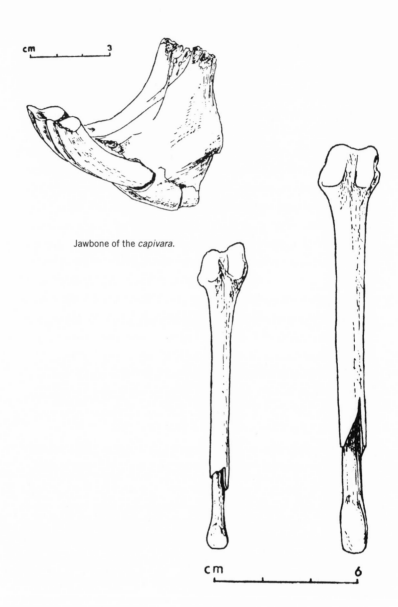

cm _____ 3

Jawbone of the *capivara*.

cm _____ 6

Prachi with a metallic tip.

when an important event occurred or a decision was made that concerned everyone, Jyvukugi took pains to visit the whole camp and tell the news to all the Atchei, family by family, commenting on it and going into great detail so that everyone would know exactly what was happening.

In the beginning, these visits surprised me very much, because the Indians already knew what was going on. When the Paraguayan had something to tell them, he would have them gather in front of his daub house and talk to them in a strange and confusing mixture of Guayaki and Guarani. Only three or four Atchei Gatu managed to understand this jargon — it was incomprehensible to the others. The speech had to be translated for them, and this was done on the spot by the few who understood. In spite of this, when the people had returned to their *tapy*, Jyvukugi would repeat at length what had just been told them in a few words. As they listened to him, the Indians seemed to know nothing about what he was saying: this was a strange comedy, in which the people paid close attention and pretended to be surprised, even though he was obviously not fooled.

What was the secret behind this game? What rule had they all agreed to obey? Why did Jyvukugi have to repeat what they already knew? It had nothing to do with the kind of news the Paraguayan had told them; the Indians adopted the same attitude whether it was important or not. They did not feel they had really been informed until they heard the news from Jyvukugi's own mouth; it was as though only his word could guarantee the value and truth of any other speech.

What this represented was the essence of political power among the Indians and the real relationship between the tribe and its chief. In his role as leader of the Atchei, Jyvukugi *was obliged to speak*; this was expected of him, and it was in answer to this expectation that he went from *tapy* to *tapy* "to inform" the people. For the first time, I was able to observe directly – for it was working transparently before my eyes – the political institution of the Indians. A chief for them is not a man who dominates the others, a man who gives orders and who is obeyed: no Indian would accept that, and most of the South American tribes have chosen death and annihilation rather than submit to the oppression of the white men. The Guayaki, who also believe in this "savage" political philosophy, make a clear distinction between power and violence: to prove that he was worthy of being called chief, Jyvukugi had to demonstrate that, unlike the Paraguayan, he did not exercise his authority through coercion, but through what was most opposed to violence – the realm of discourse, the word. And when he made the rounds of the camp, he was not telling the Atchei anything that was new to them; he was reasserting his ability to exercise the function that had been entrusted to him. His discourse, then, had two meanings, since the apparent meaning was there only to dissimulate and at the same time reveal the true meaning of another word, another discourse, that was present in what he was saying. This was a weighted discourse that attempted to maintain a proper balance between the leader and the group, and it really expressed the following: "I, Jyvukugi, am your *Beerugi*, your chief. I am happy to be chief, for the Atchei need a guide, and I wish to be that guide. I have experienced the pleasure of leading you, and I would like to prolong this pleasure. I will continue to lead you as long as you recognize me as your chief. Am I going to impose this recognition by force, enter into conflict with you, confuse the law of my desire with the law of the group in order to make you do what I want? No, because this violence would not help me at all: you would refuse this subversion, and you would no longer see me as your *Beerugi*. You would choose another man, and my fall would be all the more painful because once you had rejected me I would be condemned to solitude. The recognition that I must continually seek from you cannot be gained through conflict but through peace, not through violence but through words. That is why I speak. I do what you want me to do, because the law of the group is one with my desire; you want to know who I am: I speak, I am listened to, I am the chief."

The Indians were in some sense aware of the concept of politics expressed in Jyvukugi's imaginary speech. As proof, take the words of a man I talked to about the chief's activities. Asking him what Jyvukugi did, I used the verb *japa* (to make); he answered me with excitement: "*Jyvukugi jap ia, inandy!* Jyvukugi does not 'make' anything, he is the one who speaks!" It was not that Jyvukugi did not do anything: on the contrary, he worked very hard making arrows all the time. What my informant wanted to express was that Jyvukugi defined himself not by *doing*, but by *speaking*, and it was this that determined his difference from the others and made him the chief. The obligation to use the instrument of non-coercion — language — *every time it is necessary* gives the group permanent control over the chief because every word he speaks is an assurance that his power will not menace the society; on the other hand, his silences are disturbing. Of course, the Guayaki have not worked out a theory behind their concept of political power. They simply create and maintain a relationship that is built into the very structure of their society and found in all Indian tribes. The "power" incarnated by the chief is not authoritarian. This does not mean, however, that these primitive societies still have great progress to make in order to create a true political institution (that is, something similar to what we are accustomed to in our own civilization) but that these "savage" societies *refuse*, by a sociological act and therefore unconsciously, to let their power become coercive. The chiefs are prevented from using their position for personal ends: they must take care that their personal desires do not infringe on the interests of the community; they are in the service of the group; they are its instruments. Permanently under the control of the group, the leaders cannot transgress the norms on which the whole life of the society is based. Power corrupts, it has been said. This is a danger the Indians need not fear, not because of a rigorous personal ethics, but because of a sociological impossibility. Indian societies were not made for this, and that is why they have not been able to survive.

Toward the end of the first half of the sixteenth century, the conquistadores reached the heart of the South American continent. In expedition after expedition, the early explorers, having been massacred by the Indians, took their ships up the Río de la Plata, the River of Silver, so named by the Spaniards because they believed it led to the country of precious metals — the Peru of the Incas. They had never seen this country, but the Indians who lived on the Brazilian coast and carried copper machetes and breastplates of beaten silver had told them that these objects came from mountains lying far to the west, the Andes.

They also knew that a Portuguese sailor, Alejo Garcia, had been shipwrecked on the coast in 1521, at approximately the same place where the modern port of Santos is located, and that he had set off toward the west with a group of Tupinamba Indians. When he reached Paraguay, he had no trouble recruiting several hundred Guarani warriors, some of whom already knew the country of gold because they had pillaged its frontiers several times in the past. Alejo and his group crossed Chaco and entered Bolivia, which was at the edge of the Incan Empire; they seized a large booty of gold and silver and then went back toward the east. After reaching the bank of the Paraguay River, the Guarani killed Alejo Garcia: the booty was all theirs now, but Garcia had still been the first white man to cross South America and see the wealth of the *Caracara*, the Vultures, as the Guarani called the Incas. None of this worried the Spaniards, who were not afraid of much; on the contrary, Garcia's fate reassured them: hadn't he proved that Eldorado actually existed and was within their reach?

But things turned out differently. Between the conquistadores and the gold lay Chaco, and the Indians who lived there were fierce warriors, the mortal enemies of the Guarani and therefore of the *Karai*, their white allies, whose scalps were especially prized. When at last the Spaniards reached the mountains after several fruitless attempts, they learned from the Indians that, for a long time now, bearded white men armed with guns and mounted on horses had been fighting and shedding blood in the north of the country: this was how the Spaniards found out that Pizarro had preceded them and destroyed the empire. For them, it was too late: the gold had not been destined for them.

A long time had passed since the fearless and unscrupulous young wolves from Andalusia and Estremadura had first set foot in Paraguay, founding the small fort of Asunción, the future capital of the country. Enough time, in any case, for them to have been softened by the climate and the beautiful Guarani Indian women and discouraged by the continuing failure of their *entradas* across Chaco, so that they gave up the dream of conquering the land of riches.

Virtually isolated from Spain, which no longer knew what had become of the conquistadores of Río de la Plata, they now preferred to abandon themselves to debauchery in the arms of their mistresses. Their recent alliance with the Guarani had naturally been to their advantage: the men became their slaves and the women their concubines, and every Spaniard had a large harem. Already hundreds, and soon thousands, of *karai ra'y*, children who were half white and half Indian, ran around the houses

109

made of dried earth and in the gardens where their uncles, once proud warriors, were raising manioc and corn for the lords, their brothers-in-law.

Of course, the hidalgos did not rule all the Guarani tribes, only those around Asunción. There were many other tribes to the north and east, powerful and prosperous in their large collective houses, which could each hold more than two hundred people. There the young men were brave, the old people wise, and the great sorcerers, the *Karai* with their incredible powers, knew how to talk to the gods — this was why the white men who had come from the east were also called *Karai*, since they too seemed to have incomprehensible powers. Thanks to the chants and dances of the shamans, the crops grew in the plantations and Tupan, appeased and charmed by the beautiful speeches of the *Karai*, sent his kindly rain whenever it was needed. Game was abundant in the forests: with arrows, traps, and clubs, the inhabitants of the *tava*, the villages, were able to get all the meat they needed. Then there was also the merciless war against the Ka'aygua. Who were the Ka'aygua? "Those of the forest": this was the derogatory name given to this tribe and others by the Guarani, who used it to designate all tribes that seemed savage to them. The Ka'aygua were almost never seen except when they approached the gardens to steal food. As soon as their presence was noticed, they could be heard fleeing into the woods like maddened tapirs, who plunge straight ahead through the trees. The Guarani viewed the Ka'aygua as animals, and their reputation terrified the women. The Guarani would have been happy to exterminate them, but it was impossible: the Ka'aygua did not even know how to farm; they did not build houses but wandered constantly through their immense forests. It was impossible to get near them, even when a band of them left the forest for a while to attack a village at dawn. A volley of arrows would strike the Guarani men where they slept in their hammocks, and then they would be assaulted and beaten over the head and limbs with stone hatchets and wooden clubs. The attackers would make a quick retreat, carrying off the women they had come to take. Sometimes lookout men got wind of an attack, and they were able to fight off the Ka'aygua; and sometimes warriors from several villages would join together and pursue them, and if they managed to intercept them, they would hold great banquets at which they ate the prisoners as a way of getting back at them for their offenses and for the people they had killed. But quite often, the Ka'aygua disappeared into the depths of the woods, which they knew better than anyone else.

The Ka'aygua were not aware that this was what the Guarani called them. They called themselves Atchei, which in Guayaki means *the people*. And the Atchei called the Guarani, Machitara — Many Arrows. They had been enemies for so long that they could not remember ever having had any contact with them other than when they met in war and ambush. And since the Guarani were infinitely more numerous than the Atchei, they were given the name Innumerable Arrows.

So, on the one hand, there were the Machitara-Guarani, living in permanent settlements at the edge of the woods, which hid their villages and gardens, and on the other hand, the Atchei-Guayaki, living far back in the heart of the forest, furtive nomads defending themselves inch by inch against the gradual advance of the others. These were the two groups of Indians in the eastern part of Paraguay, forever locked in reciprocal hatred. Although the Atchei had accepted the white man's world, they would never agree to ally themselves with the Guarani. While I was staying with them, a group of Guayaki left Arroyo Moroti to establish a temporary camp one day's march away. But quite near that place was a group of about thirty Guarani. As soon as the Guarani learned of the arrival of their ancient enemies, extremely peaceful though they were, they decamped and fled twenty-five miles away to seek protection from Paraguayan soldiers: they thought the Atchei were coming to massacre them and take their women.

What was the source of this hatred? What event in the distant past had caused it? It is almost impossible to find a historical answer to these questions. There is very little archaeological evidence, and the Indians' past is therefore full of obscurity, confusion, and disorder. Yet certain hypotheses seem more likely than others. The territory occupied by the Guarani extended from the Paraguay River to well beyond the Uruguay, almost to the Atlantic coast. The Indians of the Brazilian coast, though similar to the Guarani in their language and civilization, were called the Tupi. This is why we speak of the Tupi-Guarani as a homogeneous cultural unit. All these Indians were conquerors. Their expansion across the South American continent was a response not only to religious uneasiness — which led them to make great migrations in search of *Ywy mara ey*, the Land Without Evil, the Earthly Paradise — but also to a warlike ethos which glorified the model of the warrior to the young men. Also, they undoubtedly needed more territory, probably to accommodate a population explosion.

In any case, the Guarani were certainly not the first people to occupy Paraguay — even if they had lived there for hundreds of years, as is proved by the recent discovery of pottery dating from the eighth century. The first waves of invaders probably did not settle in the deserts, though they overran them. These areas were most likely inhabited by populations that were no match for the pitiless *kyreymba*, the Guarani warriors. There were far fewer of them, and they were easily conquered. The Guarani had an expeditious way of taking control of a conquered territory: whenever possible, they killed off the men, married the women, and adopted the children. There is no evidence to prove that this is what hap-

112

pened between Paraguay and Uruguay, and yet there is no evidence against it either. It is therefore very tempting to speculate that the Guayaki Indians are the last survivors of an ancient people who lived in these regions before the Guarani.

Another reason for thinking this is that, contrary to a belief that is as widespread as it is inaccurate, most of the Indians of South America were farmers — at least in the tropical areas, where the land could be farmed — and the crops they grew were just as important to them as the food they hunted, fished, and gathered. In fact, civilizations of nonfarming nomads are very rare. Yet they do exist, as witness the Guayaki. What does this mean? The Guayaki are living fossils, throwbacks to a distant period, when agriculture was unknown. But then how did these tribes manage to survive intact for hundreds and even thousands of years while nearby peoples developed and perfected the art of farming? Were the Guayaki able to resist all outside influences, remaining on the margins of history for two or three thousand years while agriculture was being practiced all around them on the continent? It is hard to believe that they had escaped the "contagion" of agriculture (the fashion of agriculture, one might say), and this would mean that the present nomads do not really go back to ancient times. If this is so, there is only one other possibility: the nomads have no knowledge of agriculture, not because they never acquired it, but because *they lost it*. And this would mean that, like any other civilization, they were not able to avoid being marked by history.

What was the overwhelming event that led to the Guayaki's historical backtracking, to their cultural regression? It could be that some natural catastrophe drove them far away from their gardens, but it is more likely that they came into conflict with a superior military force, a more highly developed civilization. In other words, the overwhelming event was probably the war of

113

conquest that brought the Guarani into their territory and obliged the Guayaki to seek refuge somewhere else. At that point, they probably lived almost clandestinely, still trying to hide their small plantations. (As we shall see, there is evidence of this.)

But the die had been cast: there was no way for them to return to what they had been. As the Machitara exerted more and more pressure and made their lives more and more insecure, the Atchei gave up agriculture completely. This happened fairly recently. But perhaps it would be going too far to say that the only relations between the conquerors and the conquered were hostile, as though they had always coexisted without affecting one another at all. There must have been temporary reconciliations, pauses in the war, when the Guayaki had a chance to acquire and assimilate (even if in a fragmentary manner) the Guarani's most attractive cultural traits. Although they did not return to their original condition, as generation succeeded generation they adapted the language of their enemies to their own use, borrowed some of their myths and beliefs, and imitated some aspects of their ritual life. This caused the Guayaki not only to regress but also to become *Guaranized*.

Perhaps this is the most appropriate historical interpretation to give the myth that the Mbya-Guarani still recite: "In the beginning, the Mbya and the Guayaki lived together under the leadership of P'ai Rete Kwaray, the god with the body of a sun. One day, the Guayaki appeared at the ritual dance entirely naked; P'ai Rete Kwaray, furious, upbraided them, laying his curse on them, and dispersed them through the forest. This is why they have lived as wandering savages ever since." The Guarani's conscience is clear, but there are things they do not know. The Atchei only got what they deserved, think the Guarani; they should not have offended the god by disobeying the rules of the ritual performed in his honor. But there is also an underlying uneasiness here: the

Mbya cannot accept differences; unable to suppress these differences, they try to include them in a familiar code, in a reassuring set of symbols. For the Mbya, the Guayaki do not belong to a different culture, *because there can be no such thing as differences between cultures*: they are outside the rules, beyond common sense and above the law — they are Savages. Even the gods are against them. Every civilization, of course, has its pagans; but our Christian civilization never hesitated to sing the praises of a God whom other people refused to worship, though they were tortured and killed for doing so. This is another way in which the true worth of our world can be measured.

The first to come during the conquest were the soldiers; then came the priests, and, in the beginning of the seventeenth century, the great Ruiz de Montoya started a missionary venture that was to grow into the amazing empire of the Jesuits in Paraguay. The members of the Society of Jesus endured a good deal of pain and suffering, and several lost their lives. But their obstinacy and their determination not to use force to induce the Guarani to settle in the missions overcame the Indians' resistance. The Indians quickly realized that life with the Jesuits was better than slavery: they were caught between the Portuguese *bandeirantes* of São Paolo and the Spaniards of Asunción — both of whom considered the Guarani tribes an inexhaustible source of slaves. The missions were primarily refuges; and one century later, the Jesuits could pride themselves on having gained control over most of the Indians in the area and on having introduced them to Christianity. Tens of thousands of them, even hundreds of thousands, lived in these small settlements.

The Fathers soon heard of the existence of the Ka'aygua, whom the Guarani described in terrifying terms. A combination of curiosity and missionary zeal made the Jesuits want to see these "forest people" up close; their souls were particularly vulnerable to the Evil One, and the Jesuits wanted to win them over to God. They made several attempts at peaceful contact but were not successful; the Guayaki were too elusive. Then they decided to abandon their policy of nonviolence in favor of a more effective plan and organized a military expedition with the help of the Guarani, who were only too happy to go after the Ka'aygua. This time they were successful; a band of about thirty Guayaki was captured and brought back to the mission.

The Fathers, who had mastered the language of the Guarani perfectly, soon noticed how closely related it was to the language of the Ka'aygua. They even found Guayaki to be a very sweet language and attributed its musical sound to the purity of the forest streams from which the Ka'aygua drank. But they were not able to go on observing the Indians for long; these barbarians turned out to be so stubborn and so unwilling to imitate the example of the Christians that most of them preferred to die of hunger, while the rest returned to the shady woods to be tormented by the devil. The Jesuits were discouraged and had no desire to repeat such a futile experiment. Nothing more was heard about the Guayaki until the beginning of the twentieth century; their existence would have been taken for a myth if from time to time there had not been news of one of their attacks, exaggerated out of all proportion.

Although the Jesuits were mainly dedicated to spreading the faith, they were also learned men, fascinated by the strange spectacle of the New World and its inhabitants, whose customs and beliefs they recorded, interpreting them as the work of the devil. Thus the archives of the Society constituted a sort of encyclopedia of America, and all this knowledge, patiently accumulated over the decades, provided Father Pedro Lozano with the raw material for his elegant and erudite *History of the Conquest of Paraguay*, which he was commissioned to write. He worked on it for more than twenty years, visiting each "colony," examining all the documents, and questioning all the witnesses; his work was not completed until long afterward, when the Jesuits were expelled from America in 1768. This *History* is packed with information not only about the tribes which were converted to Christianity, but also about the infidels, including the Guayaki.

Until quite recently, all we knew about the Guayaki was contained in the few pages Lozano devoted to them. Yet the picture he painted, though necessarily incomplete, was very accurate, as I was able to verify. The Jesuits had been given valuable information about the Guachagui — as Lozano calls them — by the Guarani a century before Lozano made use of it. Arms, tools, containers for carrying liquids (water and honey), ornaments, the haircuts of the men and women, the setting up of camps, hunting and fishing techniques — all this was correctly described, and it is a shame that Lozano is so brief. But when he comes to the question of religious beliefs, Lozano, like all missionaries, is disappointingly banal and ethnocentric; he simply expresses the orthodox point of view of the Society and does not pass on the concrete information provided him by his Guarani informants:

"Where religion is concerned," he writes, "they have no false beliefs or superstition and they do not worship any objects; quite simply, they have an elementary knowledge of one true God, Creator of heaven and earth, and some very vague memories that the wicked are punished by flame and fire, which causes them to be fearful."

This is a complete distortion of the Guayaki's religious universe, invented to serve the cause and without much imagination. Lozano simply credits the Guayaki with a Christian conception of a creator, of good and evil, and even of hell! Much more interesting are his brief notes on the Atchei's society: "Sometimes they wage civil wars against one another; and generally the reason for this is to steal each other's women, because there are so few of them — there are far more men, something which is surely very rare in the West Indies." Here Lozano is remarking on a peculiarity of the Guayaki that is still true today: there are many more men than women, whereas the opposite is usually true in other Indian tribes. I was struck by this when I arrived in Arroyo Moroti: Jyvukugi's group consisted of exactly fourteen men and seven women. This lack of women in itself was enough to explain "the civil wars" fought by the various Atchei tribes: they were trying to take what they did not have. But why were there so few women? Lozano said nothing about it because he knew nothing about the Guayaki's religion.

There is actually no need to search for some biological anomaly to explain the imbalance in the sex ratio; the lack of women is a direct result of the Indians' ritual life, which is in turn involved with their beliefs. It required some patience for me to get to know these beliefs, and what I was able to learn was in certain respects terrifying.

For the moment, I would like to continue comparing the observations of the Guarani made in the sixteenth and seventeenth centuries with those I made a few years ago. In Lozano's book there is a very curious passage just before the section on the Guayaki. It concerns the Ka'aygua Indians, a term used by the Guarani to designate not one tribe in particular but the undifferentiated group of tribes living near them, their inferiors. But what is said about them corresponds so perfectly to the Guayaki that there can be no doubt: these Ka'aygua are the Atchei.

The most surprising point is that Lozano locates them very precisely between the Paraná and the Uruguay Rivers, whereas the Paraná was always considered the eastern limit of Guayaki territory. Except for Lozano's notation, which we have no reason to doubt, no one has ever mentioned the Ka'aygua as living in that area; what is more, no one has ever discovered a people living there who conformed to Lozano's description. What should we conclude from this? Not that these people existed only in Lozano's imagination, since I was able to recognize the Guayaki from his description, but that the Atchei who lived beyond the "great river" (which is what *Paraná* means) had vanished — either exterminated or assimilated by the Guarani at about the same time people were beginning to talk about them.

This is not unusual: there are thousands of such examples in the tragic history of the Indians, both in North and South America, except that in most cases the Indians were massacred by white men before the killers even knew their victims' names. But to continue quoting Lozano: "The customs and spirit of the *Caaiguas* are among the most barbarous anyone has discovered in America.... They live between the Uruguay and Paraná Rivers, on the lands of our Paraguay missions. There are very few people in this nation, and apparently the reason for this is that they are continually attacked by jaguars and wild animals in the woods; because they are not at all unified and each is separated from the others, they cannot help one another and are buried in impenetrable woods, forced into them by these same wild animals who disturb their tranquillity."

And now I will note something that happened in January 1963, as if no time had passed between the period in which the Guarani were giving the Jesuits information and the moment when the Atchei Gatu told me about this incident. One of the two bands that made up the tribe had been walking through the forest for several days along familiar paths marked by felled *pindo* palm trees, which had been cut down a few months earlier, before the *duy pute*, the great frost of June and July. Meanwhile, the *mynda*, the fat beetles that lay their eggs in the hollow trunks, had filled the *pindo*, which were scattered over the ground, in sections two or three yards long: to the insects, this was an invitation to make

119

their homes there; these trees had been especially prepared for them. When the warm season came, the Guayaki could gather wonderful quantities of *guchu*, the rich grubs of the *mynda*. This was the Indians' nourishing summer delicacy. Besides being sweet to the palate, the oily yellow cream enclosed in a small wriggling sack two to four inches long was 90 percent fat: "*Eaah! e gatu! Oh! how sweet it is!*" With hatchets the Indians joyously split open the trunks, which look cancerous, having been eaten away by the gluttonous grubs that feed on their sweet cores. Once the half-rotten trunks have been opened, you can see the tunnels in the mass of fibers, where dozens of enormous *mynda* grubs live. Before digging in, you put your ear against the trunk: the inside of a dead tree should be a chamber of silence, yet you will hear the hideous sound of living things swarming and crawling around. Any moment they will break through the protective bark and creep into your ear! The hatchets thump, splinters fly, a revolting smell of rot rises in the air, and the women load their baskets with pounds and pounds of grubs: the insects form a whitish mass of living matter that seems to boil at the bottom of the green baskets.

So the Atchei made the rounds of their "animal farms" or plantations — as if the insects' eggs were grain in the trunks of the trees. They feasted on the *guchu* they had gathered; but there was still a great deal left for their companions, who had remained behind in the camp, and they started back. The men walked in front; carrying only their bows and arrows, they stayed several hundred yards in front of the women, who were held back by their children and the heavy baskets they were carrying.

One of the men was Kybwyragi. His father, Paivagi, had not dared to set off on such a long walk; he was certain that his son would bring back lots of *guchu* to him at Arroyo Moroti. But his mother, Chachuwaimigi, had gone along. In spite of her age, she enjoyed the company of young men because they could give her what her old husband was hardly capable of any more. Eager to taste the joys of *meno*, love (which exasperated Paivagi), she still seemed quite vigorous. But this time she had overestimated her strength: she found it more and more difficult to keep up with the pace set by the other women, even though it was quite slow and she was not carrying much in her basket; she had to lean on a big stick. She really was *waimi*, old.

Yet she did not complain. It would have been useless; no one would have paid any attention. The others would even have scolded her if she had moaned: it would have been incongruous, even in bad taste. If you could walk, you walked; when you could not walk anymore, you stopped: as a young woman, this was what she herself had believed about the old women who were slowing down the pace of the group. She had never been bothered by the thought of what happened to *waimi* when they became too heavy a load for the band to drag around with them. Maybe it would be her turn soon; but for the moment she had to go on. The women ahead of her continued at the same pace, and little by little she was left behind; in spite of all her efforts, the gap widened: *ika mano ruwy*, her bones were almost dead, her body was exhausted. The quiet sound of brushwood being snapped underfoot by the women ahead became fainter, and soon she could not hear it any more. Chachuwaimigi was alone, and silence returned to the forest.

Kybwyragi, who was completely absorbed in looking at the ground around him, did not concern himself with what was going on behind him. It was certainly true that his mother was *waimi*, but as long as he could remember she had never had any trouble walking. Perhaps this would not be the case much longer; then someone would say: "*Wata kwa ia.* She can't walk anymore." Everyone would understand what that meant. But apparently things had not reached that point yet. Kybwyragi had already accepted

121

the fact that his mother's life would end this way. He knew that sooner or later she would have to be killed — as soon as she could not walk anymore. A young man chosen by the rest of the Atchei would approach her from behind and break her skull with one blow from his stone hatchet, after which they would proceed with the funeral ceremonies, in accordance with the teachings of their ancestors. This was the fate of old Guayaki women. Kybwyragi knew all this, loved his mother very much, and never thought about it. Suddenly one of the hunters cried out in alarm: "*Veno gatu!* Listen!" In the distance, where the women were, something was happening. Although the forest tended to muffle noises, the practiced hearing of the men quickly recognized what was going on: "*Baipu! Baipu koro!* A jaguar! A jaguar is *roaring!*" They ran back the way they had come, to protect the women and children. The women and children had heard it too, but did not feel threatened because the noise was coming from farther back. The wild animal bellowed, more and more enraged. The Atchei could easily interpret his noises; from a distance, without being able to see him, they understood the jaguar, who was telling them everything he was doing. He had found his quarry and should have been able to knock it out silently with one blow of his paw; but his prey had dodged his attack and was warding him off: this was why the *baipu* was irritated. Yet his loud snarling showed that he was not giving up; he was going to attack again. The terrified women had clapped their hands to their ears; the men listened, arrows poised on the strings of their bows, waiting. Kybwyragi waited for the jaguar to finish with his mother. She had not yet cried out; she was undoubtedly trying to frighten the animal off by waving her stick. No one said anything, everyone listened: they would have been crazy to interfere with a situation in which a woman was taking her first step out of the world of the living. They had to show respect for her. What could be done when the hour of *mano* came for an Atchei? Things had to be left to take their course. Someone would have had to kill the old woman soon anyway: the *baipu* was relieving the Atchei of this duty, and no man was ever very happy about accepting the role of *brupiare*, killer (or rather, sacrificer).

But for this very reason, the jaguar, who had happened along at an opportune time, was undoubtedly not really a jaguar. From the outside he certainly looked like one: *baipu pini pute*, a well-spotted jaguar. But appearances meant nothing. The Guayaki were able to look beyond appearances, strong in the wisdom that one hundred generations of forefathers had accumulated. This jaguar was really an Atchei, an ancestor who had changed himself into a *baipu*. There would be plenty of time to identify him once they were back in the camp; the old people would give their opinions.

But already Kybwyragi thought that his grandfather, who died before Kybwyragi ever knew him, had briefly left the resting place of the spirits — the large savanna that lay toward the setting sun above the surface of the earth. The *jamogi* had come back down into the forest to take away his daughter, Chachuwaimigi. The old balance would be restored: the daughter would rejoin her father, and the early separation would no longer exist. They would be together again up above, where there is no need to hunt anymore, where there is no forest. Or else maybe it was Kychangi, Chachuwaimigi's other son, who had been killed by the white men. Perhaps he had assumed the form of the jaguar, unable to tolerate being separated from his mother. So he had come back to get her, *ai*, mother: they were destined to be reunited.

There were cries: the jaguar had pounced on his puny adversary. The *baipu*'s snarling became briefer, as though he was panting: he had won. There was a cry of horror, but it was not an appeal for help: the woman was beyond speech, she was already far away. Chachuwaimigi was dead. Kybwyragi and his companions went on toward Arroyo Moroti: *kranve*, he was an orphan. There was no need to go and see what had happened because he could guess, he knew. And it was wiser to avoid the place because, in addition to the jaguar, *Ianve* was prowling around there now — *Ianve*, the wicked spirit of the dead people who cannot bear their solitude and try to carry the living off with them. Later, when his mother's bones had been cleaned by the jaguar and the passage of time, they would sing the words of death.

Two or three months later, Kwantirogi, Kybwyragi's younger brother, lay shivering in his *tapy*. He was sick, and every now and then he would be shaken by a fit of coughing. I offered him cold pills, assuring him that he would feel better the next day if he took them. "No," he said, "*cho kwera ia, cho manuvera.* I will not get better, I'm going to die." "Why?" "*Ianve ikemba. Ianve* has entered me completely." "Who is it?" "A certain person. She was the 'god-mother' of Chachuwaimigi, my mother." He stopped talking. He was depressed. His wife told me that he really was going to die, that soon she would be a widow, and that she would be very sad. But why? Because the *Ianve* of this woman had entered Kwantirogi's body to make him sick and kill him. She wanted him for her husband up there in heaven, in the home of the spirits. She was doing this to avenge her goddaughter, Chachuwaimigi.

One could never get rid of the dead; they were always trying to come back; *Ianve* was very dangerous, it could torment people terribly. Almost all sicknesses, all accidents, were caused by *Ianve*. The dead were clever; they waged an incessant war against the living: *Ache, ro ianve reko ju'e ia.* As for the Atchei, *Ianve* did not want them to exist. The dead had a longer memory than the living. The living easily forgot them, but the dead remained vigilant. Kwantirogi had been very moved by the death of his mother. He felt that he was condemned, and so he wanted to sing of his pain, as is customary when there is an excess of sorrow. At such

124

times, the only solace is a violent duel fought with wooden bows or a lament accompanied by a flute.

The next day he prepared his *mimby*, made up of four rosewood pipes of different lengths bound together by a small piece of creeper bark. When he was ready, I set up the tape recorder microphone in front of him; it obviously did not bother him at all. His chanting went on for a long time, broken into clearly intoned verses; between each verse, the flute sounded its four sad and despairing notes. It was quite cool and gray that day, and the only sound that could be heard in the camp was the music of the *mimby* and the man's recitative.

"My mother is no more, and for that I weep mightily. I will not go into the forest, because when I go there, I think of how my mother is no more, and I weep.

"Then I remember how when I went there I saw, I saw my mother's bones, the jaguar had eaten them, the larger bones were scattered: I saw that, just as I saw the skull. Then I shouted to Kajawachugi: 'There is my mother's skull! Strike the skull!' And then Kajawachugi struck it.

"There. I am really an orphan. And being really an orphan means that I will not go into the forest anymore: I will stay near my very weak father. I won't go anymore, I won't go running through the forest.

"My mother was the sort of person who gave a great deal, that I know. How much *guchu* she brought! That makes me cry. I will no longer go into the forest.

"My mother, my mother Chachuwaimigi, she didn't eat the *guchu*, she was bringing it for me, quantities of it, I know that. And knowing that, I cry.

"This is the way it was: my mother did not eat the *guchu*, this I know. She gave it away. My mother was someone who gave a great deal. This is why I no longer want to go into the forest.

125

"*Go!* Yes! Even though she was one of the old ones, my mother went off to look for *guchu*. I know it. And I also know that my brother Kychangi, who is dead, carried off his mother. He took her off to the sun. In the sun, near my mother, my mother, that is where my brother is; she is near Kychangi, her child. He carried off my mother, they left for the sun.

"There. I am an orphan. I saw my mother's skull struck again and again. Kajawachugi is the one who struck my mother's skull. With his bow he struck it, on the ground, he drove it deep into the earth; he beat it with his bow and drove it deep into the earth.

"The bones and the skull, my eyes saw them, my mother's head, the bones completely separated from one another, which the jaguar broke and broke again, the skull, which he ate. Then I cried, and Kajawachugi took his bow and struck the bones. He drove them into the earth, drove them deep with his bow.

"This is why I, who am really an orphan now, will not go into the forest: because an orphan who goes into the forest will be torn apart by the paw of the jaguar. The Atchei have warned me about this: 'You, orphan, if you go into the forest, the jaguar will tear you apart! Don't go back into the forest!' Well, I listened to them, and I won't go into the forest. I will stay near my very weak father.

"This flute — it is because of my mother who is no more, this flute is mourning my mother; and I, an orphan, I will no longer go anywhere.

"This flute — is the person who will no longer go into the forest, this flute; and as for me, I know very well that my mother has been eaten by the *ka jarete*, the great wildcat. I have seen it: Kajawachugi struck the bones hard with his bow, I saw it when he took his bow and buried them deep in the ground.

"I am really an orphan now, and I won't go into the forest. Even if I were starving, I would cry if I went there. Where my very weak father is, there is lots of manioc, lots of what we call *wyra-ia*, the fruit of the tree."

Day after day, and in almost the same phrases, Kwantirogi declaimed this funeral oration, which is called *ai iko ia bu*, "when the mother is no longer." Perhaps his chanting would frustrate the maneuvers of the *Ianve*, who wanted to "avenge" Chachuwaimigi by killing him, her son.

As it turned out, he survived his flu. He was not at all troubled by his recovery, nor was his wife, even though both of them had assured me only the day before that he was on the point of dying. During my stay among them, I was given numerous opportunities to observe the subtlety of the Indians' thinking and the curious reversals that were an inherent part of their view of the world.

Lozano knew that the Ka'aygua nomads were occasionally attacked by jaguars, and Chachuwaimigi's pitiable fate was a useful reminder to me that this animal poses a considerable threat to anyone who happens to run across him in the forest. Other, much more precise details convinced me that the Ka'aygua were the Guayaki: "Among them there are some deformed people whose deformity is quite extraordinary; their noses in almost every case are so flat that they look more like monkeys' noses than men's; some are hunchbacked, with necks so short that they do not even emerge from their shoulders; and others are afflicted with imperfections in their physique which accurately manifest the imperfections in their souls." This is a very Christian theory; it is even somewhat influenced by Spinoza, according to whom the soul is the idea of the body: a deformed body can only house a demonic soul. Lozano clearly never saw a Guayaki. The photographs I brought back prove that none of them was deformed; and the Guarani obviously would never have said anything of the kind to the Jesuits. The allusion to the short necks of the Guayaki was closer to the truth, however. Not that they have fewer vertebrae in their necks than we do, but the fact is that the Guayaki are not strikingly graceful, the way other Indians are. I should say right away, however, that this is only true of the men: the women have very lovely necks. And the men's shoulder and neck muscles are highly developed and are therefore very broad and thick: it would be more accurate to say they have bulls' necks rather than short necks. The Guayaki's physical strength is almost unbelievable, as is shown by the size and tension of their bows. This is all the more remarkable, considering that they are rather short. Since the average height of the men is sixty-two inches, they seem almost as broad as they are tall. I occasionally played at fighting with boys about ten years old, and I could already feel in my little adversaries the hardness and compactness that would later develop into the strength of full-grown men. If my observations were correct, therefore, Lozano's conclusions were false: the Guayaki's necks were not abnormal.

As soon as I arrived in Arroyo Moroti, my attention was attracted by the shape of some of the Indians' noses. A few of them — by no means all — seemed to have no bone in their noses, or at least such a small one that it could not support the nose. As a result, their noses seemed flattened and sunk in the face; they hardly protruded at all, and instead of pointing invisibly downward from above their lips, the openings of the nostrils seemed to be extensions of the lips, so that when you looked at them you saw two yawning orifices at the base of a minuscule appendage. This would be sure to attract attention and cause one to remark on the appearance of the faces, which were in fact rather simian even though their expressions were in no way affected by it — as witness the features of Pichugi, the Atchei Gatu woman whose child I saw being born.

It was the sight of the ritual accompanying the birth which

helped me to understand what I believe to be the cause of this anomaly, which Lozano reported so accurately. As we saw, when the newborn "falls" out of his mother's womb, he is bathed and then receives a massage over his whole body, the *piy*. As for the head, it receives special treatment: the *to papy*, "rounding the head," is supposed to give the skull the spherical shape that is considered the most beautiful. But sometimes the rough hands of the *jware*, who washes and massages the infant, press too hard on the frail bones of the *kromi*; the nose remains flattened and tilts up, somewhat like a monkey's nose. Naturally, this does not happen every time, and no doubt that is why only some of the Indians look the way Lozano described them. Yet this peculiar characteristic, which I have not observed in any other tribe, convinces me that the historian's Caaigua are the Guayaki.

But there is more. After painting the unflattering picture of deformed monsters, Lozano goes on to say: "Nevertheless, their color is usually white, very different from the dark hue of the other Indians, because they live in places where the rays of the sun cannot burn them; and when they are forced to live outside their woods, they quickly give up their hold on life, like fish out of their element." This comparison between the Caaigua and fish incapable of living out of water has some basis in fact.

The Guayaki are *completely ka'aygua*, that is, "forest people," woodsmen: they would not be able to live anywhere else; they are afraid of open spaces and avoid the savanna. Isn't the home of the dead a sinister place, a *prana wachu*, a great savanna? The Atchei only feel at ease, body and soul, in the thick shade of the *kaa*, the forest. They hardly even know how to walk on the smooth grass of the clearings. Many times I saw them swaying their hips strangely as they walked, carefully lifting their feet and turning them inward, as though they were not surrounded by all the space they could possibly need, as though there were a tree trunk in front of them which they had to step over or a creeper they had to walk around. From earliest childhood the forest had been embedded in their daily habits, the movements of their bodies, in their bones, their nerves, and their muscles, and the Atchei could not forget it; if they found themselves in the savanna, they would walk across it as though there were imaginary trees in their way — they looked suddenly like ducks. Lozano was right: how could the Caaigua survive away from their homeland, when they found it so difficult to walk in a *prana*? "*Go. Ache ro pranare*. Yes. The Atchei originally came from the savanna," say the myths describing their origin; but, "*Kaari ro ure etoa*. Our home is in the forest" is the answer given by their daily life. The Atchei are forest people: *ka'aygua*.

The Jesuit's reference to the color of their skin is significant in another way, because it implies the presence of white men in America, the presence of a white but not Western element in the New World. It also removes any doubt about the true identity of the Caaigua in the chronicle: like the others, these are Atchei. The existence of the Guayaki illustrates one of the myths about the conquest of America and at the same time gives it a basis in fact: these are white Indians — but only to a certain extent, of course, as I shall try to show.

The native peoples of the continent present a wide variety of physical types, but they all share certain recurring features that clearly group them in the Amerindian racial type and classify them as Mongoloids: large and prominent cheekbones, a palpebral fold (the "Asiatic" look), black, bushy hair — which they rarely lose — very little hair on their bodies and even less on their faces, and finally, a copper skin color, which is darker or lighter depending on the region and the tribe. The Guarani, for example, are lighter than the Chaco Indians.

From the time of the very earliest explorations in South America, there were allusions to white savages in the stories and reports brought back by travelers, soldiers, and missionaries; they were mentioned by other Indians, who almost always described them as very timid or very aggressive. But these stories were largely the result of the fact that no one knew much about the inhabitants of the immense forests. No one had ever actually seen any white Indians, and for a long time these reports were ignored. Quite reasonably, too, since there had been no direct observation of such populations to provide irrefutable proof that they existed. But now we can no longer deny the facts; Lozano was not making up what he reported: the Caaigua of the seventeenth century could very well have been white, because the modern day Atchei are white.

Not that the Guayaki all belong to the same physical type. The anthropological problem they pose is complicated by the fact that the skin color of individual members of the tribe ranges all the way from the Indian's classical copper, though less pronounced, to white — not the European's pinkish white, but a dull, grayish white, like the gray skin of a sick person. Between these two extremes there is a whole range of pigmentation, and it is hard to know whether to call them more or less coppery or more or less white. Naturally, the eyes and the cheekbones are Mongoloid. So I found it rather strange to see white-skinned "Asiatics." What is more, the Guayaki themselves distinguish between members of the tribe who are *pire i ju*, white skins, and *pire pira*, redskins, though they do not see either one as being superior to the other. Sometimes a child is born with very dark skin — *pire braa*, black skin. This unusual skin color is very worrying to them, because they think it must have been caused by one of the wicked creatures that lurk in the night and blend into the darkness because of their black skin. For this reason, the newborn child must be killed, and its grandmother strangles it.

131

Strangely enough, I saw beards on these pale faces — on the faces of the men, at least — even though Indians are usually hairless. If a man's beard becomes very thick, this attribute is sometimes incorporated into his name: Chachubutawachugi, for example, had been given the name Chachu — Large Wild Pig — when he was born, but was now (at the age of about forty) called Chacu with the Great Beard, so thick and long was the mop of hair that had grown over his face.

One preoccupation is shared by all Indians: to keep reaffirming their humanity and protecting it from the natural world, protecting themselves from being swallowed up by the savagery of nature, which is always on the lookout for human beings, always eager to reclaim them. They therefore consider it a point of honor, both ethically and aesthetically, to differentiate themselves from animals — or rather, to make the most of the differences that exist. Animals are hairy, and men are not, except in certain places on the body — the armpits, the pubic region, eyebrows, eyelashes, and sometimes on the tip of the chin in older men, where there are scattered little wisps of hair. But even though this is not much, it must be removed so that there will be no confusion between the human body and the body of an animal. Like ascetics, they do violence to their bodies. Their bodies must bear the mark of culture, the proof that they have emerged from nature and can never return to it: they must pluck out their hair. And this is no small matter: it is actually a form of torture that men, women, and even children periodically inflict on themselves. Several techniques are commonly used: the most widespread consists of tearing out the hair with tweezers made of a flexible twig. It makes the skin and eyelids red and irritated: the Indians suffer not only in order to be beautiful, but also — and this really amounts to the same thing — to make sure their faces keep a truly human identity. They get rid of everything that

132

might be a disagreeable reminder of the ugliness and stupidity of animals.

The Guayaki were not very concerned about plucking their body hair, because they had enough to worry about with their beards: *buta jupi* means shave the beard, just as *rapa jupi* means polish the bow. They did shave themselves, or at least the women shaved their husbands. They would use a splinter of bamboo and scrape it again and again across the skin, which they would keep taut between their thumbs and index fingers. In return for this, the men would cut the women's hair with the same tool.

They stopped performing these services for one another as soon as we arrived in Arroyo Moroti and handed out small mirrors to the Indians; they had never seen mirrors before and immediately called them *chaa*, eyes, just as they called my glasses *chaa beta, tembeta*, eyes. They were not merely surprised when, like Plato's prisoner leaving the cave and looking at his reflection in the water, they saw their faces in the *chaa* for the first time: it would be more accurate to say that they were spellbound. For half an hour at a time, even for an hour, they would look at themselves (especially the men), sometimes holding the mirror at arm's length, sometimes right under their noses, dumb with astonishment to see this face, which belonged to them but which they could not feel: when they tried to touch it with their fingertips, they felt only the cold, hard surface of the *chaa*. Sometimes they turned the mirror around to see what was behind it. The Atchei were very excited about the *chaa*, and they all wanted to own one. This passion even provoked behavior that was rare among Indians: the desire to hoard. Several women actually accumulated as many as five or six mirrors, which they stuffed in their baskets and brought out from time to time to examine.

When I later showed the Guayaki photographs, they almost never recognized their friends and never themselves. The children, on the other hand, showed great quickness of perception and soon learned to identify faces. One day, three or four Indians were looking at an old French newspaper I had lying around my hut; they were murmuring and touching the faces of people in photographs. I listened to them and discovered that they were naming the people: "Who is that?" "That's Chachuanegi," they answered without hesitation, pointing to a round-faced, jovial *Beeru* wearing a large hat and a tie: it was Krushchev. Acting on a whim, I asked one man if he recognized the Nambikwara adolescent on the cover of *Tristes Tropiques*. He studied it very seriously then exclaimed loudly, "*Teeh!*" And with a wide smile that clearly showed he was not going to make a mistake, as though I had been trying to catch him napping, he said: "*Go ro cho!* That's me!"

Lozano was accurate in describing the Caaigua, and his observations support the Paraguayans' legends about white-skinned, blue-eyed Guayaki. This last detail about blue eyes is untrue, but in any case both tribes belong to the same group and are racially different from the rest of the Indians because of the color of their skin. And the fact that Lozano's Caaigua lived beyond the Paraná simply means that there was a time when these people, who were of older stock than the Guarani, occupied a much vaster territory than the modern-day Guayaki. The Ka'aygua, who had no doubt been regressing culturally for a much longer time than the Atchei, already lived a completely nomadic life at the time of the conquest: "They are so lacking in the ability to plan ahead that they cannot even plan for their subsistence," the historian wrote, "since their only way of feeding themselves is by hunting and fishing when they happen to come across something in the forest or the river; but most of them feed off of grubs, snakes, rats, ants, or other vermin which they can find without any difficulty. Forest honey is their greatest delicacy and hydromel (honey mead) is their ambrosia, heating them so well that they can resist the cold of winter." By contrast, this is what he says about the Guayaki: "Although they wander here and there through the forests, looking for forest honey, fruits and animals for their food, they also plant corn; but their harvests are not abundant, because they like to eat it when it is tender, before it has ripened...." At a time when the Ka'aygua had already lost their knowledge of agriculture, therefore, the Atchei still knew how to cultivate corn. But undoubtedly they soon regressed even further and gave up planting corn for good. It had become too risky — the insecurity of their way of life forced them to flee from their gardens too often, leaving behind the ears of corn they were not able to gather to the birds and rodents.

All the latest allusions depict them as purely nomadic. And when I talked to the Guayaki about cultivated plants (which they had never stopped eating, since over the centuries they continued to steal manioc and corn from the Guarani and then the Paraguayans), it appeared that they had no word for *to plant* in their vocabulary and that they had no memory at all of their ancestors' practice of agriculture: "*Beeru ro wyraia wate rekopa; ure Ache reko ia*. The white men are the ones who have manioc and corn; we Atchei have nothing." They say this without bitterness; this is the way things have always been, ever since the beginning of time, when everything was divided up between the Indians and the white men, beteween the poor and the rich. The Guarani feel the same way; fate gave the white men the lion's share, but what falls to the Indians must remain theirs and must not be given up to the white men.

For four centuries, the Mbya (whom the Atchei call the Machitara) have resisted conversion to Christianity. Even now, when the vices and diseases of the white men, of the *Juru'a, those with large mouths*, are ruining their health and destroying their children, even now, when they might believe that their gods have abandoned them, the Mbya continue to resist. Just a few years ago, one of those rude, uncultivated, and boorish men who too frequently become missionaries as an outlet for their paranoia or their stupidity (usually these missionaries are American Protestants rather than Catholics) went to pester Vera (Lightning), the great chieftain of the Mbya. The Indian was meditatively smoking in front of his hut, dressed in stinking rags and listening to the edifying chatter of the *Juru'a*, who was talking to him about God and salvation. Tired of this absurd situation, Vera got up, disappeared into his *tapyi*, and came back out transfigured: the miserable tramp of a moment before had metamorphosed into a god, a *karai ru ete*. The white men's rags had been thrown off: on his head he was wearing a *jeguaka*, the men's ritual ornament, which was a cotton headpiece with a colorful crown of feathers on top and fringes that fell down over his naked back; his only clothing was a cotton loincloth; in his hand, he held a stick of finely polished hardwood, the *ywyra'i*, symbol of his leadership. There was a nimbus of stormy light around the chief, the *mburuvicha*: *he who is great by the strength of his faith in the gods.* And now the dumbfounded evangelist heard the thunderous voice of Lightning: "Hear me, *Juru'a*! You white men were given the savanna and an abundance of things. We Mbya were left with the forest and a few things. Let it continue this way. Let the white men stay where they belong. We Mbya will not disturb you in your homes. We are Ka'aygua, the forest dwellers. Go away from my house, go, never come back!"

I enjoyed Jyvukugi's company very much. In every respect he was an excellent informant: because he was the chief, he was very familiar with the traditional knowledge of the tribe, and he showed scrupulous intellectual honesty. When he was not sure if he had remembered something correctly, he would appeal to another

Indian. For all these reasons, I spent many hours with him when he did not have to go hunting in the forest. One afternoon I was listening distractedly to a banal conversation he was having with his wife. After a moment, I realized that I no longer understood anything they were saying and saw that, instead of talking, *they were whistling*! I should explain this, at least to the extent that I could grasp what was happening. I do not believe this was a type of communication different from ordinary language, as sign language would be, for example. Rather, I suspect that what I heard was a *whistled language* that had nothing to do with articulated language and whose tone, loudness, and modulation contained a meaning perceptible to someone familiar with the code. This is quite possible, especially since similar modes of expression have been discovered among other populations. But in this case, I think it was the normal language in a distorted form.

As I listened to this surprising dialogue (which I unfortunately did not have a chance to record), what I heard was mainly whistling sounds such as *tss, dzz, djj* — explosions interrupted by abrupt glottal stops and followed by long vocalized expirations ending in a simple expulsion of air. Naturally, I could not decipher any of this. And yet this was ordinary Guayaki — a language I could understand to some extent — but reduced to that part of its consonantal structure that could be whistled and to breathed vowels. Basically it was the language as anyone could have whispered it, reduced to its simplest perceptible expression. The small range of sounds produced did not seem to affect the liveliness of the discussion that Jyvukugi and his wife were carrying on at a great rate; they even seemed to be having a very good time, and sometimes their faces would shake with repressed laughter. I also noticed that from time to time I would hear nothing and only their lips would be moving: instead of listening to the sound of the whistling, they were reading each other's lips. It was this that led me to think that this way of talking was not a true whistled language. Why had the Guayaki created this strange way of communicating? I can only guess at the reason, but I do have one hypothesis. The main quality of this method of manipulating the language by deforming it was really its quasi-silence, which situated it halfway between sound and gesture. And I imagine that, out of fear for their safety, the Atchei had determined to minimize the chances of being overheard by their enemies: the ghosts of the dead or, more plausibly, the Machitara and *Beeru*. But perhaps, in the end, this supposition is too pragmatic, and we should instead look for an explanation in the mythological character of Jakarendy, the master of honey, who did not speak but whistled in order to attract human beings and shoot his fern arrows at them.

In any case, I am almost sure that that day Jyvukugi and his wife were "whistling" instead of talking in a normal way so that I would not understand what they were saying to each other. And they were completely successful in doing that.

At the time, I did not pay too much attention to this. It was only after I had returned to France and reread Lozano's book that I realized how interesting the incident was. Lozano says the following in reference to the Caaigua: "They make use of a peculiar language which is difficult to learn because, when they speak it, it would be more accurate to say that they whistle it; or rather they make a sort of murmuring noise in the back of their throats without forming any words." Once again, I admired the exactness of the information that the Guarani had given the Jesuits and the faithfulness with which the historian had reproduced it. Among the Guayaki I could imagine that I was living several centuries earlier, when America had not yet been discovered.

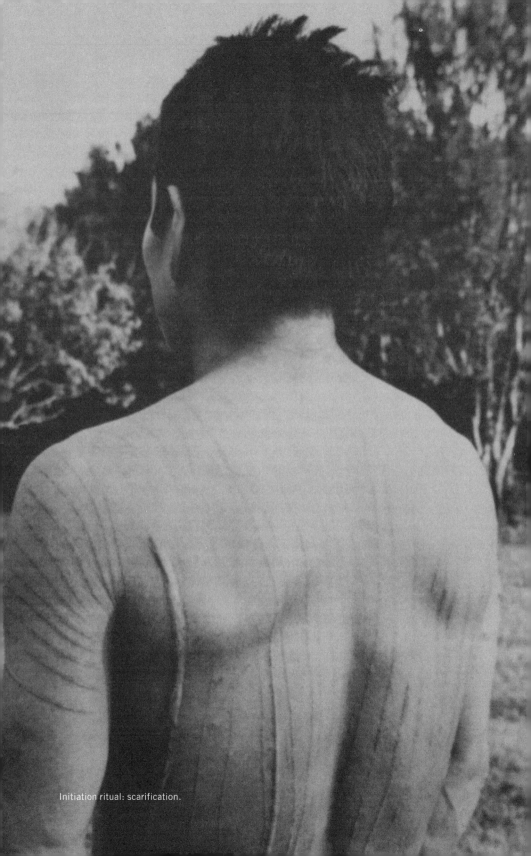

Initiation ritual: scarification.

Young Chachugi's initiation ritual.

CHAPTER FOUR

The Grown-ups

"There are no grown-ups," someone wrote recently. This is a strange remark to make in our civilization, which prides itself on being the epitome of adulthood. But for this very reason, it might well be true, at least for our world. For once we step outside our own boundaries, whatever is true for us in Europe no longer applies. We ourselves may never become adults, but that does not mean there are no grown-ups elsewhere. The question is: Where is the visible frontier of our culture, at what stage along the road do we reach the limit of our domain, where do different things exist and new meanings begin? This is not a rhetorical question, for we are able to situate the answer in a definite time and place. Earlier, when the answer seemed to be given to us arbitrarily, no one worried about the question it was responding to. Nevertheless, the answer came at the end of the fifteenth century, when Christopher Columbus discovered the people from beyond — the savages of America.

In the islands, in Montezuma's Mexico, and on the shores of Brazil, the white men crossed the absolute limit of their world for the first time, a limit that they immediately identified as the dividing line between civilization and barbarity. Much more than the inhabitants of Africa, who were in some subtle way closer to the old European world, the Indians represented all that was alien to the West. They were the Other, and the West did not hesitate to annihilate them. The redskins would later share this sad privilege with the other true savages. They were all inhabitants of a world that was no longer meant for them: the Eskimos, the Bushmen, the Australians. It is probably too early to gauge the most important consequences of this meeting. It was fatal for the Indians; but by some strange twist of fate it might also turn out to be the cause of the unexpected death of our own history, the history of our world in its present form. This does not prevent us from wondering, however, if "there are no grown-ups" among the Indians either.

At Arroyo Moroti there was a relatively large number of children in spite of the fact that the Paraguayans had carried off so many of them: twelve among the Atchei Gatu and about twenty among the *Iroiangi*, most between the ages of five and twelve. The small number of newborn babies and small children was evidence of the troubles the Atchei had experienced during the past few years. How could they take proper care of a *kromi* when they had to keep running away from white killers? The women were constantly on the alert to the needs of their babies, and at the first cry of a little one — who lay in the carrying sling that always hung at his mother's side as though he were in a minuscule hammock — his mother would silence him by stuffing a tasty little tidbit into his open mouth. But how could the women shower their babies with all the tenderness they needed when they were constantly worn down by the fear of seeing the white men carry off their children? Their terror at the approach of the *Beeru* and their dogs was so great that within a few seconds the women would go crazy, forgetting the *kromi* who lay on a mat beside them and plunging straight ahead into the forest.

The Atchei remember how one woman died: she had gone off

alone carrying a three-year-old boy on her back. She had the bad luck to come upon a group of *Beeru*, who immediately chased after her. She would have escaped them, since she was more skilled at running through the woods than they were, but she had to cross a clearing. She rushed ahead, and as she was about to reach the other side, she felt the child bounce against her and heard a loud explosion. The impact knocked her forward, throwing the child to the ground. She turned around and saw that the bullet had split him nearly in two. She had no time to mourn him. A second bullet was fired, and she joined her son in the *prana wachu* of the dead.

A gaucho told me how just a few years ago, as he was looking for stray cows, he saw a woman gathering berries. She had not heard him approach, because his horse was walking on thick grass. He promptly took out his rope and lassoed her. He returned to the *estancia* dragging his prisoner behind him. The woman remained surprisingly calm. She talked volubly, making many gestures; no one understood. She pointed to her heavy breasts and made the gesture of nursing: she was explaining that she had left her child in the camp, that he had to be nursed, and that they should therefore let her go. The men were very amused by her pantomime. They were also astonished to see a Guayaki express the same feelings as their own wives. But they kept her so that she could work for them; after several weeks in captivity, she finally managed to escape.

This was why there were few very young children in Arroyo Moroti. It was too hard for the women. They would become disheartened, and some of them, finding out that they were pregnant, would ask their husbands to perform *ykwa*, to give them an abortion. A man rarely refused to do this for his wife. He would press his fists against her belly with all his strength; sometimes he would kneel on her, and sometimes he would use a heavy piece of wood. The woman would suffer, turning and twisting under the pressure, but the pain would not make her give up what she had started. Other women preferred to wait until the child was born: they would then kill it immediately, either by striking it on the neck or by strangling it.

This should not be construed as a sign of indifference on the part of the Indians; on the contrary, it was very painful for them, but they had no choice. The white men had not been content merely to steal their *kromi*; they had even forced them to stop giving birth. These practices remained common until quite recently, but they were not caused by violence from the outside; they were carried out by choice, usually in order to avoid some future difficulty. If a girl found that she was pregnant by a lover whom she did not plan to marry, then she would perform an abortion on herself with her mother's help. Or when a married woman bore two children too close in age to one another, the second child would be killed, because the mother would not have been able to nurse two *kromi* simultaneously: Guayaki children, after all, were breast-fed until they were nearly three years old. The grandmother would be very upset if her daughter became pregnant again while the first child was still nursing: "*Nde bruaa wachu ma jove! Embogi mano vera!* You're big and pregnant again! The boy who is nursing will die!" she would scold sharply. These were actually sound practices; they safeguarded the balance of the group's population, ensured a good understanding between couples, and protected the children's health.

I spent the first weeks mainly in the company of the children, in particular with a gang of about ten of them ranging from seven to twelve years of age (the *kybuchu*) who, because of their age, were relatively independent of their parents and the adult group in general. The adults were not mistrustful of me, except for the *Iroiangi* to a certain extent. But they would quickly become tired

144

of my conversation, since it was mainly about subjects they found completely lacking in interest: who is your father, who is the sister of your mother, who is the brother of your mother, and so on. Sometimes the people whose names I wanted to know would be dead, and the Indians would find it distasteful to talk about them: "Who is your mother?" "She's dead." The answers to other questions were even more disconcerting to me: "What is the name for the brother of one's mother?" "My mother does not have a brother." Yet they knew the word *tuby*, maternal uncle.

The Indians' attention span usually did not last longer than fifteen minutes. Once this much time had gone by, they would yawn widely or keep saying *kwa ia* (I don't know), and I would see that it was useless to go on with the conversation. In vain, I heaped them with gifts of candy, which they appreciated because of its resemblance to honey. But now and then, overcome by an immense boredom, my informant would fall asleep on the ground at my feet.

I always gave out candy during these conversations, and once it resulted in a delightful exchange. Jakwachugi was already an old woman, even though her husband was no more than about thirty. Apparently the years had not diminished her taste for her husband's attentions, for when she learned one day that he had been guilty of committing adultery with a young woman, she gathered her things together in a rage, loaded up her basket, and went to join her son in another camp. I was once questioning Jakwachugi and saw that her attention was beginning to wane; she seemed more interested in the comings and goings of the camp than in my detailed questions about ancestors whom she hardly remembered. As usual, I said: "Would you like a piece of candy?" I used the Spanish word *caramelo*, which the Atchei have transformed into *kramero* and which they prefer to use over the Guayaki word for sweet things — *ee*, that which is sweet. "*Kramero?*" I suggested with an engaging smile. Jakwachugi, however, was a little hard of hearing and did not understand me, because her mouth dropped open and her eyes became incredulous: "*Meno? Meno nde jwe?* Make love? Do you want to make love?" Instead of *kramero*, she had heard *meno*, which means to make love. And she thought that I too was becoming tired of our conversation and was suggesting to her that we go lie down somewhere under the trees and forget her husband for a while. The misunderstanding was cleared up, but for several days after that Jakwachugi would look at me with a rather dreamy expression in her eyes.

In the beginning, then, it was a waste of time to go on questioning the Indians when they no longer felt like answering me — a waste of time for them and for me. The men would think about their arrows, hunting, honey, and the women about their *tapy* or their children — in other words, about everyday concerns. (A few months later, my friend Jakugi admitted to me: "When I saw you coming, *myryro jwe*, I wanted to run away.") For this reason, since I still wanted to accomplish the first stage of my work — familiarizing myself thoroughly with the language — I decided to form a friendship with the only Atchei who had enough time to teach it to me — the children, the *kybuchu*.

This project did not cost me much (a few pounds of candy, ten penknives, and a little trickery) and was crowned with success: a team of teachers was almost always available to me. Though they were sometimes boisterous and quick to tease their pupil, whose boots they particularly enjoyed stealing, they were unfailingly patient and kind. They were more realistic than their parents and understood very well that my Guayaki was rather limited, that they had to explain things to me almost as though I were an idiot, and that in the end I was what I was — a *Beeru*, who in exchange for very little would provide an abundance of *kramero*. Thanks to them, my vocabulary and my understanding of the syntax grew every day.

There were mistakes, of course: walking along with one of the boys one day, I pointed to our shadows, which moved over the ground in front of us and he said: *kapi*. I confidently made a note of this word in my notebook and only later realized that my young informant had actually given me the name of the grass that lay under our shadows. Most of the *kybuchu* — an age-group that more or less included boys from seven to fifteen — owned a bow and a set of arrows. Sometimes they were a gift from the father, sometimes from the *jware*, and sometimes even from a nonrelative: one of the Strangers, for example, had given his bow to Jyvukugi's son. Boys of that age were already well trained in handling their weapon; without going far away from the camp, they could spend hours alone in the woods stalking prey suitable to the power of their bows (which was not negligible). And it was not uncommon to see one of them return to his mother's hut and, with a false air of modesty on his face, throw one or two birds at her feet, saying briefly like a real hunter, "*Kybwyra cho eru*. Some birds that I have brought." The adults' congratulations are brief too, but highly valued by the hunter.

For the *kybuchu*, hunting is still a game, but they hunt as passionately as their elders. The day the tribe of *Iroiangi* arrived at Arroyo Moroti, the boys saw several domestic ducks owned by the Paraguayan swimming in the little pond in the center of the clearing. The boys thought that by a lucky chance wild birds had come there and, immediately forgetting that they were in the process of trying to enter the world of white men, they encircled the water and sent a shower of arrows at the ducks.

Until they are about three years old, the children never leave their mother's side — in fact, they hardly leave her for one second. As long as they cannot walk, they spend most of their time in the carrying sling or straddling their mother's hip. The mother usually carries her child wherever she goes, even if it is only to get

Dave, mat made of *pindo* leaves.

water or to collect wood for the fire. During his infancy, the baby and mother are in some sense welded together, day and night — and in almost complete silence, since the *kromi* is hardly ever given time to open his mouth and cry. In this respect, young Indian fathers are lucky: their sleep is not disturbed by angry howling. Furthermore, until the child takes his first steps, the father does not have much of a role, especially if the child is a girl, since the Guayaki almost always prefer boys. Being a father also affects the man's status as a husband, since sexual relations with his wife are theoretically forbidden as long as the child has not been weaned. The purpose of this prohibition, of course, is to prevent children from being born too close to one another, and for the most part it is respected; there are exceptions, however, as is evidenced by the women who from time to time are obliged to ask their husbands to help them abort. So, there is always at least two years' difference in age between two children of the same mother.

Besides mother's milk, the *kromi*'s diet includes adult foods: the orange-colored pulp of certain fruits, separated from the large pit; or grubs whose insides are squeezed into the little mouth (when the grubs become too large, their chitinous heads are nipped off with a fingernail). When the child's first teeth appear, he is given a little piece of meat to try them out on. The baby, sitting on a *dave*, a prettily woven mat of palm leaves, sucks it, throws it down, and picks it up again. It is soon covered with dust, twigs, and scraps of bark: it does not matter, no one does anything but shake the formless piece of food a little when it becomes too thickly covered with debris. The mother, sitting close by, is putting together a basket, or perhaps a box made of feathers, or a piece of cloth made of plant fibers, a *tyru*: this is worked as a form of crochet, since the Guayaki do not know how to weave. This *tyru* will be used as a rug, or a cape thrown over the shoulders in winter, or a cover for the basket.

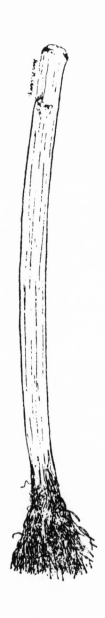

Koto, brush for absorbing liquid.

There is also the cooking to be done. Some meats are roasted, others boiled. The peccary, the roe deer, and large animals in general are first flambéed and then cut up with bamboo knives; the pieces of meat are stuck onto a pole planted obliquely above the fire and held up by a forked stick, and there they cook slowly. The fat trickles down and sputters on the embers. If the animals brought back from the hunt are fat, the Atchei are pleased; if they are lean, the Atchei are disappointed. So as not to lose such a prized food, the drops of fat are collected in a piece of palm wood whose fibers have been frayed at one end: this is the *koto*, a sort of brush that is dipped in liquids (fat, honey, etc.) and then sucked.

Other game is boiled, like the *kraja*, the howler monkey. One strange feature of their material culture is that, even though the Atchei are nomads, they make pottery. The women make crude ceramics, sometimes decorated with thumbnail imprints. These are the vessels, the *kara*, in which meat is cooked; some other foods are also cooked in them, one being the terminal bud of certain palm trees, known in Europe as an hors d'oeuvre called palmito.

When it is raw, it has a very pleasant sweet taste; cooked, it is made into a stew with grubs. The *pindo* palm also yields a sort of flour. The process by which it is obtained is not simple. The tree must be opened and the mass of fiber extracted, then soaked in water and squeezed out, handful by handful. As a result of washing the woody fibers, the white particles of "flour" adhering to them are deposited in the bowl. When the "*pindo* flesh" has been washed, the water, which has turned white, is boiled away until a sort of thick paste remains: this is the cooked flour, to which either grubs or honey are added to make *bruee*. Without waiting very long for it to cool off, everyone sits in a circle around the *kara*, molds a little ball of "puree" between his fingertips, and swallows it. To drink, there is water, which comes either from a *daity* or a large bamboo tube. The handfuls of fiber are thrown in

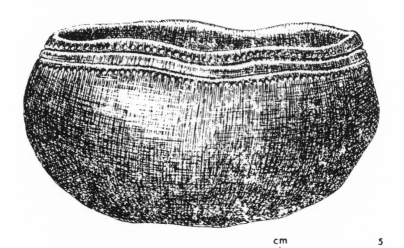

cm _____ 5

Kara, pottery decorated with the tip of a snail shell.

a pile and soon dry out; they will be used in a variety of ways —
for wiping asses, among other things. As soon as a young child
feels something under him, he stops playing with his toucan beak,
gets up on all fours, and with his rear end in the air cries: "*Aigiio,
puchi!* Mother, I've shat!"

The Atchei's day begins very early, even before the first gleam
of light appears in the sky. If there is no sign of *Beeru* in the area
and if game is abundant, they remain in the same camp for several
days. They leave when the animals become scarce. The Atchei
walk in single file, the men in front, the women behind; the
women carry along a smoldering stick, which will allow them
to light a fire easily when they stop, saving the men from the
exhausting task — especially tiring when it has rained and the
wood is damp — of starting a fire by *kyrypi tata*, a friction method
in which they make the shaft of an arrow spin around like the bit
of a drill on a piece of dry wood: the rubbing eventually ignites
the wood powder and smoke appears; they throw pinches of dry
moss on it, blow, and the fire catches. This is a serious act, almost
sacred: no one must speak, especially not laugh, or else there will
be no fire, and the women are not even allowed to watch while
the man spins the reed between his hands.

They do not walk for very long: a few hours, rarely more than
two or three. They stop in a likely place — some place where the
trees are not too high, since they attract *Chono*, Thunder, and
never in the thickest part of the forest because there is a great
deal of smoke there. It is good to be near running water, but not
too near because of the mosquitoes. Sometimes they have the good
luck to come upon an open area, where the undergrowth is full of
beautiful long-leaved ferns. Then it is easy for the men to make a
clearing and set up the *enda*, the camp. The head of each family
constructs his own shelter, which consists of four forked stakes
supporting crosspieces that are quickly fastened with creepers

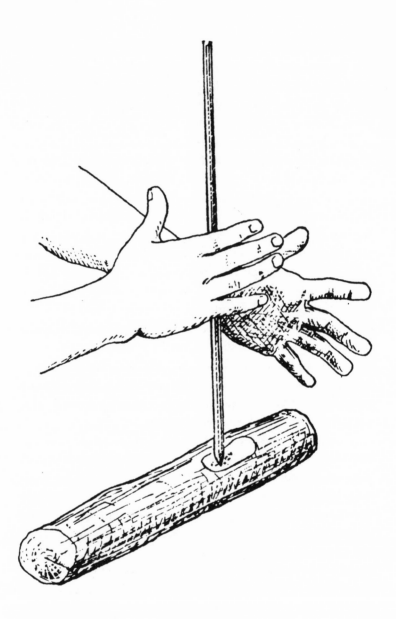

Making fire.

and on top of which they pile a thick layer of palms or ferns. The *tapy* may be small, but its roof will be impermeable. Under each shelter burns a fire placed at the edge in such a way that the rain cannot reach it.

It is best if *genipa* trees grow near the camp: the jaguar, stepping on its leaves, will make them crackle and warn the camp that he is nearby. And if there are *anbwandy* (*Helietta longifolia*) there too, it is even better: using pieces of its bark to massage the body is a good cure for various illnesses, especially *baivwu*, a disorder resulting from, among other things, eating honey without mixing it with water. When the fruit of the *genipa* are ripe, they are heated in an armadillo carapace and eaten. But many other tribes use the juice of these fruits as a blue-black dye to decorate their bodies, since it contrasts vividly with the red dye produced by the fruits of the urucu.

When the children are seven or eight years old, they are old enough for school. And little savages go through the same things our children do. Starting at this age they learn everything they need to know to deal successfully with nomadic life in the forest. In the evening, when the sun goes down, before they go to sleep, they listen to their grandmothers telling stories from the past, about the time when the first Atchei appeared on the earth and the time when darkness did not yet exist. The grandmothers explain to their grandchildren who the invisible beings are and that they must be feared; that an Atchei must always be generous to another Atchei; and that if you refuse to share the meat of a wild pig with your companions, for example, the pigs will clack their tusks together and you will not be able to shoot them.

Eating is not a simple act; you cannot eat just anything in any way you choose — and all this has to be learned gradually. Quite soon the children are taught not to eat monkey meat standing up, or else the jaguar will tear them apart, and that the same thing will

Construction of the shelter used for male initiation.

Tapy ywa, male initiation shelter.

happen if they laugh while eating a piece of anteater. It makes no difference if the low voice of the old person puts the grandchild, the *kiminogi*, to sleep. He will hear the same stories hundreds of times, they will become engraved in his memory, and when he grows up he will be able to repeat them just as he heard them.

The *jary* and the *jamogi*, the grandmothers and grandfathers, more or less take charge of teaching "letters" and ethics, while the introduction to the natural sciences — botany, zoology, climatology, astronomy, and so on — is handled by the parents. How can a boy become a *bretete*, a good hunter, if he does not know about the habits of the animals and birds, their cries, their ways of hiding or running away, the way they live and the places they frequent? And in the same way, a girl must know all about plants and trees, when they flower and when the berries and fruits ripen so that she can become a good gatherer and help feed her future family. None of this can be learned quickly. So as soon as the *kybuchu* is strong enough to walk through the forest without getting tired, he accompanies his father on the hunt. The *kybuchu*'s apprenticeship in the forest lasts for years, until he is old enough to be recognized as an adult.

He grows continuously more knowledgeable, stronger, and more skillful; he does not yet make his own arrows, but he sees his father carving them all the time. He learns that they must not be wasted and that, if a monkey or a bird that has been shot remains pinned to the trunk or the branch where the arrow nailed it, the hunter must climb the tree and bring everything back down. The tip of the shaft will be broken, but he will sharpen it again. When the tip becomes too short, the hunter will give it a longer shaft, and now that it is lighter, it will be used only for small animals shot at close range. The boy watches and listens, and the father is patient, never getting angry. The son learns that he must not catch the *bairekwa* fish with his bare hands, because the spikes

159

on its fins will hurt him; that sometimes Jakarendy, the master of honey, becomes furious with the Atchei and blocks up the hives to stop the Atchei from finding them; and that the bees will not build their hives in places frequented by the *taira barbara*, an animal who is a great lover of honey and who robs the hives.

The boy is taught to be prudent: he must be aware that the female tapir is dangerous when she has young and that, whereas the cries of the *myrokije* bird signal that its companion, the jaguar, is nearby, the cries of the *brupichu* signal that there are *capivara* to be hunted in the vicinity.

As for the animals, there are certain rules of courtesy to be observed toward them. When the hunter kills them, he must also salute them; he arrives in the camp, his game hanging over his shoulder, which is nobly spotted with blood, and he puts it down and sings in its honor. In this way, the animal is not simply a neutral piece of food; if it were reduced to that, the other members of its species might get angry and not allow themselves to be shot anymore.

Hunting is not simply a matter of killing animals; you owe them something, and this debt is paid when you bring the animals you have killed back to life by talking about them. You thank them for letting themselves be killed, but their common names are never mentioned. So that *brevi*, tapir, is called *morangi*, and *kande*, the little peccary, is called *barugi*. You have to be sly with the animals, you must pretend to be talking about someone else; by fooling the game this way, you somehow annul man's aggressiveness and wipe out the fatal act. The hunter's chanting seals the secret agreement between men and animals. The *kybuchu* are also taught this: to live in the forest one must avoid excess and respect the unity of the world in order to make sure it continues to be generous.

His respects to the anteater: "The very large one, I bring him!

The *kybuchu*.

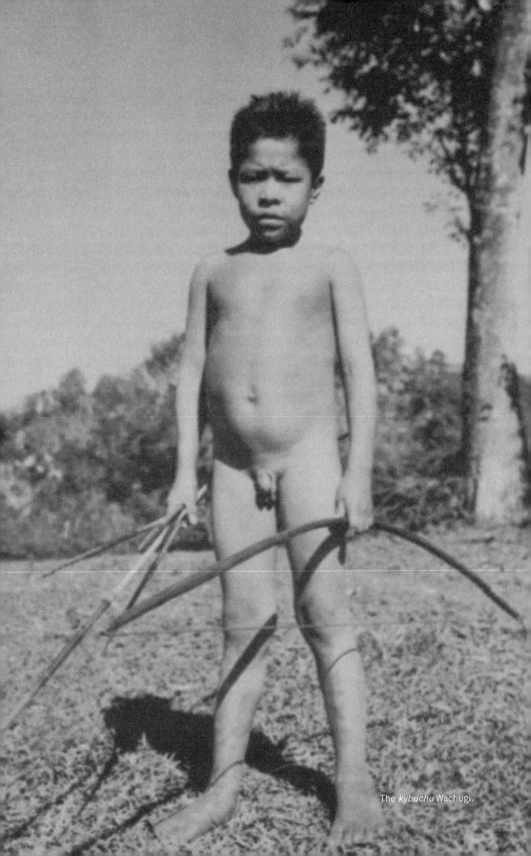

The *kybuchu* Wachugi.

I am the one who shot him with my arrow. The very large one, I killed him, I bring the target of my arrow!"

His respects to the female of the great peccary: "Yes! Let's have a fire with beautiful flames! I'm here! The beautiful mother, the old one, it is an old one that I bring!"

His respects to the deer, preceded and followed by whistling: "He who lingers a long time in the shadows, I bring him!"

His respects to the howler monkey: "Here I am back again! He whose whiskers are certainly not new, I bring him! The thickly bearded stinking one, I bring him!"

The seasons pass, the cold period returns, the *tata jemo*, the Pleiades, appear in the east, and the *kybuchu*'s knowledge grows. The things in the forest become familiar to him, they speak to him, he understands them, he is at home in the woods, he is one with the forest. One day, his father decides that the boy's childhood is over.

They felt that the moment had come. The *kybuchu* were already *yma*, big and strong. They knew all the secrets of *bareka*, of hunting, and they could not be kept away from women much longer without things getting complicated: even though they were not allowed to do it, they eyed them with more and more interest. And everyone knows what happens then: "*Dare mecha ka-ia, kana pija.* If you keep looking at young women, you soon get an erection." There were plenty of boys who followed the girls in the tribe and lay in wait for them when they walked along the streams hunting frogs. Did they merely laugh when the boys made it understood what they wanted? In the end, some of them usually gave in to the feverish attentions of the *kybuchu*. Or else the *kybuchu* would masturbate. It was clear that they were no longer children, that they had become grown-ups.

Young Kybwyragi declared to his principal father one day that he wanted the *imbi mubu*, the perforation of his lip. This would confirm him as a hunter; he would wear the labret, the sign of his entrance into adulthood, and would have free access to the women he had lusted after for so long.

His father Rambiagi was happy, and at the same time he understood that from *kybuchu ete*, an accomplished man, a hunter in his prime, he would be passing on to the following stage, that of *chyvai provi*, "he who is already a little old." There were two other adolescents in the camp about the same age as his son. Rambiagi and the other fathers had a talk and decided that the three boys should undergo the trial at the same time.

So they were three *peperove*, three companions in the initiation, and the fact that they had gone through the *imbi mubu* together would create lasting bonds among them which would cause them to help one another for the rest of their lives. Furthermore, in memory of their youth together and as a sign of friendship, Rambiagi wanted the principal role in the ceremony to be taken by his own *peperove*, Jyvukugi, who was also the brother of one of the three boys to be initiated.

Kybwyragi went to find Jyvukugi: "I would like you to be the one to pierce my lip. Thus my father has spoken." As for the younger brother, his father said to him: "Let your brother be the one to pierce your lip." And the same thing happened with the third candidate. Jyvukugi agreed to officiate, he would open the way for the three adolescents into the world of adults, and there would be three more hunters in the group: "I will be your *imbi-mubuaregi*, the piercer of your lip." The boys were happy to get his consent, because he was already a prestigious member of the tribe.

He began to give orders: "Go over there. Clear the place with your hands." All three of them spent the afternoon preparing the *enda ayia*, the initiation spot, at a distance from the camp; they cleared it carefully, cut down the bushes, uprooted all the vegeta-

166

tion: everything was nice and clean. When evening came, they lit a large fire in the middle of the place and sat down side by side, alone in the night for the first time. They had never gone without eating before; their mothers had always had something to give them. But this evening they could not eat or drink: this was how things had to be when a boy aspired to become a *beta pou*, a new labret, a new initiate. And also for the first time, the *kybuchu* chanted timidly, their as yet unpracticed voices sounding the men's *prera*. The hunters answered from a distance with their own chant, encouraging the chant of the *beta pou*. This went on for a while; the silent night and shining fires surrounded them. Then, as if in protest, as if in plaintive regret and pain, the voices of three women could be heard: these were the mothers of the young men. They knew they were going to lose their children, that soon they would no longer be their *memby* but men worthy of respect. The women's *chenga ruvara* was a last effort to hold back time, and it was also the first chant of their separation; it celebrated a change.

The chanted and wept refusal of the women to accept the inevitable was a challenge to the men: their *prera* redoubled in strength and violence, it became aggressive and almost drowned out the humble plaint of the mothers, who were listening to their sons chant like men. The boys knew they were the object of this struggle between the men and the women, and this encouraged them to hold on tightly to their role: this evening they were no longer part of the group, they no longer belonged to the world of women, they no longer belonged to their mothers; but they were not yet men, they did not belong anywhere, and that was why they sat in the *enda ayia* — it was a different place, a temporary space, a sacred frontier between the past and future of these boys, who were about to die and be reborn. The fires burned down, the voices grew quiet, and everyone went to sleep.

Early the next morning, they went to Jyvukugi again. They were hungry, but this was a big day, and they were a little afraid: "Go into the forest and cut down some *pindo*," he ordered. The boys took metal hatchets, the ones Jyvukugi had recently stolen from a camp of Paraguayan loggers. They went off; they cut down the trees, opened the trunks in order to tear out the pith, cut off the palms and the terminal bud of the young plants, and carried everything back to the camp; the boys carried the large leaves in bundles on their shoulders. Meanwhile, Jyvukugi had gone hunting, because he needed a coati.

The fathers were there: "*Tapy ywa nwa! Baky vera! Pichua!*" they said. "The large house, build it! It's going to rain! There will be *pichua!*" The *pichua* is the wind and rain, the rumbling thunder, the eloquent storm. It always comes when the Atchei perform the *imbi mubu*, and it is a good sign. Heaven and earth — and the powers behind them — are never indifferent to the fate of man. They echo whatever man does; sometimes they even intervene too much and the Atchei become frightened. Then they have to explain to the wind and rain that they are talking too loudly and ask them to go away. But the stronger the *pichua* are at the initiation, the more successful it is. This is why a special shelter is built. Without any help, the *kybuchu* constructed it in the middle of the space they had cleared the day before. This *tapy* is called *ywa*, big, because there is more than enough room to stand up straight, whereas the everyday huts are too low for that. The *tapy ywa* is high (nearly ten feet) and spacious and can shelter many Atchei. The palms that the boys brought back were laid over the roof, which was set on thick poles that had been stuck in the ground. While their sons were busy building the hut, the mothers in their turn went off into the forest to get *toi ee*, the pith of the palms that the boys had cut down. They loaded their baskets. Along with the terminal bud, this would be the future

168

initiates' food. Now the initiation house was ready, and the three boys sat down side by side in the middle of it. They waited without saying a word.

Jyvukugi came back, carrying a coati. The animal was grilled and skinned, and a piece of its fat was set aside. Everything was ready. The fast was going to be temporarily interrupted, the *kybuchu* were going to eat, eat until their stomachs bulged. For several days after, they were not going to be able to swallow anything because of their lips. So they stuffed themselves with the *tangy*, the palmito they had brought back with the palms, and with the *toi ee*, which their mothers had gone to get. They were not allowed to eat any other food except the coati's fat and skin. This would make their bellies good and full. But the Atchei know why the coati in particular should be given to the *kybuchu*: "*Karo ro Ache wywy. Kare ro Ache ove*. The coati are also Atchei. The coati are the *Ove* of the Atchei." The *Ove* is a dead person's double, the one that goes up toward the sun, whereas the *Ianve* does not wish to leave the living and skims over the earth at night near the camps. The coati, then, are people; they take charge of the *Ove* of the dead and climb to the top of large mythical trees that cannot be seen. From there they can reach heaven, raising themselves by a creeper that unites the world above to the world below.

Coati meat can be dangerous; like honey and other foods that are delicate to handle, it can cause *baivwa*, sickness. After all, aren't the coati people? But the skin and fat that Jyvukugi gave the future initiates, the boys who were at once dead and alive, dead to childhood, to the sweetness and tenderness of the world of their mothers, but about to be born into manhood, was not bad; the *kare* would fill them with strength, the same adult strength possessed by the coati. Sitting on a mat in the large house, the boys ate the skin and fat.

The meal was over. The initiation was about to begin, because the sun was almost vertical; its rays were burning the *enda ayia*. This warmth and light from the sun, immobile at the zenith, was a reenactment of another, mythical warmth and light: when the first Atchei emerged from the earth, when they became men, people, *nondete*, a very long time ago when night and darkness did not exist, it was always daytime, and the sun was always vertical. And in memory of the first event in Atchei history, they wait for high noon before celebrating the *imbi mubu*, marking the solemn origin of the true Atchei. The *Ache jamo pyve*, the first ancestors, emerged from the surface of the earth under the sun, and so the sun, sitting at the highest point in its course, also watches over the rebirth of the boys.

A man approached; he shaved the heads of the three silent petitioners with his bamboo knife. Then he rubbed them around the mouth for a long time with the coati fat that had been set aside, in order to soften the skin. When he had done this, he wiped off the fat with a handful of *pindo* fibers. Jyvukugi was sitting in the hut behind them. He got up, holding a well-sharpened monkey thighbone in his hand. This was the instrument to be used for piercing the lips, and it was called a *piju*. He bent over Kybwyragi, who leaned his head far back. Jyvukugi took his lower lip in his left hand and pulled it forward. He looked deep into the boy's eyes, kept his gaze there, and without moving his eyes stuck the *piju* into the lip with his right hand, poking it from the outside in and from the bottom up. Once the hole had been made, he withdrew the bone.

Then his place was taken by the other man, his assistant, the *kutuaregi*. He too had a *piju*, but it was blunt. Now he took hold of the lip and thrust the bone into the hole, from the inside out and from the top down: this was the *kutu* motion, whereas the first had been the *mubu*. He left the bone in the wound and wrapped it with a thin thread, which the mothers of the boys had made; this was called a *kaimbo*, and it would keep the bone from slipping and falling out. All this would be left in place until the wound began to heal; the wound would not close, and it would grow tough. The *piju* would be taken out after several days, and the thread would be left hanging through the hole, held on the inside of the lip by a little ball of *choa* beeswax. Kybwyragi had not said anything, and if he had been in pain, he had not let it show — not a gesture, not a sound. The men next operated on the other two *kybuchu*, who were also brave and did not complain. The wounds did not bleed much. All three of them were now *beta pou*, new labrets, young initiates. Before, they had still belonged to the *embogi*, the penises; from now on they would be called *betagi*, wearers of a labret.

A whole man, an adult, is defined not only by his *embo*, but also by his *beta*. Until he is initiated — until he wears a labret — a boy is only an *embogi*, a penis. But as soon as he wears a labret — as soon as he joins the *betagi* and ceases to be an *embogi* — he can begin to use his penis and seduce women — for example, when they go off alone to get water — and the *beta pou* do not wait long to try this. The hole in the lip and the labret which fills that hole give the man certain rights and reveal a truth which up to then had been hidden: a man is defined by his sex; and the moment a *kybuchu* is no longer called penis, people acknowledge that he has one. Such is the dissimulation of language, which names something absent and hides that same thing when it is present: a man is a penis as long as he doesn't have one, and he ceases to be a penis as soon as he has one.

In the meantime, the mothers had lit a fire under the initiation shelter. They were cooking the rest of the palmito in a clay pot. Each of the boys took a brush, dipped it in the soup, and stroked his lip with it: they were warming the wound so that it would heal well, so that it would not hurt. They did the same

171

thing with the *toi ee*, which was also warm. The wound always becomes slightly infected — they say that the lip stinks — but the infection never becomes very serious. Sometimes the man who pierces the lip is clumsy and tears it apart; they then have to wait until it is completely healed before they repeat the ceremony.

A delicious perfume spread through the initiation area; it was *choa* beeswax, which had been thrown on the fire. The smoke rose in the air, straight toward heaven, straight toward the sun's resting place. What message was rising in that smoke? What did the burning wax say to the sky? The Atchei would answer, *ure kwaty.* "We know very well what it says: things must be this way, because our ancestors have always taught us this, and if we remain faithful to the words and gestures that have always existed, the world will remain a reassuring place. It will write the same words, it will not be enigmatic."

This is because there was the smell and smoke of burned wax when the world began. For the world to become what it is today, an Atchei had to throw *choa* wax on the fire. This took place at a time when the sun did not move, did not bake the earth — *kyray cha endave* — there were rays of sunlight everywhere. One day a man was walking with his son who had not yet been initiated. On the path they came across Baio's large pot: "Don't touch it! Don't touch Baio's pot!" warned the father. But the child disobeyed him, and with one blow of his club he broke the pot. Then, from the hole he had opened, a flood of ashes poured out, and also the animals and birds of the forest, who are all Baio's domestic animals. Lastly, out came something that terrified the people, because they did not know what it was. This was darkness, night, which drove away the light and the everlasting day and invaded everything. No more sun! Only night, and it kept on and on! The boy's foolish act had brought on everlasting night. Then *choa* wax was thrown on the fire; the smoke with its pleasant smell rose into the air and caused the daylight to reappear, and the Atchei knew the face of the world, the face shown by the movement of the sun in its regular progress from day to night and night to day. Things never changed after that. Nevertheless, now and then the order of the world is threatened by chaos. This is when the terrible great blue jaguar who lives in the sky throws himself at the sun or the moon in order to eat it; if this happened, people would again have to live in eternal light or darkness, and it would be the end of the world. So the people become very frightened and do everything they can to keep this from happening – the jaguar must be frightened away. The women yell stridently and throw reeds onto the fire, and as the reeds explode, the men make a *jeproro*, a threat hurled against the animal. With their stone hatchets, they split the earth furiously. There is a frightful din in the Atchei camps; everyone makes as much noise as possible. In the end, the animal is frightened, abandons his prey, the sun reappears, the moon grows right again, and life in the world resumes its regular rhythm.

Herein lies the secret and the knowledge the Indians have gained from it: excess, a continuing lack of proportion, tends to alter the movement of things, and what man must do is work to prevent that, safeguard the life of the group against disorder. A man cannot be both child and adult – *kybuchu* and seducer of women – but one or the other. First he is a penis, then a labret. Things must not be allowed to become confused: the living must keep to one side, the dead to the other, the children in one place, and the initiated in another. Long ago, wax was burned, and its smoke divided day from night forever. The wax that was now burning in the initiation fire was rising up into the heart of human space and dividing it, showing that once this limit was crossed there was no possibility of turning back, that all things are united, and that the same order governs the life of the world and the life of the community of people. Long ago, a boy, an un-initiated boy, broke Baio's pot and let loose the darkness. Now, the lips of young men are pierced. Through this ritual, the Atchei are acknowledging the fact that, like day and night, the generations succeed one another in a certain order. The wound in the lip will never close, because it is also the mark of *lost time*: neither the son who has become a man nor his father nor mother will be able to recover it. *Go nonga*. This is the way it is. So, under the great immobile sun, they burn a little wax. It is a decree that assigns definite limits to space, a period for each thing, a living place for men. What does the smoke say? It says that men are mortal.

A *chenga ruvara* burst forth from the camp, which until then had been silent. This was a chorus of all the women, not just the mothers. They were sitting on their heels, their faces hidden between their hands, and they were singing. Suddenly three men got up, growling with anger; they threw themselves at the women, punching them and kicking them. They were the fathers of the newly initiated young men. Yesterday's contest had been vocal, the men chanting against the women. Now the men were hitting them. Rambiagi kicked Kybwyragi's mother violently with his heel and sent her rolling several feet away, and she cried out. Then all the other women flew to help the mothers. They hung on the arms and shoulders of the men and tried to calm them down. They immobilized them and rubbed their faces and chests with palm marrow. "Don't hit them!" They blew hard into the men's ears, as though they were trying to make something go back in.

But the men were *by-ia*, they had no more *by*, their "natures" had deserted them, and they were beside themselves. "We must get revenge! I am the avenger!" There were shouts, moans, and calls on all sides. The excitement mounted. The people were becoming delirious. Now the other men who had been watching got up. They were armed: brandishing their bows, they seized large arrows and rattled them together. "Don't shoot!" cried their wives. But they did not listen; they were doing the *jeproro* all together. They were yelling with all their strength, their faces twisted with rage, because they too were *by-ai*. They were becoming dangerous: their arrows were against the strings of their bows, and the bows were taut and ready to shoot. The women were frightened and were weeping. All the children, terrified, had fled under the trees. Hidden behind the trunks, they watched this sudden violence without understanding it. The first arrows flew on all sides of them. They passed alongside the initiation hut and over its high roof. The men approached it slowly and menacingly. The three young initiates began to be afraid too.

They knew very well that the emphatically demonstrative anger of the men was more than half feigned and that, without the *rapa michi*, the game of violence in which they hit one another's bows, without the *jeproro* and the striking, without the battle of men against women and the defeat of the women, the initiation would not be complete.

All the same, in the heat of battle the men would sometimes lose their self-control and hit harder than they should. They stood there in a line, still shouting as though the *beta pou* were jaguars and letting loose their arrows; now it seemed as though they wanted to kill the boys, as though they refused to recognize them as adults, as initiates, as though they were rejecting these new companions. But Jyvukugi was there, and he was not afraid. He was there to protect the boys whom he had just torn from childhood. He would defend them against the men and complete his task faithfully by making the group of grown men accept the young men. He too became *by-ia*, full of anger; he hurled abuse at the hunters, he threatened them. He stamped the ground with his feet, he picked up handfuls of earth and threw them at the men — he was terrifying. He made an enormous din, because he was the boys' *jepare*, their "avenger." The women came quickly; they surrounded him and massaged him, gave him a good rubdown. They asked him not to make so much noise, to calm himself: "My *beta pou* child will escape!" the mothers said. He listened, he calmed down little by little. The men had not dared to take one step farther and were now retreating. Peace returned to the *enda ayia*. The bows and arrows were laid down, the people went back to sit in their huts, and the initiation was over.

The Atchei remained in the camp four more days and nights, waiting for the lips to begin healing. The young initiates stayed in their shelter, spending the night there. Because of the *piju* in the hole in their lips, they were unable to talk or eat: all they could have was palmito soup prepared by the mothers, which they ate with a brush. In any case, most foods were forbidden to them. To eat the flesh of the armadillo would bring bad luck at hunting, *pané*; peccary would cause bad diarrhea; monkey would make their eyes fill with blood like newborn children; rattlesnake would make their buttocks flat and thin — something that is very distressing to the Atchei. All sorts of honey were also prohibited. And if they did not obey the rules, they would be unable to shoot animals. The initiates were very hungry; because of this, the mothers could be heard chanting every evening, sad at the thought of their famished sons: "My child! He has no stomach at all!"

As for Jyvukugi and his assistant, they were obliged to respect the same taboo: nothing to eat but palm marrow. On top of this, they had to refrain scrupulously from making love, as did the fathers and brothers of the boys; *meno* in these circumstances would make the lip wound sore and would delay the healing. By depriving themselves of their wives and lovers, the men were showing allegiance to their young companions, because the boys did not yet have the right to be intimate with women. They would

176

win this right later, when the wound had healed completely, when the string that was knotted inside the lip, preventing the hole from closing again, broke. At the moment the *kaimbo* broke, the boy became a real *betagi*. But as long as it was intact, he had to stay away from women: if he did not, he would suffer the worst misfortune a man could experience — bad luck at hunting. If at this time he did things that were forbidden, he would not be able to do what he had to do later. And it was a man's inevitable destiny to become a *jyvondy*, a shooter of animals. The Atchei still talk about something that they now find amusing but that angered them very much at the time — how young Bykygi disobeyed all the laws in order to satisfy his desires. He followed a young woman who was going for water and forced his attentions on her. And the string was still hanging from the hole in his lip!

When the four days had gone by, the Atchei left the camp. It was not long before the hole in the lip had a clean edge and no longer smelled unpleasant. At this point the father of each of the *betagi* gave him his labret, which the boy would wear from then on in camp. The labret was a long, thin monkey bone clearly visible to the women and was meant to seduce them, *pravo vwa*. Since they were men now, their fathers would help them to make their own bow and set of arrows. The long labret was removed when they went out hunting because there was a danger of hitting it with their right hand as they pulled back the bowstring. It was replaced by a much shorter *beta*: if they did not wear a labret, they would not be able to kill any game. And when they returned to the camp, the dead animal on their right shoulder, they would know the proper songs to sing. And as a special honor, they would take a piece of meat to Jyvukugi and his assistant, their "piercers."

Did an Atchei become a grown-up simply by having his lip pierced? Not at all: the *imbi mubu* was an important ceremony, and everyone took part in it — it was a group ceremony — but it

177

was not a sign that the adolescent had reached adulthood. There was more to come, and that was the *jaycha bowo*, the carving of tattoos, the scarification of the back. Once that had been performed, the young man would be in a position to accomplish what he had always been destined for: he would cease to be a carefree seducer of young women and become the husband of a woman who would bear him children.

They wait from six to eight years before performing this ceremony. And since a boy receives his *beta* when he is about fifteen, the tattooing takes place when he is twenty-two or twenty-three: *buta provi bu*. When one has a little beard, say the Atchei. When the time comes, an old man in the tribe, most often the one who pierced the young man's lip, says to him: "You are no longer a *betagi*. You are a full-grown man; for this reason, I want to carve the tattoos. I will be the one who carves your back." This is not a request but a statement: the thing must be done now, and the *betagi* must go through with it. The man goes off to find a stone. Sometimes he has to go far away because it can only be found in the beds of certain streams. One side of it must be very sharp, but not as sharp as a splinter of bamboo, which cuts too easily. To choose the right stone, therefore, requires good judgment. This is all the equipment needed for the new ceremony: one stone.

When he has found what he wants, the *bowaregi* cuts down a young tree with a smooth trunk in the middle of an open space in such a way that when it falls it leans on the branches of another tree and remains in a tilted position. Everything is ready; the operation (and it is that — almost a surgical operation) can begin. They wait for the sun to reach its zenith. The young man stretches out along the tilted tree trunk and puts his arms around it; he is on his stomach, with his back exposed and his skin good and tight. The "carver" takes his stone and cuts from the top of the man's shoulder to the highest point on his buttocks. The incision is not a light and superficial one, as it would be if a razor-sharp splinter of bamboo were used, for example. This is really a crevice in the back that cuts through all the layers of skin. In order to make this kind of furrow without using the knifelike edge of the bamboo splinter, one must have a strong grip, because the skin resists. The *bowaregi* presses down with all his strength; he tears the skin. The entire surface of the back is plowed this way with straight, parallel lines, from one shoulder to the other; there are at least ten incisions. The blood flows freely; the young man is covered with it, as are the arms of the man cutting him, the tree, and the ground all around him. The Atchei say that the pain is atrocious: it is much worse than the piercing of the lip, which is hardly felt. The *jaycha bowo* almost kills the person who undergoes it. But just as during the *imbi mubu*, the young man does not moan or cry out: he would sooner lose consciousness — though even then his teeth would still be clenched. This silence proves that he is brave and worthy of being considered a full-grown man.

When the entire back has been worked, the *bowaregi* takes some charcoal produced by the *Kybai* tree (*Kybai* means *man*), crushes it into a powder, and mixes it with honey. He smears this paste on the wounds, rubbing it in well. The powdered charcoal acts as a blotter, absorbing the blood and helping to stop the hemorrhaging. It also becomes encrusted in the cracks so that when they are healed the long stripes will be colored a beautiful bluish black. The scarifications must be clearly visible, good and black, or else the operation is not considered a success. And when they are, then the man is *jyvete*, terrible.

The young man leaves his tree and lies facedown on a mat. His mother is crying. She heats wood shavings from a tree and places them on the wounds, leaving them for a long time. This eases the pain; it is a sedative. She will tend to her immobilized son several times during the next few days. Until the wounds have almost healed, the group will remain in the camp, because the young man cannot move — it is too painful, and the wounds must not be allowed to open again. He eats very little — no meat, because that would stop the tattooing from blackening properly. All he is given is honey diluted with water. Of course, he is not allowed to make love as long as his back is not "dry": otherwise he would not recover. Because he has respected the rules, and because his mother has cared for him, the young man's wounds stop stinking and scar tissue forms, creating a thick relief of vertical lines on his skin. The Atchei can move on. The young man is very weakened, but the hunters will give him a great deal of meat, and he will soon become fat again.

From now on he is a *bretete*, a full-grown hunter, and a *kybai gatu*, a good adult. He bears the sign of what he has become engraved in his flesh: a grown-up, the future husband of a woman. His childhood vanished through the hole in his lip, but he had not yet passed to true adulthood; he had only reached the happy time of his youth, the time of *pravoty*, of "seducing women." But youth is no more everlasting than childhood; there is a time for everything, and every moment of time is transitory. What kind of man would want to prolong his freedom as a *betagi* beyond the proper limit, continuing to seduce women indefinitely? He would soon become a source of disturbance and conflict in the tribe, both for the married men, whose wives he was threatening, and for the younger initiates, who were waiting their turn. To want to remain a *betagi* when one was old enough to be a *kybai gatu*, to cling to irresponsible bachelorhood when one could take a wife, would be to *introduce disorder into the society*. A man must give up one condition to occupy another, the one he is destined for, and the group forces the individual to acknowledge this so that the society may endure. During the long interval between the *imbi mubu* and the *jaycha bowo*, the young man can do what he likes, because the group has said to him, *You may*. After a certain time has passed, the group decrees, *It's over*. Then the trial of pain is proof that this is really so; there is nothing to be said, the man must suffer in silence, and this silence is payment for his debt to the tribe, which has allowed him to seduce the women. The blue jaguar threatens the *cosmic order* when he tries to devour the sun or the moon; the *betagi* would be threatening the *social order* if he refused to become an adult. A bachelor is like a jaguar in the community. In order to prevent the return of chaos in the heavens, the Atchei *split* the earth with their hatchets; and to prevent a similar chaos in their group, they *split* the back of the *betagi*. They work the skin, and they scar the earth — and this is one and the same mark. It expresses the law of things and the law of men and at the same time poses a riddle: the sun peacefully follows the moon, day peacefully follows night, but this eternal recurrence has nothing to do with men.

One morning I was chatting with Karekyrumbygi. His wife, the very young Chachugi, was a Stranger. She was not simply plump, she was really fat, so that at first I thought she was pregnant even though her breasts were not very large; and when I asked her, she seemed ashamed and answered, "*Bravo ia wyte*. Not yet pregnant." We were talking with her husband, as I said, when contrary to her usual discretion she came up to us looking preoccupied, murmured something in her husband's ear, and ran off to hide in the forest. The man got up immediately and went to the Strangers' camp; he hardly took the time to explain to me that "*pira upu o*, the blood has gushed." Chachugi had not even reached puberty, there was no way she could be pregnant, since the blood that had just gushed was her first menstruation. I was in luck: I was going to be able to witness the initiation of a young girl (if the Indians did not object).

Chachugi had fled into the forest because this is what a woman whose blood is flowing for the first time is supposed to do. She must flee from the eyes of other people, letting them know by this what has happened to her. The little girl is *by-ia*, as they say, without "nature," without poise — she is ashamed and runs away to hide. After a short time had passed, long enough for everyone in the camp to know that *pira upu o*, Chachugi emerged from the shelter of the trees and with her eyes lowered very quickly went to sit in her parents' hut, which they had left. To her grandmother, who was the only one still there, she murmured: "*Cho pirama*. My blood is here." And the grandmother announced in a loud voice to another old woman sitting a short distance away: "Our little girl's blood has come." When Chachugi was born, it was this woman who had lifted her off the ground and held her in her arms; and now she would help her *chave*, who had become a woman. The mother sounded a solitary lament. Now everyone present had been officially informed. The father performed a *jeproro*; several times he shouted very loudly. "My daughter's blood fell on the meat of the peccary." They had been roasting a little wild pig when Chachugi suddenly got up and disappeared into the forest.

The two old women, helped by the girl's "godfather," performed a meticulous *biri*. This was a massage in which the skin was taken between the fingers and pinched lightly. Chachugi was lying down, her eyes closed, and all three of them were crouching over her. From a distance it looked very strange to see those six hands skimming from one part of the motionless body to another. Several men had left the camp, and the others, except for the father, deliberately turned their backs on the scene. As for the husband, he had disappeared right at the beginning. The massage lasted about half an hour, at the end of which Chachugi was scantily covered with two or three dry palm leaves. The

tapave got up and disappeared into the woods, as did the godfather. Meanwhile, the father built a fragile, low frame within the
bounds of the camp but at a short distance from the other huts:
this was the *tapy jyvapa*, the arched hut reserved for "she whose
blood has gushed." But unlike the boys, the girls have no initiation space cleared for them.

The godparents came back a little later, the godfather carrying
pindo palms and the godmother a large armload of ferns. The
palms would be used to make both the roof and the walls of the
shelter, which really was arched: it was a short upside down V.
Inside, the old woman arranged a bed of ferns, and Chachugi
slipped into the shelter, entirely hidden by the rest of the ferns.
She was totally invisible because she was *kaku* — not meant to be
seen. The godmother sat down near the seclusion hut and cried
for a few minutes, then began preparing food for her "goddaughter" — flour and *pindo* buds were all she could have.

The hours passed. The Atchei took their siestas or busied
themselves with their usual occupations; no one had said anything to me yet, and since I was there to observe (notebook and
pencil rather stupidly in my hand), I did not dare leave, in spite of
the heat, the mosquitoes, and my own hunger. I had to stay there
and be sure I did not miss anything. There would not be another
initiation of a girl for at least two or three years, since none
of the little girls was old enough for the *pira upu o*. An Indian
gave me a piece of raw palmito, which had a very delicate nutty
taste. As it turned out, nothing more was going to happen today.
Toward the end of the afternoon, the godmother took the girl her
meal of plants, which she ate quickly, keeping her eyes shut. She
not only had to remain hidden, but even had to take great care
not to look at anyone else, especially not the men, except for her
father and godfather. She was bad, a source of evil and unhappiness, a cause of *bayja*. This was what the Atchei call the extremely

dangerous situation in which men are often placed because of the blood that flows from women when a child is born or the first menstruation occurs.

I got up very early the next day to witness the rest of the ritual. But despite my haste, things had already started: the seclusion hut had been moved so that it was clearly outside the camp, because the space Chachugi had occupied the evening before was soiled, not directly by the blood but by all the aversions and terrors it had brought with it. That place had become impure, uninhabitable. The girl's father had gone off into the forest; he would bring back a load of shavings from the *kymata* vine, without which the purification would have been impossible. An enormous quantity would be needed because a great many people would have to be purified: not only those who had been contaminated by coming into direct contact with Chachugi, but also a large group of men who had carefully kept away from her. Tatuetepirangi, Red-Skinned Tatou, explained it all to me, and then I understood why the husband had gone off so quickly the day before. As he placidly sat having his breakfast of grubs, which swarmed over his plate, he asked me: "And how about you? Won't you have the *kymata tyro*, the *kymata* purification?"

"I don't know. Should I have it too?"

"You mean you have not made love yet?"

"With which woman?"

"With the *kujambuku*, the big woman." (This was what the Atchei called girls who were about to menstruate.)

"No, not with Chachugi."

"*Amai!*"

He was very surprised, and then I was too, because he seemed to think it quite normal that I might have enjoyed the favors of the little girl!

"Well, then," he said, "you're like me. When there is no lovemaking, then there is no *bayja*; and if there is no *bayja*, then there is no purification."

So it was very simple: all the men who had had sexual relations with a girl whose blood had not yet come had to submit to the ritual. Earlier I had been astonished to learn that Chachugi, the *breko* — legal wife — of Karekyrumbygi, was not yet a woman. But now I learned that not only was a husband involved but lovers too; he gave me the whole lot of them without any hesitation — he seemed perfectly up to date on the love life of all the Atchei. We arrived at a total of seven. Chachugi, who was thirteen years old at the most, had already made seven men happy. *Amai*!

Some of the seven *bayja* were here, but the others were away; they had been hunting for several days. They had to be told about what had happened so they could come back right away and have the threat exorcized. This was why Karekyrumbygi had left to look for them without delay. If they did not undergo the purification, they would fall under the claws of the jaguars, who were attracted like lovers by their state of *bayja*; or perhaps Memboru-chu, the Great Heavenly Serpent who appeared in the form of a rainbow, would swallow them. In any case, there was a great danger that the *brara*, a poisonous snake, had already bitten them.

The secluded girl lay under the palms and ferns. Women had gone to get water. The godfather soaked the shavings in the water, handful by handful. The water began to turn white and foam up. If it was emptied into the stream, all the fish downstream would die, as though they had been asphyxiated. But the *kymata* was only used by the Atchei to drive out the *bayja*. This was what they were going to do now. A long stake was fixed in the ground near the seclusion hut. The godfather went to get Chachugi; he took her out from under the ferns, covered her head with a piece of cloth, and led her to the stake, which she clung to with both hands. He took off her veil and covered her head with an *aicho*, a sort of bonnet of tightly plaited palm, which was pulled down over the head like a beret. It was used only when a girl had reached puberty and would assure her of having beautiful hair later. Several people vigorously washed the girl, who stood silently with her head bowed and her eyes closed: her parents, her godfather and godmother, and my friend Tatuetepirangi. She was "soaped" and rinsed from head to foot with handfuls of shavings soaked in purifying water. They were careful not to overlook the girl's private parts, and several times I saw traces of blood on her thighs quickly wiped away with a sponge. At regular intervals, the women crouched down, did a *chenga ruvara*, and went on with their work. Soon Chachugi had been completely washed, and she was dried with dry shavings. Again hidden under the cloth, she was led back to her secluded place.

It was now the purifiers' turn to be purified. One after another, they leaned against the same stick and were conscientiously washed down. This would last a long time, because aside from the five or six Atchei who had taken part in the ceremony, there were Chachugi's old lovers, as well as the ones her husband had gone to get. Much stranger and unusual to me was what was happening to Chachugi. She had not gone into the hut but was lying facedown on some ferns. Her *aicho* was removed, and her godmother cut off all her hair. Then two small cords made of nettle fiber were knotted under her knees: like the massage that had been given her in the beginning, they were supposed to prevent the girl's legs from becoming thin. The Atchei are horrified by thinness, which they take to be a sign of bad health, and they especially like their women to be nice and round. What is more, a woman "with dry bones" is not strong enough to walk through the forest with a basket on her back containing two or three coati, a child in the baby carrier, and a smoldering stick in her hand; a thin woman is not good, it is sad. Therefore, every pre-

186

caution is taken to make sure that the calves and thighs of the *kuja* will be as shapely as possible.

But this was not all. For Chachugi, who was still lying on the ground, was now being whipped. Two old women, each gripping a short leather thong, were flogging her with all their might from her shoulders to her ankles. With all their might, it was true, and yet the sound of the smacking on her skin was not very loud because the whips were too short and too thin for the blows to be really painful. The object of the treatment, then, was not to test the girl's resistance.

"What are they?"

"*Brevi embo ro go*. Those are tapirs' penises."

"Why are you hitting her?"

"We are hitting the *kujambuku* with tapirs' penises so that she will desire men."

This answer seemed rather enigmatic. How would being whipped by a tapir's penis make Chachugi more ardent (so far she had not shown any lack of ardor) in soliciting the attentions of men? Questioned further, the Atchei were no more explicit — *go nonga ure*, that's the way we are. Though they might not have known what they were doing, there were many other tribes that could explain it.

The choice of the tapir was not really arbitrary. For the Atchei, it is essentially a game animal, appreciated for the taste of its flesh and the amount of meat it can provide. Since its hide is too thick for wooden arrows, they catch it in traps, digging a conical pit near the streams where it usually goes, and covering the opening with a fragile trellis of leaves and grass; the heavy animal (which weighs more than 450 pounds) does not discover the trick, falls into the hole, and is unable to get out. Then all they have to do is knock it out — *brevi ityty*, make the tapir fall. But in the myths of many Indian cultures, this fat animal with its long and rather obscene nose always plays the role of seducer — in spite of his heavy, ungraceful appearance, he is an irresistible Don Juan. Husbands fear his advances toward their wives, and he frequently does fatal damage to their honor. The tapir is highly erotic, and he loves romantic adventures so much that girls are crazy about him and find him exciting. What could be better than to use this Casanova's penis to strike a young girl who has just reached womanhood, if she is to attract the advances of men instead of repulsing them? Of course, Chachugi did not need this love potion, but at least they could be sure that she would be contaminated by the tapir's penis for the greater pleasure of the tribe's young gallants. When all is said and done, the Atchei really did know what they were doing.

The purification was proceeding rapidly. The pile of shavings was shrinking, but there were still enough for the hunters whom the husband had gone to find. They arrived safe and sound, since they had not been bitten by any snakes. They signaled from far away that they were approaching by crying out sharply two or three times, and the people in the camp cried out in answer. They had to do this: an enemy would never warn the camp that he was coming, so if they did not want to risk being struck in the chest by an arrow, they did well to let the camp know who they were a little in advance. Not long ago the Atchei used to hide pointed bamboo splinters under leaves in various places along the paths leading to the camp — and the unwelcome visitor who did not know where they had been placed was quite likely to get one stuck in his foot. Without even glancing at Chachugi, the men (including her husband) went to the designated place where they were washed.

A woman was painting the girl. In an armadillo shell that had been rolled into a horn, there was a black mass: this was a mixture of beeswax, resin, and some powdered charcoal. The woman took a little of this on the edge of a highly polished wooden blade, held it near the fire so that it would become almost liquid, and then applied it to the skin. It made a shiny black mark which would not go away for several days, even if the girl bathed in the stream. Her face was decorated first, with horizontal stripes on the forehead, two vertical stripes on each wing of the nose, four on the cheeks, and six on the chin. Then the woman proceeded to her neck and chest, and soon her entire trunk down to her pubis was covered with six rows of vertical marks, which made a very pretty effect. The same was done to the girl's arms and then her back. When this was finished, the woman painted her own forearms, torso, and belly and did the same to the two old women who had taken continuous part in the ceremony.

Night fell. Chachugi had gone back into her hut, still without having eaten anything. The two children of one of the girl's lovers had also been purified, and the smaller, who was only about fifteen months old, had protested against this treatment vehemently, because the water was cold. I was told that "when a *kujambuku* gets her blood, the children vomit, they can die." A gruel made of *pindo* flour and corn had been cooking in a large pot. When it was ready, a little honey was added to it, and the godfather gave everyone present a share of the *bruee*. This was the communal meal that brought to a close the first part of Chachugi's purification.

As with the *beta pou* — but immediately after the purifying bath, instead of several years later — the girl would undergo the *jaycha bowo*. The procedure was the same and would be carried out with a stone that the godfather would choose. The *kujambuku* would lie down on her back. The scarifier would cut open the skin from the base of the breasts to the pubis, twice on each side, in the form of arcs, not vertically as for boys. Then he would fill the space in between with short cuts; these were also curved and would stripe the whole of the belly. This *jaycha mama*, round scarification, would ensure the girl of quickly becoming pregnant; she would soon have a baby. The furrow in her belly said that this flesh was destined to be fertile from now on. The wounds would be smeared with powdered charcoal. They would heal and take on an indelible black color, and the woman would be marked forever. Why did the Atchei do this? So that their women would be beautiful, so that they would be good and fat. Without this scarification, they would be *gaipara*, thin, of poor quality. And if the mother's belly was properly chubby, the *doroparegi*, the first child, would "fall" easily, and the woman would not suffer.

I was supposed to witness all this the next morning. But when I turned up, three-quarters of the Indians had disappeared. The only people there were a few old people and Chachugi's parents. Chachugi herself was still in seclusion. Everyone looked upset. I asked what was happening, and the father, who was very disturbed, said: "*Jaycha ia! Kujambuku kyrymba ia ete!* No scarification! The girl completely lacks courage." For the first time, the Atchei's law had not been obeyed. Chachugi had been afraid; she had not wanted to face the *jaycha bowo*; the trial by pain had terrified her. How was this possible? The people were furious. But what could they do? Everyone knew very well that if the "blood had come out" several months earlier, before there had been any contact with the whites, Chachugi would not have dreamed even for a moment of backing out of what had been the duty of Atchei women from time immemorial. But things had changed. The rules of earlier times and even of recent times were little by little giving way before the world of the *Beeru*. For a long time, these rules had been obeyed, and this was why the Atchei had endured in the face of everything and everyone. The basis of Atchei life was faithfulness to the law. Once this bond between themselves and their very substance was severed, respect for the law and

belief in its value could only disintegrate. This was why Chachugi
had been afraid: her fear was not only an indication of her dis-
tress, but also the first symptom of the disease that was infecting
the Atchei — despair. They should not have left the forest; they
should not have come to the white men: "Near the *Beeru*, the Atchei have ceased to be Atchei. What sadness!" With death in his
spirit, this was how Jyvukugi had sung of his sorrow during the
whole of one long night. In spite of Chachugi's refusal, there
were great *pichua* and the wind blew very hard.

For one month, until her next menstruation, Chachugi refrained
from eating meat, honey, and wasp grubs, so that her eyes would
not become bloodshot, her first child would not be a girl, her
labor would not be endangered, and her first son would not be
deformed. She also refrained from playing the flute because it
would "dry out" her arms. She did not make love either; what
was more, no man would have dared suggest it to her: a *dare
pou*, new woman, was too dangerous. For a time, all the men and
women who had taken part in the purification ritual also gave up
the pleasure of *meno*.

Chachugi had been afraid of becoming a grown-up, a true
Atchei — she had wanted to remain a "new woman." Could such
a thing last long? In any case, the fact was that one cold morning
in June, the body of the little *dare pou* was discovered, already
stiff; she had died silently during the night. No one said anything
about it. *Ache ro kwaty*, the Atchei know.

Guayaki camp in the forest.

Chapter Five

Women, Honey, and War

The days went by peacefully, especially when the Paraguayan chief was gone. He was sometimes away for weeks, getting drunk in nearby villages. When he returned, hardly able to stay in his saddle, he would fly out in an incomprehensible rage, drawing his Colt and firing it in all directions while he shouted vague threats in Guarani. The Indians would be frightened; but this did not happen very often, and all in all the white man spent little time in the forest with the Atchei. He was usually off drinking *caña* in sordid *cantinas*, the kinds of places where the drunks were always reaching for their daggers or revolvers and fighting in wild brawls.

When my provisions ran out, I would go to San Juan Nepomuceno on horseback to buy cigarettes, beans, fat, rice, and such. There was a shopkeeper there who was very well off because he had no competition and was able to capture the local trade. His customers would come on horseback from their faraway homes, tie their horses to the gate, and stay there for a long time chatting while their order was filled. The grocer, who had sharp ears, knew everything that was going on in the area. One day, this friendly and jovial man beckoned me to go into the back of the shop with him.

"Listen, Don Pedro," he said. "Everyone around here thinks

you're very rich, and I've heard that you're going to be robbed. I have a safe, and I think you should leave your money with me. Then if you're killed, at least the money won't be lost," he added, laughing loudly.

He obviously did not believe me when I told him that, sad to say, I had nothing to put in his safe. I thanked him anyway and started back toward the forest, somewhat worried since night was falling. Yet I arrived at the camp without mishap, secretly pleased that in some respects my trip had been like a scene from a Western.

As I left the world of the white man and rejoined the Guayaki in the woods, I resumed a relaxed and lazy life, once again becoming part of the Indians' slow, unbroken rhythm. When the Atchei settled in Arroyo Moroti, their life had changed radically, especially where food was concerned, since they now had to eat many more fruits and vegetables — principally manioc — and much less meat. And the Indians became extremely depressed if they had to go without meat for more than a few days. In order to ensure an adequate supply of meat, they would have had to go far away from Arroyo Moroti, disappearing into the forest for long periods, and the Paraguayan would not have liked this at all. The Indians themselves were hesitant to go very far away from a place where in spite of everything they felt safe. Anywhere else, hostilities with the *Beeru* would have started up again, with fatal consequences. Nevertheless, the Atchei could not do without meat, not for more than three days. They would become morose, inert, dozing near the fires and refusing to cooperate with me at all.

Fortunately, spurred on by hunger, they would soon take action. One man would rouse himself very early, before the sun was up. Sitting on his heels in the light of the fire, he would begin chanting, repeating the same things over and over without a break for about half an hour. In the beginning, I did not understand the chant. But it always ended the same way: as soon as there was enough light for him to get his bearings, the man would get up, take his bow and arrows, and leave. He had simply been announcing that he intended to go hunting and telling everyone how many nights he would spend in the forest if he did not return the same day. When he planned to be away hunting for several days (several nights, in Atchei language), his wife and children would go with him. But they would leave in broad daylight, at least an hour after him: his wife, carrying her basket and a child and holding a smoldering stick, would not be able to keep up with him. When a man announced his plans this way, one or two others were always ready to leave with him. They left discreetly, apparently without waking up anyone else. But the man who had chanted always left first. Through his chanting he told the tribe he was leaving, indicated which direction he was going in, and also asked for company on his trip. But he did not wait for an answer, and without bothering to find out if anyone would follow him, he would go off.

It was not a useless precaution to say which direction he was going in. A thousand things could happen in the forest, and it was just as well for his companions to know where to look for him if he and his fellow hunters were gone too long.

One night, a man chanted that he was going to hunt monkeys and that he would return to the camp three nights later. Two others were going with him, so there would be three families in all, including two children. But after a week had gone by, they had still not reappeared. "The jaguar has eaten them up," remarked the Atchei. They always say this when the hunters do not return at the appointed time. In the same way, when I said I wanted to go for a walk in the forest, they inevitably said: "The jaguar will tear your guts out." Actually, it is rare that anyone ever meets up with a jaguar, and, except for Chachuwaimigi's recent death, it had been a long time since the animal had bothered anyone.

When they invoke the threat of the *baipu*, they are not really talk-ing about the animal so much as any accident which could disrupt the flow of their daily life: the jaguar is only a metaphor for this disruption. In any case, they were beginning to worry about this prolonged absence. They decided to go see what was happening, and I joined the group, in spite of their warnings: "It's very far! Lots of jaguars! Our companions are already dead!" They were really afraid that I would slow them down. They finally agreed to let me come, and I soon understood the reason for their reluctance.

This was not like a hunting trip, in which everyone explored the terrain slowly, inch by inch, with eyes and ears; here it was a matter of going straight to our destination without losing any time — and they walked very fast. I found myself at the tail end, slowed down and sometimes stopped altogether by the vines, which made me trip or suddenly tied me to a tree trunk. Thorns caught in my clothes, and I had to rip them loose with wild thrusts of my shoulders: I was not only trailing behind, but mak-ing a lot of noise as well! The Atchei, on the other hand, were quiet, supple, efficient. I realized fairly quickly that part of the problem was my clothes; the branches and creepers slid over the Indians' bare skin without hurting them. I decided to follow their example and took off my clothes, which were already in rags, leav-ing them at the foot of a tree so that I could retrieve them on the way back. I kept on only my boots — I could not have walked bare-foot and was afraid of snakes — and a large leather belt and holster which held my .38. Except for that, I was naked as a jaybird. In this bizarre outfit, I started walking again; at least there was no risk of an embarrassing encounter.

After about three hours, having crossed two small streams — fording one and crossing the other over a Guayaki bridge (a tree trunk lying with one end on either bank) — we reached the camp. There was only one fairly large shelter; the ashes were cold, and there was no one there. The Indians examined the ground all around, pointed out to one another things I could not see at all, and without hesitation turned in a certain direction. After another half hour of walking, we found them. Why had they abandoned the first camp and established another so close by? I do not know. Maybe they felt it was *ine*, stinking, contaminated; or maybe they had been frightened by a spirit. Here, too, there was only one shelter; the freshness of the palms indicated that they had been cut the day before. A slender thread of smoke rose from the fire, which was almost out. Except for one woman, who was nursing her little girl, the people in the tent were lying down. They were so sick that they hardly opened their eyes when we arrived. Normally, the men would have had their arrows in their bows, since we had prudently refrained from announcing our approach with the usual shouts: when you find signs of another human being in the forest, you never know who you are going to meet. They lay on the ground, feverish, no doubt suffering from flu.

"During the night," they groaned, "Krei came. He tried to smother us." When you feel a weight on your chest, when you find it hard to breathe and your dreams are bad, then you know that Krei is there.

"You should come back to the camp," we said to them. "You'll be taken care of, there are medicines there."

There was no answer. They were apathetic. To my great surprise, the men I had come with stayed there ten minutes at the most. They did not insist that the others leave. Picking up their weapons, they started back: their mission had been accomplished — they had found the hunters and had talked to them; they had not wanted to come, and so the others would go back. You might think this was an indication of profound indifference on their part, of total insensitivity to the fate of the sick people, even of cruelty. But this was not the case.

197

In fact, the reason they did not press their companions to follow them was that they respected their freedom. The sick people had apparently decided to stay there, and so they should not be urged to come. When an Atchei is sick, he prefers to remain alone, waiting for the sickness to leave him. If Krei's victims had said, "We want to go back, but we cannot," there is no question but that the others would have done their best to help them. And this is what happened. As we started to walk back, old Tokangi turned toward the *tapy* and shouted, "When you're dead, *briku u pa modo*, the vultures will devour you!" The Indians find it a repulsive prospect not to leave the world of the living according to the rituals. They would do anything rather than offer their bodies to nature and its animals, particularly vultures. "We're coming," we heard them say. With tired motions, the women gathered their things and put them in their baskets. Tokangi and another man took the children on their backs, we divided up the bows and arrows that belonged to the sick hunters, and we left. We walked slowly, because they could not go very fast. Several hours later, at night, we reached the camp; the Atchei did not make a big fuss over it. Aspirin was handed out to the sick people, fires were lit, and everyone went to bed.

I did not go with the Atchei very often when they went hunting. It meant spending one or two nights in the open and lying on the soft, wet forest floor next to a fire whose smoke hardly repelled the swarms of mosquitoes. It also meant having to go hungry, since I could not force myself to eat grubs. Besides, except for becoming tired, I did not gain much from these outings — only the observation of certain hunting techniques and tactics: what happened, for example, when a group of men surrounded a band of monkeys yapping in the treetops or a troop of wild *chachu* pigs, and the big ones began clacking their teeth at our approach, not in fear but in anger. There were also collective coati hunts, because the Indians were very fond of coati meat. Only married initiated men took part in this kind of hunting, which consisted not of shooting the animals down from the trees but of forcing them to come down to the ground where they could be caught by hand. To do this, the men would spread out around a clump of trees where coati had been seen, shoot arrows into the branches, throw pieces of wood or clumps of earth, shout and make such a racket that the animals became completely panic-stricken and could only think of one thing — to flee from the noise. They would scurry down headfirst. But at the bottom would be a man, his left forearm bound in a thick cord made of plant fibers and women's hair. A woman makes this *pabwa* for her husband using her own hair — obtained during a period of mourning, for example, when it is shaved off. The hairs are set aside especially for making this rope, which is only used for hunting coati. It has a symbolic as well as utilitarian value, however.

When the coati reaches the ground, the man pushes him against the trunk with his protected left arm, takes him by the tail with his right hand, swings him in the air, and smashes him against the tree with all his might, which breaks his skull or his spine. With this technique, the hunters can also capture the coati alive and use them as guard animals in the camps. But the *pabwa* is not always an effective protection against the ferocious bites of the coati, and several men proudly showed me the large scars left by these wounds: "Because of this, there will be great *pichua* when I die!"

All this was beautiful to watch; the Indians were so agile, so skilled, their gestures so precise and efficient — this was total mastery of the body. But just because of that, and because I could not match them, they were not very eager for my company when they went hunting. They would have been reluctant to have any white man along. The reasons were purely practical: they know how to move around quickly and silently, and a white man does

199

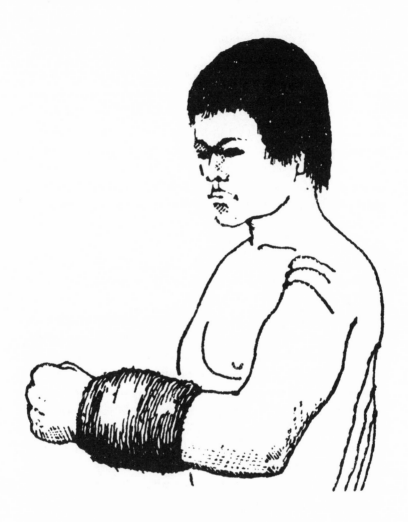

Pabwe, cord used to hunt coatis.

not. A white man wears shoes, he crushes twigs underfoot and makes the branches crackle, he shakes the creepers and makes so much noise that for hundreds of yards around the animals hear him and run away or hide. The hunt is jeopardized. I did not want to interfere with the Atchei's most important activity and did not try to impose myself on them. I had no trouble passing the time at Arroyo Moroti, because not all the Indians would leave at the same time; there were always people around with whom I could chat, joke, let the days flow by. It was never boring.

I was always informed of just about everything that went on in the camp, thanks to the *kybuchu*: when they were not following their fathers in the forest, they would stroll around or play in the clearing. One of their greatest games was spying on the adults in their private activities. They watched their movements and followed them when they went off into the woods, hid and observed them, and then commented at length on what they had seen, stifling their laughter. They were everywhere at once, intolerable and yet appealing. They had no illusions, because for them the adult world was completely without myths, without secrets, transparent. You had to watch out for the *kybuchu*. When the young women went off to pee together, calmly certain of being alone, they would suddenly hear bursts of laughter echoing around their secluded spot and the usual risqué remarks: "*Kyrypy pira! Kyrypy pira!* Red ass! Red ass!" The boldest of the boys would shout: "*Nde pere pira!* Your cunt is all red!" And then they would scamper off through the underbrush followed by the insults of the young women.

By the age of seven or eight, the children know everything there is to know about sex, for two main reasons. First of all, the adults are naturally very interested in it, and this does not escape the attention of the ever alert youngsters. Secondly, though the "grown-ups" are not in the least exhibitionistic, they make no effort to hide sexuality or the subject of sexual activities from the children. In their presence, and without any embarrassment, they discuss *meno* (making love), the adventures and experiences of various lovers, and the jokes made about these matters are understood by everyone. They have no taste for censorship, no feeling of disapproval of the body, and they make no effort to disguise the fact that they value this pleasure highly. The adults are willing to live under the children's eyes. No one tries to deceive them, and they are not deceived. But there is never any ambiguity. A man never allows himself to be familiar with his usual partner in front of anyone, young or old. Freedom and restraint: this is the atmosphere among the Indians. One might think that the total absence of repression could lead the *kybuchu* to precocious exploration, but this is not the case. Everything is very clear to them: *meno* is good, because the grown-ups say so; we will also do to women what the grown-ups do, but not before they give us the right to imitate them, not before our lips are pierced and we are called *betagi* instead of *embogi*. Women are for the initiates.

Occasional quarrels broke out among the *kybuchu*, though they never came to blows. From time to time, I would see one of them coming toward me. For a minute, he would walk around the hut, stealing glances at me, and then he would make up his mind. "So-and-so has done *meno* with such-and-such a girl!" he would murmur, his face full of pain at having to report a thing like that. This was pure slander, of course, inspired by the desire to avenge himself for some offense. There were three or four girls, but they were older than the *kybuchu* and were interested in young men and married men. In answer to my questions, the boy who had been accused was quick to say, "*Kybuchu* do not make love. Only when one has the *beta*!" They were well aware that any transgression of this rule would have been punished by *pané*.

Still, they found it very amusing to watch the adults. One of the boys, for example, would emerge from the forest and say to me, out of breath and in a great hurry to be off again. "Come quick! Chachugi and Baipugi are making love! They're in the forest! *Juja ury pute!* We're laughing, it's so much fun! Come on!" And to convince me, he writhed around wildly, mimicking poor Chachugi who was busy making love to Baipugi and unaware that he was the object of so much attention. I did not push my indiscretion (or professional conscience) so far as to respond to these pressing invitations. But this infallible system of information allowed me to find out what the adults would probably have hidden from me: clandestine love affairs, adulterous intrigues, and illicit pleasures rounded out a life that was as ordinary as any other. The *kybuchu* were not moved by any desire to denounce people; this was simply a good way to amuse themselves a little at the expense of the adults. On the other hand, it meant that I was in on the Atchei's secret life completely and could therefore understand its impact on the stability of the couples and on the way matrimonial conflicts were resolved.

The Atchei were as discreet about their love life as they were about taking care of their bodies. If they wanted to make love during the day, they had to steal off into the forest. A man would go off with a false air of nonchalance that gave him away completely; a few moments later a woman would get up and walk off in the same direction: they had a rendezvous. In general they would choose the warm hours of the afternoon, when everyone was asleep . . . but there were always the *kybuchu*. At night, no one ever went into the forest; the darkness was too dangerous, full of spirits, ghosts, phantoms. They stayed in the *tapy*. But even though I often slept right in the middle of the Indians, I never heard the slightest sign of abandon: it seems they performed the thing very quickly. Nevertheless, Kybwyragi once told how when he was a little boy he awoke in the middle of the night and saw his parents making love: "Terrible fear!" he said. On the other hand, it is quite common to see young couples caressing one another, though quite casually. Sometimes the husband will rub his cheek against his wife's face, but without kissing her — the Atchei do not kiss. They coo and murmur sweet things to each other. Less frequently, there is specific touching. A young woman, sitting on her folded legs, is making a bowstring, rolling fibers along her thigh; beside her, her husband dozes; but he is evidently only half asleep, because suddenly he plunges his hand into the predictable place. The woman cries out in surprise, but she has no objection. She bursts out laughing every time he returns to the attack. They play around this way for a moment, then both return to what they were doing before with no visible sign of emotion. What is more, during the year or so that I spent among the Atchei, I never saw an erection.

In spite of their obvious taste for it, I did not come away with the impression that the Guayaki were experts in the art of love, except perhaps for one or two of the *Iroiangi* men. It seemed that they conducted their own experiments, because everyone spoke with surprised amusement about a young husband who was encouraging his wife to perform fellatio on him — proof that this was not common practice among the others.

Among the few young women in the tribe, there was one very attractive girl of about fifteen who made no effort to hide the fact that she liked men. Nor did the men neglect her ("This girl," they said, "gives her hole very freely"). But she seemed insatiable and always let her desires be known. When there was no convenient *betagi* around, she and the other girls her age played games that made them laugh a great deal: one would tell a story, distracting the attention of another, and then suddenly touch her sex. Surprised, perhaps delighted, the other would cry out sharply and then try to pay the first one back. But this was not as good as having a man. One warm afternoon when everyone in the camp was taking his siesta, this girl wandered idly around. Her body was driving her crazy, and she seemed in a rather bad humor, undoubtedly because she had not immediately found what she wanted. But then she spied Bykygi; he was asleep, stretched out on his stomach, his head between his elbows. Without more ado, she went up to him, lay down on top of him, and without any self-consciousness began assaulting his rear end with vigorous thrusts of her body, as if she were sodomizing him. The poor man, torn so wildly from his sleep, groaned with surprise. She paid no attention and pinned him to the ground, clasping him between her legs. As if this was not enough, she now slid one hand under the man's belly and tried to catch hold of his penis. The two of them writhed around on the ground, one on top of the other, the girl silent and stubborn and the man crying out (though not very loudly), "*Poko eme! Poko eme!* Don't touch! Don't touch!" It did no good, because this was just what she was after. And she succeeded. The victim soon stopped protesting; a few minutes later, they both went off where no one could see them. She knew what she wanted, and she got it.

The *kybuchu* always let me know which husband or wife was deceiving his or her mate and with whom. Sometimes the affair was casual — a little lovemaking in a secluded spot in the woods could not be taken very seriously. At most — and even this depended on how irascible he was — the deceived husband would claim the right to take revenge, not real revenge — in which case he would have broken his bow over the head of the lover — but symbolic revenge, in which he would brandish his bow at the lover without hitting him: this was *jepy rave*, feigned vengeance.

I only found out about one crime of passion among the Guayaki: old Tokangi had killed a man when he was young by shooting him with an arrow. But Tokangi, broken down as he was, still had a reputation for being an *yma chija*, a naturally violent man. The women are less tolerant than their husbands, especially when the man is a well-known hunter: obviously, they are not willing to let him be stolen away by another woman. They punish their husbands either by refusing to sleep with them for a certain length of time or by immediately paying them back by doing the same thing: they offer another man the favors the husband had spurned. Things did not go any farther than this, and the couple's understanding would not be very harmed by these escapades.

Sometimes, too, a little humor helped to calm the anger of the offended partner. One day the camp was more lively than usual, and one of my small informants ran to me, explaining that "Kandegi has hurt himself! There is blood! They're going to perform a purification!" What had happened? Kandegi had made love with a woman who did not belong to him. They had seen him come running back, his penis all bloody: he had wounded himself. There were many people around, and everyone discussed it. Several men said that the reason the penis was "torn" was that the woman was too thin, her vagina was too narrow, and as he forced his way in, Kandegi had cut himself. (I thought the cut was not caused by the vagina but by the vigor of the man's assault; or had he simply scratched himself on some grass or a twig, since they had made love on the ground in the forest?) But in any case, an accident was bound to happen, the Atchei said: Hadn't the woman been just recently widowed? And didn't Kandegi know that such women were to be avoided, at least for a while? *Ianve* had punished him and would also punish the woman: he would carry her off over his shoulder like a piece of game, far away from the Atchei, and make her sleep alone in the savanna for several nights. To avoid these dangers, both would have to submit to a purifying bath. Kandegi was shamefaced and uneasy, because *Ianve* would try to smother him that night. On the other hand, it was also said that *Ianve* tormented a man who was satisfied with only one woman. It was therefore better to sleep with several, just to be left in peace. While Kandegi was being sponged off, his wife, who was sitting nearby and looking on, made fun of him: "*Ocho pa!* He is all torn up. That will teach him to make love with such a thin woman!" This was enough vengeance for her, and the two were soon reconciled.

These escapades, which added spice to the lives of the people involved and enriched the chronicle of the tribe, did not have any ill effect on the unity of the group; the social order was not threatened by it.

Eight or nine years earlier, long before contact was established with the *Beeru*, a split occurred within the Atchei Gatu. Jyvukugi, who was already the leader of the group, had a beautiful wife named Kimiragi. One day she went off alone some distance from the camp while her husband was away hunting; she went quietly, intending to gather some fruit from a *guaviju* tree. Around her the birds were singing fearlessly. Her attention was attracted by the insistent cry of a *mere*. The bird seemed to be hidden in the thickets. Curious, she approached, parted the underbrush, and discovered not a *mere* but a man who had imitated its cry in order to attract her attention: it was Kybwyragi, a grown man who had undergone scarification just a few months before. Forced to remain a bachelor because of the lack of women among the Atchei Gatu, he lived in his parents' *tapy*, eating food prepared by his mother and resolving the problem of *meno* by having quick liaisons with married women. "When there are no women," the Atchei explain, "we share other people's women." Jyvukugi's wife was there, at his mercy; he caught her and made her lie down, and then and there he consummated the *piaro* — what could be called

207

rape. Actually, they say that Kimiragi did not put up much of a fight. Who knows? Perhaps she went off in search of fruit hoping this would happen! In any case, the affair did not end there. It even took on dramatic proportions.

It turned out that Kimiragi had enjoyed this adventure and wanted to prolong it. It soon became generally known, and when Jyvukugi found out about it, he flew into a fearful rage, because he really was *yma chija*. He was all the more angry because he was his young rival's *jware* and *jepare*: he had assisted at his birth and had pierced his lip. He was in some sense a father to Kybwyragi. What was more, the Atchei condemned the young man's misconduct severely: what he had done was almost incestuous! Beside himself, Jyvukugi seized his bow and began shooting off arrows blindly. He was out to kill, and the men ran behind trees and the women cried out. At last, when he had shot off all his arrows, a few old women, including his mother, succeeded in quieting him; with hasty motions, giving him a *piy* and imploring him, they managed to calm him down.

But the harm had been done; he decided to leave, and several families, including those of his brothers, decided to follow him. This was the end of good relations among the Atchei Gatu. The separation lasted several months, and tension between the two groups could have turned into open hostility, even war. Fortunately Bywangi, Jyvukugi's father, foresaw what might happen and wisely resolved to try to mend matters.

He went off after his son; he went very far, walking through the forest for many days. He found the group and set out to convince Jyvukugi that he and the others should come back, that the tribe needed its chief in order to face the white men's attacks, which were occurring more and more often. Jyvukugi was calm now; the months he had spent away from his wife had quieted his rage. He was no longer beside himself, and the bitterness that remained in his heart did not prevent him from listening to reason. So he heeded his father's advice, because as chief he felt responsible for all the Atchei Gatu. In addition, he had no wife: there were no others available, but in any case he wanted Kimiragi, his own wife, back. But then there was the problem of Kybwyragi, the lover. He resigned himself at that point to accept the solution that men always adopt in cases like this, since there is no other choice: when a bachelor becomes the rival of a married man, rather than let the situation deteriorate in semi-clandestinity, which would sooner or later disrupt the society and pit the respective relatives and friends of the two rivals against one another — rather than run a risk that could be fatal to the tribe — they decide — with the help of public opinion — to make the "secret" lover the official "secondary husband" of the woman he has been running after. The rivalry between the two men is thereby suppressed; they are both husbands, and the multiplicity of opposing desires is resolved in the unity of the polyandrous marriage.

The Atchei Gatu were reunited, songs and tears celebrated the reconciliation, and Kimiragi, triumphant, now lorded it over two husbands, the principal one — *imete* — being Jyvukugi, and the secondary one — *japetyva* — being Kybwyragi. Once the decision was made, peace descended on the ménage à trois. When the *japetyva* — the less important husband — is a widower, already old and not very demanding sexually, the daily life of the couple is not much affected. The secondary husband takes charge of the smaller tasks — cutting wood for the fire, fetching water, taking care of the children. In exchange for this, he escapes loneliness and shares his family's meal. If the two husbands are young and strong, their wife's position is even better, both materially — since the two husbands compete zealously with one another to bring back more game to their wife — and erotically, since she can always count on both partners being favorably disposed to her.

This situation can become delicate, for it is possible that both men might want her at the same time, and it is always the wife who decides which to take, being careful not to favor one over the other. Sometimes she goes off into the forest with the *imete*, and sometimes with the *japetyva*. The husbands have no complaints about this arrangement. As for the children, they consider all their mother's husbands to be their fathers, though they distinguish among them according to how each stands with their mother. The principal husband is the true father (*apa ete*), and the secondary husband is a partial mixed father (*apa miro*). Eventually, a certain degree of paternity is granted to a man who made love with a woman while she was pregnant. He is called the *apa perombre*, the father who has done *pero*, that is, who has slept with a woman pregnant by someone else. All these men claim with equal conviction to be the children's father, and no one challenges them.

Kimiragi had a son, a *kybuchu*. There was a striking resemblance between the boy and Kybwyragi, who had to be his biological father. Nevertheless, the boy considered Jyvukugi to be his *apa ete*, and Jyvukugi for his part assumed the role of father. One time, Jyvukugi was discreetly teasing his wife in the boy's presence. The boy became furious and began punching his father in a rage. The parents laughed and said, "You are very *kyrymba*, very brave."

During the day, there is no special rule governing the positioning of the family members in the *tapy*. At night, however, the position in which everyone sleeps around the fire is assigned in advance; you cannot lie down just anywhere. The Atchei sleep right on the ground, if it is not damp, or on palm-leaf mats; they are naked. During the night they could not stand to wear the clothes given them by the white man and would take them off as soon as the time came to go to sleep. The woman is the center of the sleeping space. First of all, there is the fire, burning at the edge of the shelter. Then there is the first row of sleepers, the children — up to the age of seven or eight, after which they are already somewhat independent of their parents and sleep together next to their own fire. Behind the children is their mother, facing the fire so as to benefit from its warmth. If she has a baby, she holds it against her body in its carrying sling, well protected from the cold. And lastly, behind the woman lies the husband or husbands, sleeping farthest away from the fire, as is only fair. Eventually, when the temperature drops very low as it does in June and July, a second fire is lit opposite the first. The woman is thus metaphorically divided from top to bottom in accordance with her twofold nature: her front is her *mother* aspect, where the children sleep between her and the fire — she forms a sort of border between the child space and the adult space; her back is her *wife* aspect, reserved for her husbands.

When there is only one husband, there is no problem — he stretches out next to his wife. But what happens when there is more than one? In this case, the woman is divided again, not longitudinally this time, but transversely, so that she compromises three sections (since apparently a woman cannot have more than three husbands). Each of these "areas" is occupied by one husband, depending on his position in the marriage hierarchy. First there is the lower part of the female body, from the waist down; the second part in a descending scale of "values" is the woman's head; and the last lies between the first two — the middle consisting of the woman's back. Naturally enough, the most privileged section of the woman, her very femininity, belongs to the principal husband: lying more or less perpendicularly to the woman, he sleeps with his head against her thigh; this is his right, for he is the *imete*. The secondary husband sleeps at the other end from the principal husband, with his head next to the wife's head.

And if there is a third husband, he takes the place in the middle, which is the most neutral sexually, since he was the last to come, even if in her heart of hearts the woman secretly prefers him to the others. This is how the Atchei sleep. What is more, the husbands are identified by the part of their wife's body which is assigned to them. Graphic and precise, these terms realistically express the division of the woman into three parts. They are worth recording.

The principal husband can be called by three different names:
kyrypytywaty: he who is accustomed to being near the anus.
kymakatywaty: he who is accustomed to being near the leg.
aivirotywaty: he who is accustomed to being near the behind.

As for the *japetyva*, they are respectively:
totywaty: he who is accustomed to being near the head.
jyrukatywaty: he who is accustomed to being near the ribs.

Among the *Iroiangi* there were no polyandrous households. When the tribe came to Arroyo Moroti, the chief had two wives: one of them was given to the Atchei Gatu and reinforced the alliance between the two groups. But the absence of this form of marriage did not mean the Strangers were unaware of it. They were just as familiar with it as the others and practiced it whenever necessary. Since the proportion of men to women was more or less balanced, there was no reason for a woman to have more than one husband. Nevertheless, one day the problem came up. Since Chachuwaimigi's death in January, her last husband (young Japegi, whom she had substituted for old Paivagi) had been without a wife. He had gone back to live with his parents, and his mother cooked for him and made the strings for his bow. Naturally, he tried to obtain the favors of the young women, and he managed

212

to form an intrigue with the wife of an *Iroiangi*, Krajagi, the very beautiful mother of two young boys. As far as the lover was concerned, this was undoubtedly just a brief escapade; but the woman took the thing much more seriously. This happened in June. A good portion of the Atchei left Arroyo Moroti (and I went with them) to camp rather far away next to a grove of orange trees (probably the site of an old Jesuit mission), whose branches bent under the weight of thousands of ripe oranges. For the Indians, there were two benefits to be gained from this move: not only the succulent oranges, but also the animals attracted by them, especially the monkeys and even wild pigs — and this made the hunting easier. The woman left with her lover, without bothering to worry about her husband and children, who stayed behind at Arroyo Moroti. The two men had already been involved in a rather violent quarrel in which they had shot at one another several times. The husband was one of the strongest men in the tribe, and the lover became afraid. This was why Japegi had seized the opportunity presented by the trip to put some distance between himself and the husband. But he found himself in an embarrassing position when Krajagi decided to go with him — she was furious with her husband because he had pinched her cruelly again and again: this is what the men do when they are displeased with the way their wives are behaving. Japegi was not anxious to continue the affair, which had started off so badly, but what was he going to do with the woman? She did not want to go back to Arroyo Moroti. It was decided, therefore, that Kajawachugi and the two children would be sent for so that husband and wife could be reconciled. And the Indians unanimously appointed me to go get the husband and bring him back to his inconstant wife.

I was not very pleased with this decision — it was a good day's journey on horseback between the two camps — but I could not refuse: I had to do what was asked of me. So I left. I found Kajawachugi sad, very depressed. I was not sure what arguments to use to convince him to join the others: "Here, you are like a widower. No women. Who does the cooking? How are you going to eat? Your boys want their mother. Come with me." In vain I described his situation here in the blackest terms and contrasted it to the very agreeable life at the other camp ("The oranges are very good. There is game"). He stubbornly persisted in answering: "*Ape ro cho enda.* This is my home." And he was right: it was up to Krajagi to come back; he should not have to join her and her lover. I did not go on insisting and set off again, certain that I had failed. I had hardly gone one mile when I heard someone walking behind me: Kajawachugi was catching up to me, his younger son on his shoulders and the other trotting behind him. I was relieved. He had made up his mind to come. I took the boy on my back. As we walked, I asked the *kybuchu* about his mother. He knew everything about the affair she and Japegi were having. Without showing any emotion, he said, "*Kuja meno jwe.* The woman wanted to make love."

We arrived in the middle of the night. The next day Kajawachugi made a proposal, couched in a few brief sentences: he would agree to let the other man become Krajagi's secondary husband. This was the only solution to the conflict, since the woman did not want to give up her lover. Japegi would come to live with them under the same roof, and he would have the status of *totywaty* — he would sleep next to Krajagi's head. It was an honest proposal; Kajawachugi had no ulterior motives. But Japegi clearly did not see eye to eye with him. He was afraid of the husband's physical strength and as an Atchei Gatu felt reluctant to live in a position to relative inferiority among the Strangers. He chose to decline the offer and returned to Arroyo Moroti, somewhat upset. Kajawachugi was not at all disappointed; for him the affair had turned out very satisfactorily. Krajagi, however, was distressed. She sulked and would not even speak to me anymore, as though I had been in some way responsible for what had happened.

Sometimes people are named after their sexual organs. One very old, skeletal *Iroiangi* grandmother whom I once saw calming her grandson by giving him her breast, which was as thin as a pancake, was now known only by the name of Perechankangi — vagina of dry wood. Everyone called her that, even the children; it was not disrespectful, but simply objective, and she was not offended. All the Guayaki are named after animals, and nearly all the animals can provide names for people. The only exceptions are a few birds that are not eaten because they are pets of *Chono*, Thunder, and the agouti. The Atchei have another term besides the word *embo* to designate penis, and that is the expression *tavwa jaka*, which means head of an agouti. If a boy is gesticulating and his penis is bouncing in all directions, a woman will cry out to him, "You, boy, don't shake like that, it makes your agouti's head jump!" Also, a pregnant woman will avoid eating the meat of the agouti: otherwise, she would give birth to a child swollen like an erect penis.

The Atchei appreciate sexuality at its true value: freely and discreetly exploited, it can open the way to pleasure for men and women. Why go without what is so good? There is a certain order, however: no one substitutes the demands of his desire for the law of the group — the law is always triumphant because it is never broken. The community of the Guayaki Indians is liberal enough so that anarchy is not a temptation. And these people are savages.

The month of June was very cold. An icy wind blew from the south, and the wall of vegetation barely managed to contain it. I would not have thought I was near the tropic at all, and more than once we woke at dawn to see what amounted to a polar landscape: white frost on the grass of the *campos* and frozen puddles. This was the time of the *duy pute*, the great cold. For the Atchei, it marked the passage from one annual cycle to the next; it was in some sense their new year. The fires were kept burning day and night, and at the end of the afternoon we would all spend some time in the forest cutting wood to burn. In this way I was able to learn from the Indians which was the best wood, which would give off a great deal of heat and very little smoke. The *kybuchu* had got into the habit of sleeping next to my fire, which saved them the trouble of going to get wood; but even so, they did help me a little. The ones who had clothes did not lie down without taking them off.

Surrounding me, then, were seven or eight *kybuchu*, who were sometimes joined by two or three adults, forming an incredible pile of naked bodies — arms, legs, heads, all mixed up together, warmed as much by animal heat as by the heat of the fire. From time to time, one of the people sleeping would change position, grunting as he turned over and upsetting the structure. Then there would be silent agitation for several seconds before the structure settled into place again. It was a miracle that during these nocturnal upheavals no one lay directly on the embers. And yet it never happened, even though no one woke up during this commotion.

In the morning, the bodies would be completely gray from the ashes. The Indians would brush themselves off vigorously, since they hated to have ashes touching them. They said that certain children were born with *pire krembu*, ashy skin. These children would be killed. They also hated to see me covered with ashes and would smack me all over trying to clean off my clothes after I had wallowed in ashes during the night: "Ashes! This is to get it off!" they would say, annoyed. A pregnant woman will never eat the flesh of the *braa* snake: the child would be born with ashy skin. What is the source of this antipathy? Maybe it has

216

something to do with the myth about the origin of the night, in which the boy broke Baio's great pot and let loose darkness and ashes, which made him dirty. Are the Atchei afraid that contact with ashes will cause the return of chaos — continuous night — which the foolish action of the uninitiated boy brought about? It is possible. In any case, the only situation in which contact with ashes was tolerated was when they were used as a cure. If someone was seriously ill, he would be entirely covered with ashes; the sick person would lie there a while, all whitish, and then he would be washed. So the month of June was chilling us through; several nights in a row the temperature fell below freezing.

At the end of the month, all the *Iroiangi* except for a few *kybuchu* disappeared without saying anything, taking their belongings with them: we simply woke up one morning and found them gone. They had gone east, into the heart of the forest, where they would not be in danger of meeting anyone. The Atchei Gatu stayed in Arroyo Moroti. For a moment, I thought the Strangers had suddenly decided to resume life in the forest for good. "They're doing it for the *to kybairu*," the Atchei Gatu explained to me.

When the Guayaki were free and masters of the forest, each tribe controlled its own hunting territory, either unaware of its neighbors or prepared to drive them off with bows and arrows if they attempted to invade. But not all the members of one group lived together. Each unit, politically independent of the others, was subdivided into small bands of twenty to twenty-five people, comprising a few families. The Atchei Gatu, for example, included two bands, and the Strangers, who were more numerous, included five or six.

It was economically necessary for the Indians to be scattered through the forest this way. Since they were so dependent on

217

hunting, they had to take into account the fact that in any one place there would not be much game. It was not every day that they were lucky enough to come upon a herd of wild pigs and wipe them all out within a few seconds. Since the animals were dispersed over vast stretches of land, the men had to be too. In places where the whole of the tribe could not have survived because of a lack of food, a small unit could manage without any trouble.

The tribal area, in other words, was divided up into subareas in which these bands roamed. Each band had a sort of proprietary right over the territory it lived off, which was enormous in proportion to the number of people who occupied it: about twenty people would need more than a hundred square miles of forest in order to follow the yearly cycle in peace. They simply could not stay in the same place all the time.

After being in the presence of human beings for a few days, the animals go off somewhere else to find peace and quiet. The men must therefore follow them, step by step. From one camp to the next, they cover the whole of the area. By the end of a year of wandering, they are back where they started.

But their movements are not completely random; they must retrace their steps to gather the grubs that have been multiplying in the palm trees they cut down several months earlier. These grub "farms" mark the fact that a particular area is owned by the band. "These are Chachugi's palms, and these are Pirajugi's," they would say, when we chanced across some fallen trees. Naturally, no one would touch them, since they belonged to their companions.

The bands within one tribe had friendly relations with one another, since they were made up not only of *irondy*, companions, but also of blood relatives. From time to time, two bands would meet, camp together for several days, and then go their separate ways. But as a rule each little group wanders alone, within the limits of its own area nearly all year long, leading a life that is in every respect the same as the life its neighbors are leading. Of course, they give a sympathetic welcome to other bands when they are being too closely pursued by white men and come to take temporary refuge with their companions. Sometimes, too, a messenger from one band will come to tell the others that something important is happening that requires their presence. But this did not occur often, and long months would go by without news of other Atchei. This separation could have been permanent; nothing prevented it from continuing indefinitely.

Yet once a year all the bands would converge on one camp, the tribe would be reunited, all the *irondy* would light their fires side by side: this was the Atchei's great festival, the *to kybairu*, and this was what the Strangers were going off to celebrate in June 1963, far away from indiscreet observers.

As soon as the first cold days arrived, everyone talked a great deal about the change in the weather. Its progress was followed closely: first there was the *duy pou*, the new cold, which was not yet very sharp; then there was the *duy provi*, fairly cold; then, at the end of the month, the *duy pute*, extremely cold. This was the sign that it was time to leave. At the same time, they were watching the changes in the color of the flowers growing on the *kymata* vine: they gradually turned from light yellow to red, which coincided with the most severe cold. "The cold is the *pichua* of the creeper when it is all red. The great cold is avenging the red creeper." In Guayaki thought, "vengeance" is the counterbalance of things, the reestablishment of an equilibrium that has been temporarily upset, a guarantee that the order of the world will not change.

What does the *jepy* avenge? Every event, positive or negative, harmful or beneficial, that takes place in the world of things or the world of men, whatever adds something or takes something away from the community of Atchei. Things and people must be subject to the rule; the limits of every deviation must be drawn or revealed; the sometimes shifting face of the world must be kept unified and serene. This is the basis of the Indians' concept of *jepy*, for they are uneasy when faced with *movement that distorts lines*. It is a means of at once doing away with change, abolishing differences, and continuing to exist in the light of Sameness.

But what was it about the vine that caused the cold to become its avenger? In June the *kymata* is *pregnant*, about to give birth to an unexpected child: the *myrynga* bee's honey. This is, of course, a metaphorical motherhood, which leaves the nectar in the secret hollows of trees where the insects have accumulated it. Nevertheless, the Atchei consider it a mother, thus assigning the honey a family place in the plant world. But it is only the mother of the honey of that particular time, when the cold indicates that it is time to gather it: the new honey, the first honey, whose return is a sign that underground nature is trembling, big with its renewal. It is the new year. When the creeper flowers and there is frost, that means there is fragrant honey, that young birds are being born in the nests, that the female tatou are pregnant, and that the snakes, asleep under the leaves between the tree roots, are beginning to stir.

The creeper is flowering: this is what the happy songs of the *kyrypreta*, *jeivi*, and *avia pyta* say. How pleasant it is to hear them, perching on a branch, and how exciting to know that they are summoning everyone to the *to kybairu*!

The word for honey is *ai* or sometimes *tykwe*, which means juice — *myrynga tykwe* means juice of the *myrynga* bee. But the first honey, the child of the creeper, is called *kybairu*. It is named after the main festival of the Atchei, who celebrate the regular motion of the world, the exact return of the same seasons, by coming together — all the *irondy* at once — and eating nature's first fruit, the new honey, the *kybairu*. The honey celebration is a good time to recall that the true society is the tribe, not the band, and as such the *to kybairu* — a game for adults only — clearly embodies a desire to reconstitute the larger community, even if only for a short while. *To* means head, or rather human head, since there is another word for the head of an animal. *To kybairu* is a game in which the men and women put their heads together in such a way that they form the same pattern — and achieve the same unity — *as the cells that make up the layers of a beehive loaded with honey*. The beehive is a metaphor for society. This is why the Strangers did not need the Atchei Gatu, who belonged to a different hive. This game is only played with one's own kind.

"When the *kyrypreta* bird sings joyously, it is a sign that we are going to visit the *cheygi*'s camp; it is time to gather. We are pleased. We are going to be happy to see our companions again. Everyone will laugh a lot, it will be fun. There will be women there." Who are the *cheygi*? People in other bands, people they have not seen for some time. They enjoy seeing their brothers or sisters or mothers and all their friends.

But they especially enjoy seeing the women, the daughters and sisters of the *cheygi*. They miss women; and the game they play not only celebrates the festival of honey, but also the festival of love. It is a chance to abandon themselves to the joys of *pravo* — of seducing women. "Visits to the *cheygi* are for courting young women." Festival of honey and court of love.

It was most important to be presentable, not to look sloppy, for this would have shocked people: the men carefully plucked their eyebrows, because the women did not like a coarse man who had hair around his eyes like an animal. They arranged their hair, shaving it on their foreheads and the top of their heads so that it formed a crown and letting it hang down a little on the backs of their necks. The ones who felt like it and who had been able to kill the necessary animals also made headdresses out of jaguar skins shaped into a cone and ornamented with a bunch of coati tails, which trailed over their shoulders. It was very beautiful. Dressed this way, a man was a true Atchei, a great hunter. The men in all the different bands took these pains so that they would be pleasing to the women.

They were all readying themselves to make love. Married or not, they were all counting on having intoxicating adventures with the beautiful daughters of the *cheygi* they would come into contact with during the game. But for the young men who were still bachelors, there was not only the pleasure of anticipating brief intrigues but also the possibility of finding wives. As a rule, the Indians did not marry within their own bands but took their wives from other bands: the *to kybairu* is also the time and place for the men of different bands to exchange women. So in the midst of the cold of June, the hearts of the young Atchei men were warmed by the sound of birdsongs.

On to the women! This might have been the marching song of the Indians as they walked to meet one another. But the gravity of the occasion — which does not in the least diminish its joy — requires that everything be done with a certain circumspection. There are obstacles to overcome. Along the way the men keep an eye out for hollows in the trees where there might be hives. Since it is cold, the bees are torpid and not at all aggressive. It is easy to extract the honey, and the women fill their large *daity* with it. There will be a great deal of *kybairu* to give their companions. The wax is set aside: after it has been thoroughly chewed, it is made into balls and arranged in the baskets.

The day before the meeting — they will know how close the *cheygi* are by traces of smoke in the distance, tracks, or a barely audible cry — the men prepare a mixture of wax, pulverized charcoal, and resin. It is very thick and smells good. The women paint the men with it. First the face — they apply the black charcoal powder over their foreheads, cheeks, and all around their mouths — and then the whole torso, in front and in back, and in long strokes down the arms. Some men have the women add fine lines over that and then put white *urubu* on top of it. Still others have their shaved skulls ornamented as well. The men are ready, and everyone knows that the *cheygi* will be painted in the same way. The charcoal hides the whiteness of the skin, and the whites of the eyes shine through the blackened faces. The men look terrifying! They would fill their enemies with fear. And in fact, this is the war paint the Atchei cover themselves with when they go off to fight. "When they see us all black, the *Iroiangi* are very afraid and run off. We terrify them!"

This is the way things are done: a peaceful meeting, held for the sake of strengthening the political alliance among all the *cheygi* through the marriages that will be arranged there, begins with a show of violence. The women and children hang back a little; the men arrive at a pleasant clearing, their bows and arrows in hand, superbly decked out: they stand face to face, warriors prepared to attack one another. Are they actually going to do it? Not at all. There is no feeling of hostility; everyone is peaceably disposed. Then what is going on? They are not really capable of expressing it very well, yet they know what they are doing. The fact is that the exchange of women, the establishment of the matrimonial relationship, does not concern only the man and woman who are going to get married.

Marriage is a social act involving two groups: the group taking the woman and the group giving her up. An inequality arises from the fact that one is taking something away from the other (even if now or at some future time another woman comes to take the place of the first): one suffers a lack, the other an excess. A mar-

Ambwa, hunter's ceremonial headdress.

riage is not neutral; it causes things to be different, and this can sometimes lead to conflict: to violence, to war.

The Guayaki tribes fought among themselves in the past, sometimes to conquer a hunting territory, but more often to capture women, as Lozano remarked. This was necessary because there were almost always more men than women. Even if the problem was handled by allowing one woman to have several husbands, polyandry did not always succeed in guaranteeing every man access to at least one woman. The life of the tribe would be endangered by this general uneasiness, and the tribe would decide to attack the Strangers and steal their women. The oldest Atchei Gatu remembered that several decades before they had wiped out part of another tribe that lived far away to the east near the Paraná River. Almost all the men were killed and the women were taken. The demographic situation was reversed: several men had more than one wife.

There is a secret relationship binding marriage and violence, women and war. Why do the men open the festival of *to kybairu* with this bellicose display, dressed up as warriors? Because they are well aware — and careful not to forget — that along with the bond which the exchange of women will soon create between them and the *cheygi* there is an opposition between the men who are soon to be brothers-in-law, and this opposition must be recognized.

This confrontation between the men and the future husbands of their sisters is resolved either by the violence of combat or the alliance of marriage: you can either capture the women after a war in which you have been victorious — and dispense with the brothers-in-law, who are now your enemies — or exchange wives peacefully, so that the groups become allies. War is an aggressive visit; peaceful visits are like a war that you have managed to avoid. But in both situations the object is the same: to get women. Of course, among *cheygi*, among men of the same tribe, there is no

225

question of stealing one another's wives. But it is best to behave according to the nature of things, to bring the element of violence in the matrimonial exchange into the open rather than hide it. They are not going to make war, *they are going to mime it.*

This is why the two groups of men, painted and armed, stand watching each other in the clearing where the meeting is going to take place. It only looks violent, but nevertheless it must be taken seriously. After the feigned declaration of war must come the ritual of *reconciliation*: it will be taken as proof that the path which has led to the *to kybairu* was not the path of war. Bows and arrows are laid down on the ground. The men walk toward each other and divide up into pairs: one man from one band and one from another. The couples can remain standing but generally prefer to sit down. This is the only time the Atchei allow physical contact, which is strictly forbidden in everyday relations. At this moment, however, it is even encouraged.

I was very aware of how extremely repugnant the Indians found the idea of touching one another; it was clear when food was given out: instead of passing the food directly from hand to hand, whoever is giving the food puts the fistful of grubs or piece of meat on the ground, and the person he is giving this gift to picks it up. This reserve is certainly a kind of good etiquette. But there is something else in it: the conviction that physical contact is a form of aggression. Now if you want to deny what seems to be an aggressive appearance, what better way is there than to accept what would ordinarily be interpreted as an act of hostility — bodily contact? If the men welcome this now, it means they really are not enemies. So they enter into a ceremonial game, the necessary prelude to all phases of the ritual, the *kyvai*: the tickling. Two by two, putting their arms around each other, the warriors run their fingers into the armpits and down the ribs of their partners. It is a sort of competition to see who will be the last to laugh. They try to hold back as long as possible and endure this tickling, which is a form of torture they are not used to. By allowing men to touch each other, the true function of the *kyvai* becomes clear: to establish or strengthen friendship between two men. Fairly often in the camps, an Atchei Gatu would approach a Stranger and ask him to sit down beside him. The two men would put their heads together and begin the *kyvai*, murmuring in wheedling voices like lovers: "You see, *cheygi*, we are doing the *kyvai*. We are doing it so that we will laugh, so that we will be happy. I am tickling you, and you will not be able to resist. You will burst out laughing and free yourself. We are friends." The man being subjected to this hunches up, squeezes his arms against his sides (he would have trouble trying to tickle the other man), holds his breath, and contorts his face with great effort, but he does not fight it for very long. All of a sudden he explodes, he is shaken by a spasm and breaks out in hysterical laughter. This is too much, and he gets up and tries to escape; the other man tries to stop him, and this goes on for a few minutes. At last the *cheygi*, hiccuping, sick with laughter, and nearly suffocating, manages to ask for mercy in a shrill voice: "Enough! A lot of tickling! It makes my stomach hurt!" They are friends. When I had a favor to ask, it was better not to risk the embarrassment of being refused. I would therefore address myself to a *cheygi*, and in order to establish a friendship I would imitate the Indians and give myself up to the pleasures of the *kyvai*. The happiness would be shared by everyone. The partner I chose, whom in other circumstances I would certainly never have challenged, would collapse after several minutes of tickling, a Hercules flailing about on the ground and whimpering like a newborn child.

One time I wanted to show my sympathy for a young *Iroiangi* woman who was several months pregnant. But I had hardly touched her when she very abruptly moved away, more upset

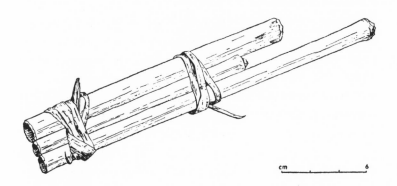

Mimby, flute.

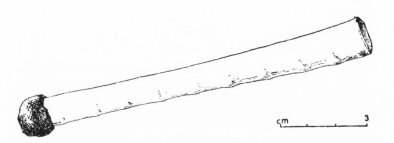

Whistle made of vulture bone with a wax stopper.

than angry. "*Bayja vwa!*" shouted another woman, "it's because of the *bayja!*" And she explained to me that because I had done *kyvai* to a pregnant woman I would become *bayja* when the child was born. The jaguars would eat me up unless I was purified with *kymata* creeper. When the time came, I was purified and I never ran across any jaguars.

The act that starts the *to kybairu* has taken place. The men have performed a good *kyvai*, everyone is pleased, everyone is now *cheygi*. The camp, which has been quickly set up, swarms with Atchei — the entire tribe is there. The men go to the river to wash off the paint, which is no longer needed. The women sing the ritual greetings. The *daity* are full of honey, giving off a rich fragrance, and the *pindo* brushes are ready. Quarters of two kinds of wild pig are grilling over the fires. This is the favorite meat when the Indians gather for the festival, and the men have been successful at their hunting. And here they are at nightfall, singing of their exploits, or rather declaiming them.

The stories are all identical, emphatically narrated without embellishment, and they all end with the same words: "I am a great hunter! As for me, I am the greatest killer of animals!" In this way, the women they are going to have fun with the next day will know everything about their suitors' good qualities. The women listen to the men's singing and keep time by beating a large piece of hollow bamboo on the ground in unison. *Poom! Poom!* It echoes well and sounds pretty. After the men, the young women sing or play the flute, and the boys answer them, because they have made *mimby* especially for the occasion. The older women blow into their whistles, which have been carved out of vulture bones. Shouting, singing, laughter, music, good food; all the friends are there, and the women are beautiful. *Juja ury pute!* They are so happy that they laugh. The next day they will take the *proaa*.

To grab the *proaa* is really the objective of the gathering, the climax of the ritual, and everyone waits for it with impatience. A *proaa* is a sort of large bean similar to the European bean, and it grows in pods on a forest vine. In the game known as *proaa mata*, a person puts one of these beans under his armpit or in his fist. The object of the game is to force the person to give up the bean: he is tickled and sooner or later gives up, and whoever has managed to get the coveted *proaa* brandishes it in the air. But whereas in the earlier reconciliation ritual there were only the two partners, here, in the *to kybairu*, all the adults gang up to tickle whoever has the bean. The game begins with everyone sitting around the person with the bean. He is tickled by dozens of hands at once. He rolls over the ground, the people fall on him, he tries to escape, they catch him. Piles of people collapse on top of one another. It is a wild scuffle, with women crying out sharply and men grunting softly. The children do not take part in the game, because people get so carried away that they might be hurt in the general violence. Anyway, it has nothing to do with them. This is when the men and women choose each other. If they are married, they can find an extramarital partner; if they are single, they can declare their love and eventually get married, if the passion lasts.

The whole time the tribe is assembled this game is played, and each person in turn holds the bean and is then robbed of it. It is simple for a boy or girl to give up the bean to the person he or she chooses; to capitulate under the tickling of a certain person is like a declaration of love. I will let you take the bean so that you will let me take something else; I try to rob you of the *proaa* because I desire you. The *to kybairu* is the festival of the body. Anything is a pretext for touching it and using it. If the women are singing, a group of men will descend on them, and an intense *kyvai* will be organized. Everyone is in a good mood, unrestrained, moved by joy to seek pleasure. You would have to be an unusually sour person not to give yourself up to the general happiness.

The *to kybairu* is a general ceremony celebrating two things: the fact that the whole society has come together and nature as a place of order. New honey is eaten together, friendship is measured in various amusements, and almost everything is permitted in the love contests. The *to kybairu* fulfills everyone's secret expectations and answers the sacred call of the joy of living — it is the Festival.

It is also the occasion for arranging marriages. After two young people have sized each other up during the many ticklings and bean games and decide to continue sharing the joys of *meno* — which they have already experienced more than once — they think of getting married. As soon as the choice has been made and the decision taken, things go very fast; the marriage is arranged without more ado. "*Cho reko jwe*," says the man. "I want to possess you." "*Nde reko vera*," the young woman answers. "You will possess me." In this context, possession is meant not so much in the sexual sense as in the sense of a husband's right and privilege to own his wife. The young husband then builds a *tapy*, which will become the new couple's home. Up until then, the man and woman had lived with their parents. From then on, they will have their own fire, and the young woman will cook for her husband.

Once the hut is ready, the man goes to his parents-in-law's hut. Their daughter is sitting there. The young man catches her roughly by the arm and drags her away behind him: "Come to my *tapy*, come sit next to me." Reduced to pure gesture, this is a mock abduction of a woman: *breko mata*, to carry off wives. And since every offense calls for revenge, the father of the girl does *jepy*. How? By punching his own wife. The marriage has been consummated. All that remains is for the son-in-law to carry game to his father-in-law and grubs to his mother-in-law

231

the next day. When the bands part company, the new couple can join the wife's band or the husband's, as they like. In any case, if they are not happy where they are, they can easily go off to find the *cheygi*. But most often they will decide to live with the wife's relatives.

Whom does a man marry? Anyone, apparently, except for the women who fall under the chief prohibition: mother, sister, and daughter, as well as "godmother" and "goddaughter." In the past, the choice of mate was probably governed by a collection of more complex rules. But the drop in population—mainly due to persecution by the whites—along with the small number of women made it impossible to hold to a more rigorous system. In order for every man to have a wife—even one to be shared with another man—the prohibitions had to be reduced to a minimum. Otherwise there would have been too many bachelors, and the very existence of the society would soon have been endangered.

For a man, therefore, the choice of possible women was narrow. This difficult situation resulted in some strange marriages. Not that of a man with his sister's daughter, which was the favorite, almost classic marriage of the ancient Tupi-Guarani, but the sort of marriage in which, for example, Jyvukugi married unfaithful Kimiragi, his mother's youngest sister. It may be that a few decades earlier such a marriage would have been impossible, would have been considered incestuous. But now it is not looked upon that way at all, and only the five cases mentioned above are considered incestuous by the Guayaki. I should add that the last two are not very serious. On the other hand, it would be unthinkable to disobey the injunction concerning the first three women. Incest carries its own punishment.

Even if the guilty man is not punished by the rest of the tribe, his fate will be irreversibly decided. Whoever sleeps with his mother will be changed into a tapir; whoever sleeps with his sister will be changed into a howler monkey; and whoever sleeps with his daughter will be changed into a roe deer. When a man commits incest, he is wiping out his own humanity and violating its most important rule; he is turning his back on what is, he is exiling himself from his culture, he is reverting to nature: he is becoming an animal. One cannot introduce disorder into the world with impunity. The various levels that make up the world must be left in their places — nature with its animals here and culture with its human society there. There must be no crossing over from one to the other.

The Atchei come to the *to kybairu* by paths that are known by them alone. The great cold gives them the signal. Will they be the only ones to go to the meeting place — they, the living, prepared to return to the fatherland — to the place where hymns are sung only to the opulence of life? No. The cold, the frost, and the wind *are also the pichua of dead Atchei.* From their home in the sky, the souls of the ancestors descend, nostalgic for the world below. Are they hoping to disturb the meeting of the living beings, to weaken their desire to continue to be what they are? Perhaps.

But the *to kybairu* is stronger: it symbolizes the reconquest of universal life, it expresses its spirit, it celebrates its victory. What are the dwellers of the night looking for? What do these pale ghosts want from the living who are no longer frightened by them? Yet they are there — the great cold attests to it. But what about the *to kybairu*? It is the festival of the people who live below, a challenge to death, a declaration that death has no more hold over the Atchei. The *to kybairu* is against death. The great cold is an important sign: at once *pichua* of the creeper pregnant with honey and the dead souls returning, it says that this returning is in vain. There is no question that mortals are bound to die: this is the road they must travel. But they do not travel it in the opposite direction. Here as everywhere else there is an order, which keeps the world of the living and the world of the dead separate. Then why are they both here? Because this is the happy bantering poem of the living: no subversion will ever be able to bring together what is destined to remain apart.

A month later, at the end of July, the Strangers reappeared at Arroyo Moroti. They were a little thinner. They did not talk much the first day back. They stayed by themselves and did not mix with the Atchei Gatu. The festival was over, the *to kybairu* was finished. It was the last one. Little by little, pleasure and the desire to live left the hearts of the Atchei.

Song for his mother's death.

Jakugi.

CHAPTER SIX

Killing

For a Guayaki tribe, relations with Others can only be hostile. White men, Machitara-Guarani, and even strange Atchei are all potential enemies. There is only one language that can be spoken with them, and that is the language of violence. This stands in surprising contrast to the Atchei's clear and consistent desire to eliminate all violence from relations among companions. These relations are characterized by unfailing courtesy, rejection of any hierarchy of roles in which some would be inferior to others, and the general desire to understand one another, to talk to one another, to dissolve with an exchange of words whatever aggressiveness or bitterness inevitably arises within the group in its daily life. *By-ia* means without calm, beside oneself, and they do not like to see *irondy* fall into this state. It must be ended quickly, and the women intervene immediately to calm the furious men. The adults never strike one another unless it is necessary for the performance of a ritual. Even less conceivable to them is the physical punishment that children receive elsewhere in the world.

The *kromi* and *kybuchu* are really the masters of their parents — who are willing slaves — and though the children do not make the adults the butt of their jokes, they sometimes try their patience sorely. Yet there is never any roughness, no involuntary slapping out of annoyance, only whimpers of complaint from the women and totally ineffective groans from the men. The children always win out. There was one little girl's obstinacy with her father: she wanted to go for a walk, but only with him and only on his shoulders. He did not want to, but gave in in the end, tired of hearing her say over and over again: "*Jachi raa! Jachi raa!* Carry me on your shoulders! Carry me on your shoulders!" The poor man obeyed the whims of the little tyrant who was riding him and for a long time walked up and down the camp, muttering under his breath.

Once Pichugi returned from the forest, very pregnant. On her back, hanging from her forehead, was a basket heavily loaded with grubs, fruits, and all the family's goods; and above the basket, on her shoulders, sat her five- or six-year-old, unwilling to walk. Indignantly, I went up to them and scolded the little boy: "Look at you! You're a big boy and you don't know how to walk?" He looked at me with complete indifference, and his mother apologized for him: "He's a child! His head is still soft! His bones are weak!" Once again I had got mixed up in something that did not concern me — like the day when I saw a woman bathing her feverish little girl in spite of the cold. The little girl was screaming at the touch of the icy water. I thought it would kill the child. But the mother very crossly put me in my place by remarking: "When the body is warm, we bathe in water! This is what we do, we Atchei!" She was right. It was inevitable that I should make mistakes like this, but it did not affect my relations with the Indians and taught me to know them better.

One thing that was certain was that the Atchei had a horror of violence, especially when it seemed to threaten their children. The Paraguayans' persecution of the young people, capturing them and selling them as slaves, had caused the adults' worry to become obsessive. It was touching, almost comical. The *kybuchu* had a soccer ball. They knew nothing about the rules of the game but loved to run after the ball. Sometimes the men joined them, and the boys, who were infinitely more skillful than the adults, perversely enjoyed preventing the grown-ups from touching the ball, taking it out of reach at the last minute. There would be scuffles and tumbling, all this amid the children's enthusiastic shouts. While this was going on, the mothers, far from looking on at the game calmly, would quickly sink into terrible uneasiness. And I would regularly see coming toward me a delegation of weeping women, who would beg me to intervene immediately and put an end to what was obviously about to become a general massacre! "I do not have many children! Only two!" and she would shake two fingers under my nose to urge me to save them. "We are not happy! Great fear! We do not want to see the *kybuchu* hit one another!" They were not hitting one another at all. In short, the mothers were making such a racket with their supplications, angry orders, and funeral songs that the game would soon stop. In a sense, the roles had been reversed and the children would capitulate, less because they were obedient than because they wanted some peace, as though their mothers' protests were for them only a whim that had to be indulged.

On the other hand, I was sometimes astonished by their indifference or even cruelty. One day two brothers took their father's machete and went off to play. The older one was clumsy and hurt the younger one's foot, which bled profusely. The little one began crying, and the big one got scared and ran off. The mother heard the commotion and came to where the boy was. I would have expected her to lament loudly, but no: she went up, looked at her son for a moment, murmured something, and turned on her heels, leaving him where he was. We cleaned him up and put a bandage on the cut, making him lie still for a while, though he wanted to go join the other *kybuchu*. Then I carried him two hundred yards to his parents' hut. The mother, who was sitting peeling manioc,

239

watched us come with indifference. She was the same woman who a short time before had told me that she had only two children and who had been so upset to see them running behind the ball. It seemed that her son's wound had not affected her in the least. The child was set down beside her, and immediately she burst out in a *chenga ruvara*, whose almost hysterical violence seemed to express the most profound grief. Which was real? Her apparently indifferent silence or the ritual clamor of the *chenga*? There was no telling.

But here is a different kind of story. The Atchei had appointed me peacemaker for Kajawachugi and his wife, and I had gone to get the husband at Arroyo Moroti. I returned to the camp in the middle of the night and to my great surprise learned that the man and his younger son (I had taken the older one on my shoulders) were not there, even though they should have arrived before me. They could not have got lost, because Indians do not get lost. I was soon reassured, because they silently appeared about ten minutes after us. What had happened? He explained it to me the next day. Between Arroyo Moroti and the new camp, the forest was broken by a clearing which several Paraguayan families had made in order to plant their corn and manioc. One of the houses was a *boliche*, a very modest country "store" where you could get liquor, tobacco, batteries for flashlights, salt, and sugar. I needed more cigarettes and despite the late hour decided to go a mile or two out of my way to buy some. I explained to Kajawachugi what I was going to do and told him to go on and that I would arrive after him with his older son. He agreed, and we went our separate ways. I bought what I needed by the light of an oil lamp, chatting politely with the owner in Guarani. Suddenly his dog began barking furiously in the direction of the trees, which could hardly be made out in the darkness. "A forest animal. It's nothing," the man said. I departed with the *kybuchu*, who had not left my side for a moment. But what had his father been doing? He told me about it, rather ashamed of how little confidence he had had in me. When I had told him I was going to buy some tobacco, he had not believed me. We were alone in the twilight, far away from the Atchei but quite close to the *Beeru*; he had been sure that I was lying to him and that I was really carrying off his son to give him to the white men!

What did he do then? Determined to prevent this from happening, he followed me in the dark and hid under the trees, watching what was going on in the *Beeru*'s house. The dog had smelled this resolute Atchei, who was determined to save his older son even though he was alone and encumbered with his younger son and had only his bow and arrow as a weapon. He waited a moment, saw that nothing was happening, was reassured to see me moving off in the right direction and then left himself. I did not resent the fact that Kajawachugi had not trusted me, because I was all too well aware of the thousands of unfortunate incidents which had taught the Indians that the white men were deceitful and cruel. It was even an act of great courage on his part to have ventured without hesitation into the territory of the white men, whom he did not know and who he believed might loose their dogs on him, capture him, even shoot him dead with their rifles. This incident increased my respect for Kajawachugi but also had an unexpected sequel that put me in an embarrassing position. Though I had no wish to assume this role, Kajawachugi regarded me as the person who had arranged things between him and his wife. At the same time, his confidence in me increased tremendously because I had protected his son by not giving him to the white men. Was he trying to show gratitude? Did he feel indebted to me? In any case, his wife, who had been disappointed in her affair with Japegi, came to me two or three days later with a proposition that was very clear and very dishonest ("Let's go into the forest! For *meno!*"). I answered her, laughing, that I would like it very much but that I was afraid of her husband. Without wasting a minute, she went to get him, brought him back, and in my presence asked him: "*Cho pravo!* I choose him! *Nde ro jepy vera?* Will you take revenge?" And the man, who was loyal to the tradition but also full of goodwill, wanting everyone to be satisfied, answered: "No vengeance! Only a *jepy rave.* Only a show of vengeance!" I had been put on the spot; couldn't a show of vengeance easily turn into a real punishment? You never can tell, and anyway, even if being hit with a bow is part of a ritual, it is still being hit over the head with a bow. This was the situation, and I refused the woman's offer. Kajawachugi did not show much emotion. He had just eliminated Japegi and was not overly eager to share his wife with me. She, on the other hand, took that as another reason to scorn me and to sulk. But her son really spoke the truth when he commented on what had happened: "The woman wants to make love."

The fate of this very *kybuchu*, whose father had run such real risks for him, made a deep impression on me because it seemed to contradict the love and affection of his father, which I had witnessed on that occasion. The Strangers went off to the *to kybairu,* and Kajawachugi went with them, taking his whole family, including the older son, who had a bad cold. He did not want to leave him at Arroyo Moroti. Two days after they left, about half a day's walk from the camp, a peasant who was working in his cornfield heard the sound of weak groans. He went toward the sound and found out where it was coming from. There he discovered lying among the roots of an enormous tree a boy of about ten years old: it was Kajawachugi's son. He had hardly enough strength to moan, and he was unconscious. The man picked him up and took him to the nearest Paraguayan village; the people tried to save him, giving him injections, but it was no use. He died three days

242

later, no doubt of fulminating pneumonia. He had spent three days alone in the forest, at the foot of a tree, sick and without a fire. It was a miracle that an animal had not attacked him.

Strange. The same man had risked his life — the danger may have been imaginary, but to him it was real — to save his son and had then abandoned him when he was sick to die alone. When Kajawachugi had returned, I asked him about it. "*Achy pute, mano ruwy.* He was very sick, almost dead." *Mano* means to die but also to be seriously ill; for the Indians, it amounts to almost the same thing. Sometimes people can be cured, and other times they cannot. Certainly they are still alive, but death is already in them, brought in by the sickness, which has already torn them from the group of living beings. From then on, they are only living on borrowed time, which will soon be used up. But what can be done with people who are not yet corpses but who are no longer living? It would not only be ridiculous to persist in hoping they would get well, since they are *mano* — already on the other side — but it would be dangerous for the others: their death might be contagious, and no one wants to get near them. To linger near death is to expose oneself to attack by its people: souls, spirits, phantoms that seize on the slightest excuse to torment the living. This was why Kajawachugi laid his son at the foot of a tree and went on with his journey. Was he being cruel? The Atchei did not think so, and none of them would have dreamed of reproaching the man for what he had done. We Westerners might find him cruel, but that is only because we always believe that illnesses can be cured. And what if they cannot be? This was true for the Atchei: flu was an illness unknown to them, a white man's illness that did not exist before they came into contact with the whites. It decimated them. They did not know what to call it. There was nothing they could do about it. Kajawachugi was not surprised when he was told about the *Beeru*'s futile attempt to save his son.

And didn't the spectacle of daily life demonstrate an almost exaggerated affection on the part of the adults for the children? They were never even severe: then how could the Atchei be cruel?

Their children were precious to them. And yet, they sometimes killed them.

I was just as surprised as the ancient chroniclers had been to discover that there were fewer women than men. How could such a situation be explained — one that had been reported as early as the beginning of the seventeenth century and verified as late as the second half of the twentieth? It could not even be attributed to some genetic anomaly that caused the women to give birth to more boys than girls, because, when I drew up genealogies of the present-day Atchei, it was obvious that just about as many girls as boys were born. But a good number of the girls would disappear later, and when I asked about it the answer was always brief and evasive: "She is already dead, because of vengeance." What had happened to them? Were the Atchei trying to hide something?

No, it had nothing to do with secrets. It had to do with their religious beliefs. Guayaki religion was based on the conviction that the dead are invisible phantoms and do not want to leave the living. Everyone knows this; it has been clearly proved by past and present experience: the dead are determined to remain in inhabited areas. Then how does one go about sending them on their way toward the resting place of the spirits? How does one get rid of the dead? There are several ways. First of all, when someone dies, everyone immediately leaves the camp and establishes another quite far away. By doing this, the Atchei hope that the *Ianve* of the dead person will not be able to find them again. This is usually what happens, and they are safe. But if a child dies, they stay where they are. Children are not dangerous, they do not yet have an *Ianve*, the aggressive and clever "soul" that hovers around the fires at night. They can even bury the little body under their shelter, and nothing will happen. This is what the new arrivals did when they reached Arroyo Moroti. One of the children was sick and died several days later. The parents dug a hole under the *tapy*, and it became their child's tomb.

Spirits must not be underestimated. They do so much damage among the living that they are considered responsible for almost all deaths. The dead are very good at assuming different appearances. Sometimes the Atchei recognize them in time to escape their attacks, and sometimes the spirits are too quick for them. One day, for example, Tokangi and Karekyrumbygi went off hunting and found themselves face-to-face with an enormous jaguar standing on a tree trunk that a storm had toppled. The wild animal was not in the least frightened and prepared to pounce on the two men. But Karekyrumbygi, a good hunter whose arrows never went wide of the mark, fired two arrows, one after the other, which pierced the *baipu*'s breast. Tokangi knew what had happened; he immediately recognized his mother, who had been dead so long that few people remembered her. She had not yet managed to forget her son, even though he was now an old man. She had tried to kill him so that she would not be alone in the *beeru prana*, the savanna of dead souls. And to do this she had assumed the guise of a large jaguar. Luckily, the young *bretete* (great hunter) had been there; otherwise, that would have been the end of Tokangi. Jakugi, however, was not so lucky. One day he ran into the camp pale and dumb with fear. He was rubbing his shoulder, which had been wounded by a blow. Someone went off right away to get a load of *kymata* bark, and Jakugi was purified. He had been cutting down a *pindo* when a branch of a nearby tree, shaken by the June wind, fell down, barely missing the man's head and landing full force on his shoulder. He had been the victim of his first wife. Women often prefer to attack

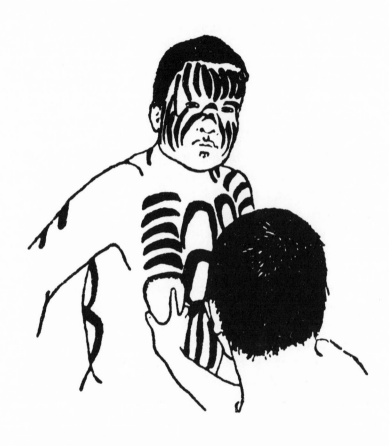

A woman applies paint to her sick husband.

their widowed sons-in-law, in order to "take revenge" on their dead daughters, they say, but also to try their luck with them and make them their husbands in the resting place of the dead. Apparently, the dead mothers-in-law want to make love with their young sons-in-law.

When Tokangi and his rescuer appeared in the camp loaded down with the jaguar, their exploit was greeted in an appropriate way. Jaguars are not killed every day. The women honored the *baipu* with loud *chenga ruvara*, the men yelled frightening *jeproro*, and Karekyrumbygi, who had killed him, was massaged with the bark of the *piry* tree. Killing a jaguar was not like killing any other game; it endangered the hunter. This was why he was also rubbed with a large snail shell — so he would not meet up with other jaguars out to avenge their fellow jaguar.

Once the jaguar was skinned, he was cut up and his quarters were arranged on a large wooden grill. The Atchei love jaguar meat, and everyone can eat it. The fat is saved and later used as a cure for pains in the bones. But some Atchei think it wiser not to use it, because according to them it causes eruptions on the skin that make a man look like a spotted fawn.

Hardly a day went by when a spirit did not interfere with their lives. It was immediately obvious when it happened, because the sign of its presence was illness. Someone was always getting sick, whether the sickness was serious or not: it might be a cold, a case of indigestion, or a heaviness in the bones. Even when they knew that a certain person was ill because he had eaten honey or monkey meat when he was not allowed to, they were quick to identify the dead person who had sent his soul into the patient's body with the disease. It was not very hard to drive it away: they would perform the *kymata tyro* ritual, sometimes painting the body with a mixture of wax and resin — whose pleasant smell would make the *Ianve* uncomfortable — and sometimes plastering every inch of the body with ashes or mud. Pregnant women are very skilled in curing people. The child they are carrying endows them with much more effective curative powers than those possessed by other Atchei. Their saliva, which they spread over the affected part of the sick person, is very potent. To be cared for by a pregnant woman is almost a guarantee that you will get well. These women also know many things that others do not know and know them much sooner. It is the child inside them who tells them everything. If a herd of wild pigs is roaming in the area, they are the first to know. They tell the hunters, who immediately go off in the direction indicated, find the animals there, and kill a good many of them. There is another reason why it is good to have at least one pregnant woman in the band: the unborn child can hear the approach of enemies, especially white men, before anyone else. He then tells his mother, and the Atchei, forewarned, can get far away from them. And lastly, these creatures who are not yet alive have one more power: they can see into the future, they can foresee death. When an Atchei has an incurable illness, they realize it immediately and let it be known that such-and-such a person is going to die. They are rarely mistaken. In August, Karegi became sick; she grew thinner and thinner, and her breathing was noisy. She was cared for until the day that young Brikugi, who was pregnant, announced what the child in her womb had told her: Karegi was going to die. Everyone stopped taking care of her, since it was useless. She really did die several days later, and her husband, Bykygi, who was now a widower and therefore threatened by his wife's *Ianve*, left his shelter and went to live farther away, with his brother. But the *Ianve* picked up his trail, and for a while Bykygi's life was in danger, because the *Ianve* had managed to enter his body. A few aspirins and the application of very black and smelly paint succeeded in driving off Karegi's spirit.

The Atchei do not know that this dialogue between the mother and the child she carries in her belly is familiar to the Guarani too. Not as part of their daily life, in which the children are silent, but in their mythology — in the great myth of the origin of all the Guarani tribes, which tells of the adventures of the divine twins, Our Older Brother and Our Younger Brother.

All the unhappiness of men and the fact that they inhabit the Bad Earth arose because the mother of the twins, pregnant both by her husband, the god Nanderuvusu, and her lover, Our Father Who Knows Things, refused to listen to her children, who spoke to her from inside her. "What! You who are still unborn, you talk to me?" she said. And she violently slapped her tight belly. Embittered, the children said nothing more to her; she lost her way and came among some jaguars, who devoured her: the story of the world had started, and it is still going on.

As for the Atchei, they listen to what the children say. They could not do without it. Even the dead need *kromi*.

When a man dies in the prime of life, he feels great sorrow at having to leave the tribe, his family, and his children. He sadly lingers around the camps. The songs and the weeping of his relatives and companions do not persuade him to go away — quite the contrary. The *irondy*'s grief helps keep him nearby. "He was a great hunter! He killed quantities of animals!" What yearning! And yet what danger for the people who survive him! His absence is mourned, but at the same time everyone wishes he would go home, to the savanna of the spirits in the west. Knowing that he is shyly and invisibly flitting around the fires terrifies the Atchei. The dead man must be satisfied. He must be given what he wants. For a *kybai gatu*, a beautiful boy, to die is unthinkable; it creates an excess, a disorder. He has been the victim of an injustice, and he knows it. That is why he stays there waiting for the debt that is

249

owed him. He will not leave until it is given to him. What has death condemned him to? Solitude. He is *jaro*, alone. This is his greatest loss but also the way he can be compensated. The offense he has received from the world demands revenge: there is always *jepy* when a man in the prime of life dies. He is avenged, but in accordance with what he wants; his desire is satisfied, and this is the guarantee that the dead man will finally leave a place where he no longer belongs. What does the *kybai gatu* want? He wants to do away with his solitude; he wants a companion to go with him on his voyage to the home of the spirits. If he is given this companion, he will go. Who will be the sister spirit, the one to console him as he weeps in the night, saddened by his abandonment? Not someone he did not like, naturally; he should be able to find one of the people he had loved and who had made him laugh with happiness. One of his children is killed, almost always a girl. This is the hunter's *jepy*, the vengeance with which the Atchei honor him. He carries his daughter off crouching on his shoulder, just as he carried her so many times when he was alive. Through eternity, she will be her father's faithful companion.

When she was born, the curse was on him: he was *bayja*, and the jaguars came in invisible crowds to answer life with death. They wanted the father, in order to do away with the excess that had been introduced into the world by the presence of the "soft head." Things must remain equal, and the addition of one calls for the subtraction of another. Now the man is no longer. He knew he was mortal: wasn't this exactly what his children were announcing when they came into the world? In return, they leave the world with their father, whom they have already killed and who is now being avenged. At least the girl is killed; they avoid killing the boys. Since they are future hunters, the tribe would miss them later. Nevertheless, they too are sometimes destined for *jepy*.

Jakugi was a peaceful man. At certain times, he suffered from the knowledge that he was being deceived. The alluring Baipuangi, his young wife, did not know how to say no, and she often forgot what a good husband she had: he was always in the forest, tracking game, spotting beehives, and gathering grubs. She had everything she could wish for and yet she was not satisfied. He could have beaten her, but he did nothing. Who was playing the flute sadly, after nightfall? The five pure notes escaped from the tubes of rosewood. Prettily, they called out to the woman who no longer wanted to sleep next to her husband and who had taken refuge at a distance in her parents' *tapy*. When he was troubled, Jakugi did not become violent. He would take up his flute. And yet he was called *Brupiare*, Killer.

The Atchei Gatu were moving ahead quickly, in spite of the heavy rain that meant summer was approaching. The dogs were more likely to lose the trail, and the *Beeru* who were following the Indians' tracks would not be able to find them. The Birds of Thunder were returning to the earth, which they had left several months earlier, bringing water and fog. Chono, their master, was annoyed by them, and his continuous rumbling filled the whole of the horizon. His great anger was also expressed by the terrifying lightning that flashed across the sky again and again. They had to take advantage of it and flee. As they advanced, the straggling line of people came upon a small clearing. Kimiragi, who was then Wachupirangi's wife, was carrying her baby as best she could in a sling. Under different circumstances, she would have taken the time to cover the *kromi*'s lower abdomen with resin so that the lightning would not frighten him. But she did not have time. Then Chono, Thunder, redoubled his ferocity. He threw his flames all around the Atchei — he wanted to kill them. Kimiragi was struck and immobilized, but she was still alive. The child had been killed, blasted on his mother's breast. This was the way angry Thunder made the Atchei pay for the return of the birds. When they felt they were safe, the men set up camp.

They were shattered. First they had had to flee from the white men, then suffer the hatred of Chono. Their bitterness was increased by the funeral songs of the women. But little by little, rage filled the heart of Rambiangi, Kimiragi's brother: his *tuty*, the son of his sister, was dead, and he could not bear it. He was not able to control himself, no one had time to calm him down—he was too *by-ia*. In despair, he took up his bow and ran in all directions across the camp. He wanted to avenge his favorite nephew, and the Atchei knew he was going to do it. Chono, the powerful on high, had seriously offended him, and the Atchei were disarmed by the force that moved Rambiangi. There was nothing they could do, they could not try to oppose him, and they did not even think of it. The weight of unhappiness was lying too heavily on them. Even the cruelest of men, like the white men, can be confronted; but when the enemy is supernatural, when the whole life of the world becomes hostile, then *ete iko ia*, one is without body, without courage, one is resigned.

Bad things were in the air. Rambiangi did not stop chanting all night long. Everyone heard the death words, and when the man got up at dawn, everyone knew exactly what he was going to do. It was as though the actions had already been accomplished. There, stretched out on a mat, was little Achipurangi, asleep. He was Baipugi's oldest son. He was going to die. Rambiangi had taken his large bow in both hands. The *kromi*'s frail neck did not resist the blow. The mother was not looking, her head was in her hands. At the dull sound of the blow, she began lamenting loudly: the *doroparegi*, the oldest son, the pretty penis who was just on the point of walking, had been killed as vengeance! But there was no hostility toward Rambiangi—everyone was beyond

feeling anger or resentment. Once the murder had been committed, the man stood there openmouthed.

At this moment, he would have accepted any form of death
without defending himself. Yet no one was going to attack him.
On the contrary, people in the camp began to get busy, because
the man was in danger: he had to submit to the purification ritual. What was threatening him? Not the *Ove* of his little victim, a
slight and inoffensive ghost, which the coati had already raised to
the upper world of the Invisible Forest, but *Ianve*, the nocturnal
phantom. Rambiangi had to be saved, and this is what the woman,
Wachugi, and her husband, Krajagi, loyally set about doing.

The *brupiare* would not eat anything for several days. He
would only have a little water and would not come into direct
contact with it. If he forgot that precaution, he would unleash the
universal flood that attacked the First Ancestors in ancient times.
In order to drink, therefore, Rambiangi took a *koto*, brush, soaked
it in a container, and then sucked on it. As for *meno*, he had to
abstain from it completely; anyway, what woman would dream of
taking her pleasure with a *brupiare*? He was a marked man, and
until the ritual removed that mark, he would be surrounded by
an aura of danger that would make him a marginal being, the
temporary inhabitant of an area beyond men. The two purifiers
covered Rambiangi's face and chest with a thick layer of mud.
They smeared it carefully all over and rubbed the body until it
was hard with mud. The woman took a handful and squeezed it
into the mouth of the patient, who was hiccuping. But it was necessary for him to vomit, because *Ianve* might already have entered
the body of the killer by way of the anus, as he often did. To keep
him from completely invading the whole of the inside, he had
to be forced out: that was why the man had to vomit. Wachugi
thrust her fingers far back into Rambiangi's throat several times.
Ianve comes in by the anus and leaves by the mouth — just the

253

opposite of food. In fact, the phantom wants to make the victim his food, he wants to eat his body, devouring it from within. Rambiangi vomited. He was exhausted, but *Ianve* had certainly been driven out. Then the man and woman freed the *brupiare* from his shell of mud by washing him with water in which *ky-mata* shavings had been soaking. Several days would have to go by before Rambiangi, remaining absolutely motionless outside the camp, could consider himself safe. Then order would prevail again, and he would once again be what he had not been for a while — *bretete*, a true hunter.

When night fell, Kimiragi and Baipugi sang. This was the time of their grief. Chono had taken Kimiragi's child, and Rambiangi had killed Baipugi's child. But it was Chono who had driven Rambiangi out of his mind. In their song, there was a single sadness, and Rambiangi listened to their lament. There was no hatred, no remorse. No one was guilty and the cause of all this lay far away. But one could still grieve, and this was the women's role. Kimiragi and Baipugi wept.

Yet more unhappiness was still to come. It was Jakugi who ended the series of murders that Chono had begun. Joylessly, tense with sadness, Jakugi told how he became a *brupiare*. The *kybuchu* listened in silence. They were not surprised, because several of them had already witnessed similar acts.

Rambiangi had killed a child dear to Jakugi. This was why things did not end with his death. The child's name was Achipurangi, Beautiful Horns. When his mother was pregnant, a hunter had given her meat from a cow he had shot. She had then decided that the unborn child would have a *bykwa*, or nature of Beautiful Horns, and that that would be his name. But people can have several *bykwa*; there are very few Atchei who have only one. The second *bykwa* of Baipugi's son came from coati meat. Jakugi had

254

killed a coati and brought the meat to the woman for her to eat. In this way, he became the child's *bykware*, the "one who furnished" his nature — in some sense, his father. The *bykware* and the *bykwapre* feel they are tied by bonds of affection and respect. When he is old and weak, the man can count on being given game by the boy whose *bykwa* he has determined. Jakugi's grief was profound, just as profound as Rambiangi's. Rambiangi had killed the child in revenge for his *tuty*. Now Jakugi was contemplating the same action; he had to take revenge. Why should the death of one child be punished by the death of another? After all, they are not grown-ups and their *Ove* do not need company in order to leave, as a hunter's does. And the Atchei confirmed this: no *jepy* for a *kromi*. Then who had Rambiangi been avenging?

And who was Jakugi preparing to avenge? Not so much their respective nephew and "son" as the common hurt they had suffered. Chono and the *Beeru* were driving the Atchei beyond grief. More and more, their most faithful companion was death. Why else would Chono have struck the "soft head" with lightning, if not to show that he no longer wanted to let the Atchei live? After that, what good was it to persist in the struggle, to try to help the *kromi* grow up, if Chono himself was killing them? Sometimes the Atchei felt they were lost, and in such destitute situations, people go crazy. There was nothing ahead of them but death. Men were killing children and destroying themselves. This was the misfortune of the Indians, this was the tragic festival of their end.

A few days went by. Rambiangi had escaped the *Ianve*, and the Atchei could start off again. Jakugi spent all his time hunting. He shot enough animals to feed his old wife, Pampingi, very well and to give the rest to the *irondy*. But when evening came, he did not celebrate his exploits in the forest with any *prera*. He remained taciturn and allowed the strength necessary for the *jepy* to gather in him: you must be *kyrymba*, bold, to kill. Killing an enemy is

255

nothing, you feel happy; but killing someone within the tribe is very demanding, you must be really *by-ia*, you must be able to pronounce the irreversible words, the words that will make you and everyone else prisoners. "One evening, I sat down next to my fire and began to sing. *Ja bykware oo wachu gatu ware, kyra wachu uare, by-ia; cho bykware jepy vera cho!* The one who had bestowed the *bykwa* because plump and succulent meat was eaten, because good fat was eaten, the man is beside himself; I who bestowed the *bykwa* will take revenge!"

It seemed as if the group was asleep, but everyone was listening; they were waiting. Was Jakugi going to kill? The name of the victim had already been chosen. A secret way of reasoning had guided Jakugi in his choice. But had he really decided whom he was going to kill? It would be closer to the truth to say that that mortal spot had for all time been reserved for the girl who was going to occupy it. Only the condemned girl could prolong and bring to a close the progress of things that were ruling the Atchei, of the subterranean powers that had taken possession of Jakugi. The murder of the little boy had only taken the man halfway down his road. The loss of the boy had crushed him, but it was not enough. Pain would have to be exalted again. It was Jakugi's wish to inflict another wound on himself, a mortal blow, the coup de grâce which would obliterate a sorrow that was too great to bear.

He chanted, saying that the next day he would avenge the death of the one whose being he had endowed by killing Kantingi's daughter: she too was his "daughter," she owed part of her "nature" to him, he had helped form her when he offered a wildcat he had killed to the pregnant woman. His "son" had been killed, and now he himself would kill his "daughter." Confused but unmistaken, Jakugi was trying to bring about his own death.

"I chanted for a long time during the night. I explained that out of revenge I wanted to kill the daughter of Wachugi and Krajagi. I said that the next day, when the first light appeared in the direction of the rising sun, I would take up my bow." The two Atchei he was talking about were the man and woman who had purified Rambiangi after he killed the little boy. They had saved one *brupiare* from *Ianve*'s attacks, and now another one was chanting near them, saying that he was getting ready to kill their daughter. By protecting Rambiangi, they had been contaminated; they were now inside the fatal circle that they thought they had only brushed against; they were now bound up with unhappiness.

"I chanted very loudly, and the girl's mother heard me from where she was lying under her shelter. She listened carefully to what I was saying, she knew I wanted to kill her child, whose *bykware* I was. As for Krajagi, the father, he also heard me saying that I wanted to do *jepy* on his daughter. I continued to chant. After a long time I saw the woman Wachugi sit down in the light from her fire. She had begun the *chenga ruvara*."

She was crying alone. Usually, the women sustain one another by singing together. But this time, no one came to help Wachugi. She spoke of her pain alone. This was why she did not sing very loudly; her *chenga ruvara* was not for other people. The words came between two bursts of sobbing: no rejection of what was going to happen, no protest against such an unexpected thing. Simply a mother who was going to lose her child in several hours confronting her helplessness and grief. Chono had started something that could no longer be stopped. The Atchei knew this very well. Krajagi was there. He was strong, and he loved his daughter. Then why didn't he stop Jakugi from killing her? He knew this had nothing to do with Jakugi: powers that hated the Atchei were moving through him. *Ure kwaty*, we know very well.

Jakugi, lying on his mat, had stopped singing. Now the woman sang: "The one who had endowed her with her nature is going to kill her, the beautiful girl." She recalled the bonds between Jakugi

257

and the one who was going to be sacrificed and what he was going to do to her. Was this a timid appeal to him to give up his plan, for the sake of this relationship? Perhaps, but there was no response: Jakugi could not kill anyone but his *bykwapre*. Soon the mother's lament was followed by the father's song. They were letting Jakugi know that they had heard his terrible message. This was a sad night for the Atchei — death was present among them. But what about the girl?

Lying next to her parents in the welcome heat of the fire, her delicate body just emerging from childhood, she was resting. Who was she? Not a baby, certainly, not even a little girl. She already belonged to the group of *kujambuku*, big women. This is the name given to little girls whose breasts are beginning to swell, whose blood should soon start flowing: almost a woman. She was not a woman yet, and yet she was, since she had already been introduced to the pleasures of love. Everyone knew it, and there was some disapproval on the part of the tribe. No one reproached the girl for her precociousness in love. Almost all the *kujambuku* do the same thing and do not wait for the first flow of blood to choose lovers and sometimes even a husband. But are they really the ones who do the choosing? Actually, it is the men who plunge into *gaita* — girl courting — at the first sign of a girl's budding womanhood. "Come, *daregi*, sit next to me!" a man says. Flattered by the interest that a *kybai gatu* is showing in her, and by being called a woman when she is not yet a woman, she goes to the man. "*Cho pravo!* I choose you!" he says. They enjoy themselves; it is a game. But a hand strays over the young girl's thighs and even beyond, and the caress is received calmly, is not rejected. "Beautiful thighs! They're nice and fat. I'm going to touch them a little!" The clever seducer knows very well that this kind of compliment is always welcome. All around him no one is paying any attention to what he is doing. This is the way it starts, and it ends at the bottom of a tree. One of these days, Kajapukugi will ask the little girl to go into the woods with him. These flowering girls do not make the first overtures, but they quickly catch on.

The Atchei found fault with Jakugi's "daughter" for having paid too much attention to someone she should not have: the man who ignored all the rules and boldly did *gaita* with his own *chave*! Pretty Kantingi had allowed herself to be seduced by her *jware*, by a man who was almost her father, the one who had bathed her when she was born. He never should have done this; he was much more at fault than she, since she was still a child and did not know any better. But this kind of wrongdoing was not punished — that was not necessary. And besides, it would quickly be forgotten.

So this was the girl Jakugi said he would kill the next day.

"I sang loudly, so that all the Atchei would hear me: out of revenge, I am going to kill the beautiful girl and she will die." They all heard him very clearly, including the girl whose name Jakugi kept pronouncing all night long. Lying motionless under the palm shelter, how could Kantingi sleep when she knew she was going to be killed? She was alone in the face of the immense terror mounting in her; her father and mother, kind and generous, sang their sad acceptance of her death sentence.

"*Kwe bu ro*, at dawn I got up and took up my bow to go and kill the girl while she slept. But she was awake, she had not slept at all during the night." Kantingi had fought against sleep, knowing that Jakugi would take his revenge at dawn. She waited, so that she could see what he was going to do. As soon as she saw him get up, she jumped to her feet: "*Pacho eme! Pacho eme!* Don't hit me! Don't hit me!" She fled under the trees, light on her feet. Jakugi ran after her, and the pleading girl ran straight ahead without turning around. "She was gone! I was not able to strike her. I was completely without courage!" Jakugi gave up for the moment.

But the *jepy* had only been postponed. Later, the girl returned to the camp. No one said anything to her; everything seemed perfectly normal. Jakugi went off hunting. The day went by, and night fell. The families settled down next to their fires. All the Atchei were asleep except for Jakugi and the girl. As she had done the night before, she was waiting for the morning to come, so that she could run away again. The two of them watched each other in the firelight, he sitting on his heels, she lying down. But she was not as strong as he was; she did not have the strength to stay awake the way he did. She was too young to hold out during that long wait, and little by little her eyes closed. She slept.

"I killed her at dawn, striking her on the neck. She did not see a thing, because she was asleep. Her mother was asleep too. Not her father. Krajagi saw, and said: 'He has killed the one whose nature he endowed. It was a wildcat he shot with an arrow for my daughter's *bykwa*!' "

The Atchei Gatu faithfully went on to perform funeral rites for the dead girl, as a way of separating themselves from her. She too was avenged, but the vengeance was only a *jepy rave*. The guilty *jware* lifted l᷈ ᷈ bow over the head of an Atchei but did not lower it. Life became peaceful again. As for Jakugi, he had to undergo the same treatment that Rambiangi had been submitted to some time earlier. He was purified by his sister and the mother of his victim. "She whose child was killed, she did the *piy* for the killer." They covered him completely in mud and put mud in his mouth so that he would vomit and *Ianve* would not cause *baivwa*, so that he would not have terror in his breast, so that he would feel good. The mother, Wachugi, was the one who stuck her fingers in his throat and brought on the spasms. One man went to get vine shavings and washed Jakugi. The women sang, both in mourning for the dead girl and to protect Jakugi, who was in danger from *Ianve*.

"When my body had become good and white again, the women took a wooden blade and spread fragrant resin all over it. The pleasant smell would stop *Ianve* from entering it. After that, my wife, Pampingi, stuck some pretty white vulture down to the resin. The body of a killer has to be very light; *urubu* down would keep the body from becoming heavy. Once I had been purified, I threw away the labret made of the bone of a little wild pig that I had been wearing when I killed the girl. You must not keep the *beta* after you have killed. Otherwise, *Ianve* will try to enter you, he will cause *baivwa*: your blood will become very thick and start to smell. Something will sink into your belly as though into a hollow in the ground. This is the sickness of the Invisible Armadillo."

During the days that followed, Jakugi ate nothing—no meat, no honey, no water. In addition, he took the precaution of remaining completely immobile in his hut; his wife did the same, and people brought food to her. As long as he was there, surrounded by his companions, he did not run any risk. But if he left the camp, *Ianve* would seize the opportunity. After five or six days, he began drinking a little honey diluted with water, using his brush. Wachugi, the mother of his victim, was the one who prepared it and brought it to him. She took care of her daughter's killer as though he were her own child, as though in her eyes Jakugi now had to take the place of the girl he had robbed her of. This is the way it is among the Atchei. A man kills a child out of revenge: he immediately steps in to fill the void he has created, he becomes the mother's *chave* and from now on calls her *chupiaregi*, my godmother. This is why she feeds him.

Upiaregi is the woman who lifts the newborn baby up off the ground just after he has "fallen" there. She loves her *chave* as she loves her own child. The *brupiare* kills another Atchei: he himself is killed by the mortal blow, he dies at the same time as his victim. The days that Jakugi spent in silence, fasting, and immobility were the days of his death — he was no longer one of the living but remained far away from them. Who would open a path for him to return, who would undertake to end his exile, to *cause him to be reborn* — him, the killer? None other than the grieving mother, whose head was now shaved. She gave the *brupiare* his first food, she helped him to be resurrected; he faced her like a "soft head," she was his "godmother," *chupiaregi*. He had killed her daughter, and now he became her "godson." Was this asking too much of the mother? It was the Atchei's rule. Beyond the strange bonds that form between the executioner and his victim and create a secret space in which they are reconciled, there is a guarantee in the tribe that there will be no hostility between families associated with the same misfortune.

The deepest kind of gulf separated Jakugi and Wachugi. It was so deep that only they could cross it. This was why he died from killing the woman's child and why he was reborn in the girl's place, in her mother's eyes.

Jakugi's story lasted one whole morning. Sometimes he interrupted it with long, tense silences that no one dared break. Then he would go on. He could have got up and left, saying, as he usually did, that he was going hunting or that he was sleepy. But this time he persisted, compelled to go on in spite of himself. A stranger had asked him to recall certain things that wanted to be said, perhaps for a long time now. But how broken his words were, how reluctant, almost inaudible! And once the words had been irrevocably spoken, how anxious he was to repeat them, his hands clenched nervously.

"I ran behind her a little ways. The *kujambuku* was fleeing into the forest, she was shouting: 'He wants to kill me! Don't kill me!' And there I was without boldness, without courage! But I had sung, and I had to do *jepy*!" He left, perhaps surprised after all this time at the weight deep in his chest that was blocking his words. Jakugi, in whom there was no violence, was a *brupiare*. He was waiting for night to come, so he could let his flute sing of his pain while his wife went her fickle way.

Although the Atchei Gatu and the *Iroiangi* were distant at first, the former full of arrogance and the latter rather humble in spite of their greater numbers, in the end they bowed before the course of events. The day-to-day life they shared at Arroyo Moroti and their joint hunting expeditions broke down their reticence: they felt themselves more and more to be one another's *cheygi*, and marriages between members of the two tribes gradually led to an honest reconciliation. In their periods of idleness, they talked; with "the skin of the belly good and tight" with tasty fat meat, their feeling of satiety made them agreeable and inclined to carry on conversations. What did they talk about? Most often of their recent conflicts with the *Beeru*, of fights in the forest between bullet and arrow, or sometimes of the extraordinary things they had seen: a snake so enormous that it was frightening, a black jaguar, incredible numbers of wild pigs. Less frequently, they would encounter invisible beings, but it did happen from time to time.

Sometimes Jakarendy allows himself to be seen, armed with his bow and his arrows of fern; and then it is just too bad for the unlucky Atchei he takes by surprise. But Jakarendy is not too mean. What he enjoys most is frightening people. But sometimes he shoots off his arrows. He once shot Chachubutagi in the leg. He did not bleed very much, and yet he thought he was dying. Jakarendy announces that he is there at the end of the afternoon. He whistles to himself as he walks, and the sound cannot be confused with the sound of a bird. He and his wife have strange habits. She tries to carry off young boys to make love with them, and when she does this, he becomes jealous and tries to take the *kybuchu*'s penis. When an Atchei cannot find a bee's nest that he spotted earlier, he knows what has happened: Jakarendy has stopped up the opening of the hive in order to make fun of him because Jakarendy is the master of honey.

Paivagi, who was not usually very eloquent, now and then would tell the story of how he met Japery one day. Japery is the master of water. When it is light, you can see him near streams or waterfalls. He is dark-skinned and talks very softly; there is no flesh on his chest. Paivagi knew that it was best not to run away; otherwise Japery would have struck him a sound blow on the neck with the very black club he carried. He stayed where he was, and Japery offered him a *capivara* skin; the *capivara* is a rodent as large as a pig. It lives near the water. The gift had to be accepted, and then he would be free to go. "What fear!" The audible chuckling came from Paivagi, who was trying to stifle his laughter as he thought back on his jitters in front of Japery.

The Strangers loved to talk about the northern Atchei, who were terrible and wicked cannibals. Not long ago they came down almost as far as Karewachugi's territory. There was a great battle, because they had to be stopped: "Lots of arrows! Big arrows! *Zzz, zzz, zzz!* We were very frightened. Everyone shouted, we insulted them: 'Atchei cannibals, we are going to kill you, and we are going to take your wives! The vultures will eat you! We are very brave!'

"There they were with their *beta* in their lips, all covered with black paint. Terrifying! Then we ran away. One of us was shot in the stomach with an arrow. We left him there. He could not walk because his intestines were running out onto his legs. It stank." "*Teeh!*" said the people listening, who knew about these ferocious Atchei, even though they had never seen them. They were fascinated, forgetting that theoretically they had nothing to learn from the ignorant Strangers. But it was just as well that they were not always haughty, because in this way there was enough entertainment to pass the long evenings.

Everyone, even the children, knew about Terygi's exploits and how he died. He was an ancient chief of the Atchei Gatu. Only the oldest of them had known him when they were young. At that time, Terygi was still *yma wachu*, a very strong man. He had a *tery* "nature": the *tery* is the giant otter, bigger than a man, who fishes in the forest streams. Terygi's strength and courage had become legendary. Under his leadership, the Atchei Gatu were fighting both other Atchei, who lived in the east, and the white men, of whom there were fewer than there were now. In those days, Terygi's people were powerful; there were enough bands to occupy vast stretches of the forest. Again Paivagi recalled how he had accompanied his father on an expedition against the Atchei Kyravwa — the Atchei who ate human fat. Terygi was leading. His men had surrounded a large band of the enemy at dawn. Almost all the Kyravwa were killed and their women captured. There was a large feast, and the Atchei Gatu divided up the wives of the conquered men. Terygi took three young ones for himself; added to the one he already had, that made four wives. "The Atchei knew how to hunt then! When you're a great hunter, then you can have lots of wives and feed them all. We are also *bretete*, but there aren't very many women."

One of Terygi's wives was named Urugi. She should not have been his wife, since she was his half sister — they had the same father. But there were very few women in the tribe. In any case, it was less serious than marrying a half sister who had the same mother. That would really be incest, and Terygi would have been transformed into a howler monkey: "The *kraja* is making love with his sister." It was in order to correct this lack of women, which had become very annoying, that Terygi had led his people to attack other Atchei and get some wives for themselves.

265

One day Bujagi, Urugi's brother, was late returning from hunting. The next day, they followed his tracks and found his body torn to pieces. The men recognized the terrible wounds that the great anteater could inflict with the claws of its front paws; they say it is capable of scaring even the jaguar. Urugi was singing her grief for her brother. Irritated, a man threatened her with his bow. Terygi then became *by-ia*, mad with rage, against his *vaja*, his mother's husband. With one blow of a stone ax, he killed him. In revenge for the man who had been killed, Chimbegi, Terygi's brother, killed all the dead man's children with his bow and arrow. One of them was a *beta pou*, a new labret, and he tried to run away. But the long arrow was swifter; it landed in his back, and the tip of it stuck out through his chest.

Terygi had disappeared a long time ago, but people still talked about him. Because the strange fact was that he was killed by his own *ijagi*. An *ijagi* is a companion. All the inhabitants of the forest are escorted by a companion; and if he is killed, he has someone to avenge him. For instance, the *ijagi* of the wild pigs is the *kweve* bird, whose song tells the Atchei they are nearby, and the jaguar is the one who avenges them, as he does almost all the animals when they have been killed by hunters. The fly is the companion of the howler monkey; the *pindo* palm is the *ijagi* of the *guchu* and *pichu* grubs. The *pipi* bird indicates the movements of the coati, and the *pana* butterfly those of the *tatou*. The jaguar's companion is the *myrokyje* bird, but he who is the supreme avenger is the only one who does not have a *jepare*. As for the Atchei, each of them has his *ijagi*, too: it is always the animal whose meat endowed him with his *bykwa*. Chachugi's *ijagi* was *chachu*, the great wild pig; Jyvukugi's was *jyvuku*, the dark cat. The animal companions know very well whether they have been shot by a man who bears their name or by some other hunter. Every animal that is killed is greeted with a song, but a special precaution

266

must be taken when you have killed your own *ijagi* — you must dedicate longer songs to him. It is something like killing a relative. It is rare that a woman does not begin lamenting when a hunter comes into the camp, because the man has brought in a roe buck or a coati and there it lies on the ground, the *ijagi* of a dead child or brother. The woman sees the animal and thinks back on the Atchei she lost, so she cries over the animal.

The *ijagi* of the great otter *tery* is water, because it lives in streams. This animal shares the jaguar's function as avenger, but only for the *krombe*, the river tortoise. Tortoises were just what Terygi was trying to catch. He was walking in the water near the bank. Suddenly he was attacked by the *tery*, which had swum silently up to him. The man, armed with half a wooden bow, tried to defend himself, but the animal lunged at his arm and tore it in half. When they heard his cries, the other Atchei ran up, the otter fled, and Terygi was carried back to camp. A large piece of his flesh was gone, and he had lost a great deal of blood. The wound was covered with flies, and he soon died, killed by his *ijagi*. He was very thin, there was no fat on him. Then they knew that this *tery* was the spirit of a strange Atchei whom Terygi had killed some time in the past. Chimbegi, who was wandering far away with his band, was told the news. He arrived full of sorrow at having lost his brother. He sang about all the hunting they had done together, all the enemy Atchei they had killed, and their attacks against the *Beeru* who were beginning to penetrate into Atchei country. "*Ja pave mano bu, jepy*. When a brother dies, we avenge him." Terygi had had three daughters by Urugi, and they were already big. Chimbegi killed all three of them with a metal ax, booty from an attack on white men. And so they went with their father into the Invisible Forest.

Tokangi told this very well, because he knew all about it: he had been there; he had seen his father, Chimbegi, kill Terygi's three daughters. Unlike Paivagi, he liked to talk, to recall things from the past. He was not doing much now, he was rather weak and hardly hunted anymore. Pichugi was the woman who cooked for him; he was her secondary husband now that his own wife was dead. She did not often make love with him, because the *imete* was very strong. He would try his luck, though without much hope, with other women: *"Poko mivwa! Tara ia!"* he would say. "Let's touch softly a little! Not much!" in a tone of voice that seemed to say, "You won't refuse me that!" And he would put out his hand toward a nice round breast. He was rarely successful but did not get angry. *Kibjoo* means to tell stories, and that was what he enjoyed doing.

He readily explained that he was a *brupiaty* — a man who was used to being a killer. The truth was that he had sacrificed several Atchei, at least three. He was not like Jakugi; he enjoyed telling about all this — it reminded him of his youth. He had committed the first murder long ago, his back had not yet been scarred, and Terygi's mother, whom the Atchei called *jarygi*, the grandmother, was still alive. But she was becoming so feeble that she could not walk anymore. This was very annoying to Urugi, one of Terygi's wives. Finally, when it became clear that she was losing all her strength, Urugi spoke to Tokangi and told him to kill her. This kind of thing was always asked of very young men. Tokangi immediately took up a metal ax and went up to the old woman who had her back turned and was sitting with her face between her hands — in just the right position. With the heel of the ax, he broke her neck with one blow. Then he was purified, and one of Jarygi's daughters made him vomit. *"Wata kwa ia pute!* She couldn't walk anymore at all!" Tokangi explained jovially.

Later, when Urugi was a widow, she was given to her brother-

268

in-law Chimbegi, since a man always takes his brother's wife. But she found Tokangi, her husband's son, to be a *kybai gatu*, a pretty boy, and she let him know it. He did not wait to be asked. She had the father for her husband and the son for her lover. Perhaps she was already thinking of that when she asked Tokangi to kill Jarygi.

The other two murders were out of revenge. Jaivigi was Tokangi's younger brother. He was hunting, and he did not see a *chini* who was sleeping under some dead leaves. The rattlesnake uncoiled like a flash and bit him in the ankle. Jaivigi returned to the camp. Women quickly went to look for the leaves of a certain tree and heated them before applying them to the bite. But it was no use; Jaivigi died, because he was not *paje*. There is no way of knowing beforehand whether you are *paje* or not. Only the bite of a venomous snake will tell you that. If you survive, then you are *paje*: there is something in you that causes the venom to have no effect. Otherwise, you die. The two chiefs, Jyvukugi and Kare-wachugi, were both *paje*. Both of them had been bitten by a *chini* or a *brara*, and they only reacted with a little fever. Sometimes, when the Indians are hollowing out a trunk to gather the larvae that are in it, they see one grub that is entirely black among the others, which are entirely white. That one is called *paje*, and only the *paje* men can eat it.

So Jaivigi died, and since brothers were supposed to avenge brothers, it was up to Tokangi to do the *jepy*. His father, Chimbegi, went to tell him what had happened. He broke in the skull of a little boy, and the victim's mother then made the mud *piy*.

When Terygi died, the Atchei Gatu had a new chief, Kyrypyragi. Kyrypyra is a bird; its name means "hairs on the ass." The new chief was Terygi's "godson." Along with Chimbegi, he inherited his *jware*'s wives. The Atchei did not show the same attachment to him that they had to Terygi. They said he was a very violent man who made everyone afraid. They did not like him very much: *berugi ia, Achete*, not a leader, the opposite of an Atchei.

A half brother of Tokangi's died, having been torn apart by a jaguar. In order to avenge him, Kyrypyragi killed one of the women he had been alloted. She was the youngest. But in revenge for her death, even though usually there is no *jepy* for women, an Atchei killed Kyrypyragi's daughter by another wife. Now this girl was Tokangi's *chave*, and he was very grieved. He became *by-ia*, sang, and killed the sister of the little girl by hitting her with his bow. So their mother, Piragi, had lost two of her children. But she was the one who performed the purification ritual on Tokangi, so that *Ianve* would not smother him. The *brupiaty* told about all this with great animation. He imitated the gestures and made the *huh!* sound which went with the action of bringing the bow or the ax down on someone's neck.

The *Iroiangi* were listening carefully. When an Atchei Gatu sang a greeting to an animal and they recognized the song, they were happy: *ure wywy go nonga*. With us it is that way too. And when the customs were different, they were surprised and explained how they did it. Each group learned to know the other little by little, exchanging information. The differences that were discovered were not always greeted with enthusiasm. Jyvukugi's people in particular were very severe: "The Strangers talk too fast! They are idiots, they do not know how to talk." They actually did talk more rapidly than the others. "What did so-and-so (a Stranger) say?" "I don't know," an Atchei Gatu woman would answer. "I'm not even listening; they don't know anything." The *Iroiangi* had metal labrets, which the others found very shocking. Also, the men wore necklaces of jaguar teeth or the teeth of other cats, whereas among the Atchei Gatu only the women did this. "Only the women have necklaces! We great hunters don't want them!"

These ungracious comments were not made to the Strangers' faces; the Atchei Gatu waited until they were alone. They could think whatever they liked, but they were always courteous. A Stranger would grind some corn then cook the meal. Since he was a bachelor, he had to do his own cooking. When the pellets were ready, he would offer one to an Atchei Gatu: "Wouldn't you like to eat a little of this cornmeal? Here, have some." "No, really," the Atchei Gatu would say. "I won't eat any. My stomach is enormous. I'm not at all hungry anymore, see!" And he would tap himself on the belly, puffing it up in an exaggerated way to show the other that there was not the slightest room left. The fact was that he was sure the food was rotten and that the Strangers were filthy. What was more, if he accepted something, it would make him vulnerable, since he would not be able to refuse anything to the person who had given it to him. And as Jyvukugi said, "The Strangers are always begging! It's incredible how much they can eat! Afterward, they have diarrhea and shit all over the place!"

This was quite natural. You cannot be enemies for generations and then all of a sudden become close companions. Besides, the Strangers did not like everything about the Atchei Gatu either, even if they did not say so openly. The proof was that they forgot to invite them to the *to kybairu*. But that did not stop them from comparing their habits. The *Iroiangi* did *jepy* too, when a hunter died. But their vengeance took a different form from the Atchei Gatu's. They put the body in a ditch they have dug in the earth. To persuade his spirit to leave, they offer him one of his children as a sacrifice, as often as possible a very little girl. Or it could be a *kujambuku*, just about to go through puberty. She is put into the grave on top of her father. The men stand around the hole. One after another they jump in on top of the child, crushing her with their feet until she dies. When the child is a *kromi*, this happens quickly; she dies almost right away. But when she is a "big woman," her bones are harder and she takes some time to die; she cries out that she does not want to die and tries to get out of the grave. *Go nonga ure.* This is the way we do it.

The men are sad, the pain in their chests is great. While the women's *chenga ruvara* gloomily resound, the men hit one another with their bows. The large wounds they inflict will earn them enormous *pichua* when they die.

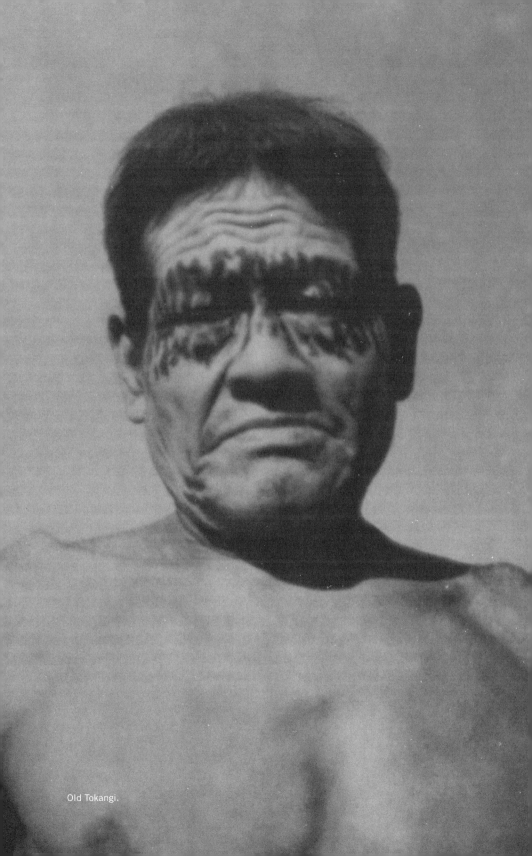

Old Tokangi.

Krembegi.

CHAPTER SEVEN

The Life and Death of a Homosexual

"You will die, and the vultures will feed on you!" said Tokangi as a warning to the sick Atchei who did not want to return to Arroyo Moroti. These were familiar words, and they were spoken fairly casually. They were not really meant to be upsetting. On the contrary, the point was to reassure the other person before he set off by referring to the worst possible dangers that lay in store for him — dangers that were so improbable that their quasi-unreality would almost be enough to put him at ease. It was a matter of politeness: you did not let someone go off into the forest without a friendly word. "You're going to hunt wild pigs? The jaguar will rip out your guts." "No jaguar! I'm very brave!" What you are doing is putting him on his guard. "You're going into the forest? All right, you're a great hunter. But be careful anyway." The dangers of the forest must never be forgotten, but there is no use in giving advice, because everyone knows what he has to do. Exaggerating things, however, you discreetly remind him of the situation.

To show the aggressiveness of nature, three kinds of animals are often mentioned: the jaguar, who is lord of the forest by day and by night; the vultures, who pose no threat if a man is alive and in good health, but who are already on the lookout for a sign

of weakening in someone on the ground; and finally the poisonous snakes, especially the *chini* and *brara*, whose green, black,
and gray spotted skin blends easily into the vegetation, whether
they are on the ground or in the low branches of the shrubs. By
the time you realize they are there, it is often too late; the wicked
little fangs are already buried in your foot, your ankle, or your
calf — seldom any higher than that. And if you are not *paje*, then it
is all over for you, you die. The vulture in the sky, the snake on
the ground, and the *baipu* are the forest's fatal metaphors. You
must therefore be careful in the *kyvaity*, the dark-green thickness
of the woods. But you are careful because you know your way
around. The Atchei are comfortable there, they feel at home.
They can be patient in this world, which to others is confusing
and frightening. It speaks to them in a familiar language, with its
thousands of different sounds, the smells of the plants and the
soil, the murmur of the wind and the water. It is not like the
savanna. There, they are afraid, they feel vulnerable, exposed to
everything: the space is different, foreign, hostile. This is the
white man's world and the world of dead souls.

When you see dozens of vultures flying together, wheeling in
lazy circles closer and closer to the ground, you know that they
have spotted something — a decaying animal killed by a hunter or
by another animal, or else a dying animal in its last frenzy — and
that they are getting ready to swoop down on it. We assumed this
to be the case when we were told by a hunter who had wandered
off from the camp one day that he had seen a great number of
vultures circling above. When there are many vultures together
waiting for an animal to die, they are especially vulnerable to
attack by bow and arrow. Several men went off with their weapons. The Atchei are fond of vulture meat; in addition, they use
the long feathers to make arrows and the long bones are used for
hunting whistles. We walked on; it turned out that there really

were vultures. Noiselessly, so as not to frighten them away, we reached a small treeless hollow. Quite a few of them were perched in the branches right above us, like sinister black spots. Others were moving around something on the ground, and as they pecked away with their beaks, their half-opened wings hid what they were eating from view. There was a sudden cry, and they all took off with a gentle beating of their wings and perched nearby, completely unperturbed.

There was no sweetness in the air that day; the corpse they had been eating gave off a terrible stench. The man had been dead for only a little while, but the *briku* had opened his belly, which accelerated the process of putrefaction, attracting numerous swarms of flies, and the flies had become drunk with everything oozing and flowing from the gashes. There were blood-splattered holes in place of the eyes, which had been pecked out by the birds. The mouth was enlarged; the birds had forced their way through the teeth to get at the tongue. But even so we could recognize him; the length of his body left no doubt. It was a Stranger whose height had surprised me; he was four or five inches taller than the tallest hunter. And now he had become food for the vultures. The Atchei did not like to see this happen. He had left several days before, saying that he was going to meet up with two families who were hunting. He had been rather ill and had probably changed his mind on the way; but he had not been able to return to the camp. He had died all alone and no doubt had seen the vultures gather in the sky above and then swoop down on him one by one. The birds were motionless; bloody slivers of meat hung from their beaks. The place was quiet. Hundreds of little yellow butterflies dryly beat their wings around Krembegi's corpse.

Unusual in many respects, Krembegi was immediately striking because of his exceptional height, which made him almost a giant compared to the little Atchei. But he was not proportionately more vigorous. He gave an overall impression of flabbiness. He had a broad, fat belly, whereas the bellies of the other men were hard and compact, even when relaxed. He was a strange hunter, to say the least.

But was this all? The members of his tribe did not like to talk about him, and when they did talk, it was only with reticence. As for the Atchei Gatu, who were hardly more loquacious on the subject, their knowing looks and crafty smiles showed that even though they would not say anything, they had certainly devoted some thought to the matter. It seemed clear that Krembegi was not just anyone.

Because he wore his hair long like a woman (the men wore theirs short), I wanted to take his picture one day and asked him to hold his bow, which was standing nearby. He got up politely but refused to hold the weapon.

"Why?"

"It's not my bow."

"Take it anyway."

"I don't have a bow, I don't want to touch this bow."

He spoke firmly and seemed disgusted, as if I had asked him to do something obscene. And then, to show that he did not feel any ill will, he pointed to something that I thought could not have been his.

"I'll hold my basket."

This was the Atchei world turned upside down: a man with a basket and no bow! Who was Krembegi? As soon as I learned the secret of this man's strangeness, people were quite willing to talk to me about him. His story was told to me little by little, first by the Atchei, who were delighted to have another chance to show

278

that they had good reasons for scorning the Strangers and that they would never allow someone like Krembegi to live among them. Later, the *Iroiangi* agreed with the portrait drawn by the Atchei Gatu and added details to it. But from the man himself I could get nothing. Timid and reserved, he would avoid talking to me. He died without having said anything.

The insistence of the Atchei tribes on instilling in their young men the idea of *bretete*, the great hunter, is the basis both of the group's moral law and of individual honor; but it also arises from economic necessity. Since they are nomads in a forest that is rather limited in edible vegetation, the Guayaki cannot subsist on gathering. Roots, berries, fruits, hearts of palm, honey, and larvae unquestionably account for a considerable portion of their food, and this should not be forgotten; it is the women's responsibility to gather this hidden food, and all around their stopping places in the forest they are constantly foraging for it. But not all areas are rich in trees with edible fruit, and the forest is generous only during certain seasons. That is why the *kuja* sometimes return to the camp without their baskets pulling on their necks. There is very little to be found in the *naku*: a few larvae reserved for the children, especially the "soft heads," because it is very nutritious, a rat, one or two frogs, and sometimes a snake, which is caught by the tail, quickly dashed against a tree before it can bite, and then roasted. Eating like this is all right once in a while, but if you make a steady diet of it you lose weight, and that is depressing.

The major portion of the food is produced by the men. In Guayaki society, it is they who have the task of supplying the people with meat and fat, which are indispensable. *Bareka*, to hunt: this is their function; they identify themselves with it and define themselves by this activity. A man can think of himself only as a hunter, one cannot be a man and not a hunter at the same time. The entire symbolic space of masculinity unfolds in the act

279

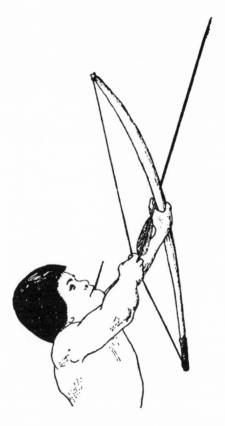

Archery position.

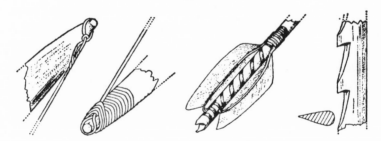

Attaching the bow's cord; feathering the arrow; notching the arrow on one side.

of *jyvo*, shooting an arrow, and from their earliest years the boys are prepared to enter their normal place, to fulfill their natural role. The long years of apprenticeship running along with their fathers through the woods, the initiation that confirms them as hunters, the women's preference for the best *bretete*, the night songs of the men loudly celebrating their exploits as archers — all these combine to make the young men take on the collective will of the group as their own personal desire. They must become true hunters, for the survival of the tribe will depend on them. They know it, and in this knowledge lies their truth, their destiny as men: either one is a hunter or one does not exist. There is no choice.

Is this to say that the men in this society are in some sense victims of economic alienation because they are completely identified with their function as "producers"? That they are somehow constrained or forced to resign themselves to the inevitable? Not at all. Hunting is never considered a burden. Even though it is almost the exclusive occupation of the men, the most important thing they do every day, it is still practiced as a "sport." There is work involved, of course, in endlessly tracking animals, in sitting still for hours watching the movements of a roe buck or a band of monkeys, in holding the bow poised for several minutes so that they will be ready for the brief instant when a bird or coati can be seen through the thickness of the foliage. They know it is crouching in the branches above, but they can't see it; they have to wait until it shows itself, keeping their arrows at the ready. They must also dig holes for the tapir to fall into and expand the armadillo's hole: the man digs, and the animal tries to escape by burrowing further into the tunnels. It is a race that the hunter usually wins but only after considerable effort — sometimes he makes an excavation so big that he can disappear into it.

And then the hunters must keep replenishing the supply of arrows. The tips are made of very hard wood tempered by fire,

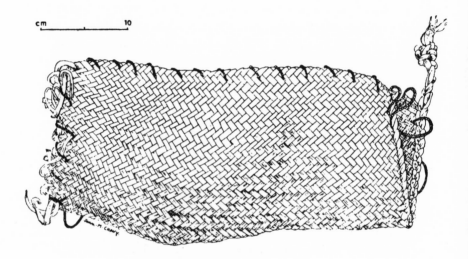

Pepo, feather holder.

but as they are used they wear out and break. They are often lost, either when a wounded animal gets away after being hit or when an arrow misses its mark and flies off into the vegetation and disappears. Whether the men are in the woods or resting in the camp, then, they are always involved with the work of hunting.

Hunting is always an adventure, sometimes a risky one, but constantly inspiring. Of course, it is pleasant to take sweet-smelling honey from a hive or split a palm tree and find swarms of delicious *guchu* left behind by the scarabs. But everything is known in advance, there is no mystery, nothing unforeseen: it is absolutely routine.

Tracking animals in the forest, proving that you are more clever than they are, approaching within arrow's range without revealing your presence, hearing the hum of the arrow in the air and then the dull thud as it strikes an animal — all these things are joys that have been experienced countless numbers of times, and yet they remain as fresh and exciting as they were on the first hunt. The Atchei do not grow weary of hunting. Nothing else is asked of them, and they love it more than anything else. Because of this, they are at peace with themselves. They feel no internal division, no bitterness troubles their souls. They are what they do, their self fearlessly achieves its fullness in doing what the group has always done since the beginning of time. One might say they are prisoners of fate. But from what point of view? The Atchei hunters themselves feel that they live in complete freedom.

To be a *bretete* requires strength, poise, and agility; you have to reach a state in which the body and mind feel at ease, are sure of themselves. This is *pana. Pana: pané-ai*, the opposite of *pané*. And *pané* is what frightens a man most. For once you have fallen victim to it, *bareka* is finished. Your arm has no strength, the arrow flies far from the target, useless and absurd. You can no longer kill anything. The return to camp is grim when your right shoulder is not straining under the weight of some animal. Instead of celebrating his catch with a sonorous chant, the empty-handed hunter sits in silence beside his fire. If *japa* — shooting wide of the mark — happens several times in a row, then measures must be taken, for *pané* has befallen the hunter. This is, of course, a painful humiliation, since it is an admission that he is incapable of being what he is: a hunter.

But it could be even more serious. A man never eats his own game: this is the law that provides for the distribution of food among the Atchei. A hunter kills an animal and his wife cuts it up, since he is forbidden to do it himself. She keeps a few pieces for herself and the children and the rest is given out, to relatives first, brothers and brothers-in-law, and then to the others. No one is forgotten, and if there is not much meat, then the shares are small, but each person gets something. In exchange, the hunter receives a portion of the game brought back by the others. He feeds them with what he has killed, and they do the same for him. A hunter, then, spends his life hunting for others and eating what others have caught. His dependence is total, and the same is true of his companions. In this way, things are equal, no one is ever wronged, because the men "produce" equivalent quantities of meat. This is called *pepy*, exchange.

But if a man is *pané*, what can he give in return, how can he pay another man back for the game he has given him? You cannot receive without giving. It is impossible to be *pané* and to respect the law of reciprocity at the same time. In the end, your companions would grow weary of always giving without receiving anything in return. An old man who is too weak to hold a bow is given food. He deserves it, and a son never lets his father go hungry. If this parasitical existence goes on for too long, however, one day he will be left at the foot of a tree beside a fire. There he will wait patiently for death. But a strong male is not an old man.

If he is *pané*, it is because he deserves it: he has done something wrong. Every act against the order of things must be paid for, and this is how the imprudent man is punished. Why help a man who has been found guilty and condemned? It would not do any good.

Fortunately, long-term cases of *pané* are rare. Every man has his periods of bad luck, his arrow leaves too soon or too late, his hand does not draw back the bow with enough force. But this can be remedied. The young men's lips are pierced and their backs are scarred to confirm them in their condition of *pana*. If *pané* should occur, the operation is repeated. This can be done by a companion or by the man himself. New scars are made, but much more superficial ones than the cruel stripes that were dug out of the skin before. They go around the biceps and crisscross with the old cuts; some men cut their forearms, others their thighs. Very little blood flows, and once the wounds have been smeared with wood ashes and have closed up, the shallow scars have the effect of attractive embroidery on the skin. This treatment is almost always successful: the *pané* leaves you, and once again you become *bretete*. And if you become *pané* again, you begin all over. The causes of this type of bad luck are mysterious. It can happen to anyone, and there is not a single Atchei hunter who does not have therapeutic tattoos in addition to the *jaycha* on his back. Even Jyvukugi had several of them.

While the cause of *pané* is unknown in some cases, in others it is very clear. One cause — and this would be so fatal that no one even dreams of attempting it — would be to eat your own game, to refuse to participate in the exchange. To insist on keeping the animals you have killed leads to a total and permanent separation from the world of animals, since the *pané* will prevent you from ever killing another one again. When you do not mediate your relationship with food through your relationship with other people, you risk being completely cut off from the natural world

285

and placed outside it, just as you are pushed out of the social universe by refusing to share your goods. This is the foundation of all Atchei knowledge. It is based on the awareness that an underlying brotherhood binds the world and men together and that what happens among men is echoed in the world. A single order rules them, and it must not be disrupted.

The Atchei therefore avoid doing things that will attract *pané*. Young hunters, for example, never eat animal brain. Although it is a great delicacy, it causes bad luck. For this reason, it is reserved for the *chyvaete*, who hunt little or not at all and therefore run no risk. Some kinds of honey are also forbidden to the young men because they bring on *pané*, such as the honey from the *tei* bee. The honey of the *tare*, on the other hand, only prevents the *kybuchu* from growing pubic hair. But there is something else. For what does it mean to be a great hunter but to identify one's very existence with the bow? And doesn't *pané* separate a man from his bow so that it becomes exterior to him, as if it had rebelled against its master? The bow is the hunter himself: a "new labret's" first task is to make his first adult bow by himself. This weapon is much more than a tool. When its owner dies, it becomes *ove enda*, the dwelling place of the departed soul, as do the arrows. The bow and arrows have now become dangerous and are discarded. The bow is the sign and symbol of the man, the proof that he exists and the means of his existing. When he dies, then, his bow disappears as well, for it is that part of the man which could not survive him, just as his last labret could not survive him. Conversely, if the bow abandons him when he is *pané*, then he is no longer a hunter, he is no longer anything.

The very strength of the bow makes it vulnerable. It is not difficult for *pané* to affect a hunter: it has only to affect his bow; he will immediately suffer from it and be *pané*. A bow is the essence of virility, the irrevocable metaphor of masculinity. Because of

286

this, it is one of the things that must be protected from its opposites. How far does the hunter's space extend, what is the boundary of the masculine world? The boundary is the feminine world.
An order presides over the lines of force in this geography and
keeps the different regions separate. If some disorder causes them
to interpenetrate, masculine space is contaminated, weakened,
and degraded by this contact with feminine space. In other words,
if a woman touches a bow, *pané* befalls its owner. For this reason,
there is a severe taboo against women having any contact with a
bow. They themselves run no risk, but for the men it can be fatal.
Inversely, the equivalent of the bow for the *kuja* is the *naku*, the
basket, which is the quintessence of a woman's femininity. When
a *kujambuku* becomes *dare* after the ritual of seclusion and the
scarring of her stomach, she celebrates her entrance into the
world of adults by weaving palms into her first basket. She knows
how to do it because her mother has taught her; she made little
ones when she was a girl. Now it is up to her to make it by herself, and until her death she will carry a basket. Just as the bow
is the man, the basket is the woman. So that if a hunter touches
a basket, or even thinks of carrying one — which would be even
more absurd than comical — the result would be the same: *pané*
would be his punishment for having contact with the basket.

It is always the men who suffer the consequences. The unwar-
ranted overlapping of masculinity and femininity affects only the
men. Only they can suffer. Of course, the *kuja* will also suffer
from *pané* in the sense that the hunters will no longer have anything to give them to eat. But the women's power is so strong
that it can be harmful to men. To be a hunter, that is to say a man,
you must always be on your guard against women, even when
they are not menstruating. You cannot be a man except by opposing yourself to women. When the distance separating men from
women vanishes, when a man crosses the dividing line, a conta-

gion is produced that makes him lose his worth, that wears away his masculinity: he finds himself within the sphere of women. Bow-man, basket-woman, this is how people are divided up. What happens to a man without a bow? He becomes a basket person.

This was what had happened to Krembegi. He was not joking when he said "my basket," because it really was his, made by his own hands with the help of one of the women. Why did he have a basket? Because he did not have a bow. And why didn't he have a bow? Because he was *pané*. But this had been the case for a long time; in fact, it had always been the case. He had never been able to kill an animal with a bow and arrow, and the matter became clear rather quickly: he was *pané* in the same way that the others were *bretete*. This was not an accident. It was his nature. But still, why, when circumstances had taken away his bow, did he provide himself with a basket? He could have had nothing at all, have remained, so to speak, between bow and basket. But is it possible to be neither a bow person nor a basket person?

Only in early childhood is there any space in which the difference between the sexes remains negligible. And Krembegi was a grown-up — he was no longer a *kromi*. He could no longer exist in this neuter universe. When one is an adult, one is either a man or a woman, a bow or a basket: there is nothing in between, no third possibility. What, then, is a man without a bow? He is a non-man, and for this reason he becomes a basket carrier.

There were two basket-carrying men at Arroyo Moroti and both were *Iroiangi*. The second one was named Chachubuta-wachugi, the Great Wild Pig with the Long Beard. A very hairy beard covered his face. And since it often took him a long time to find a woman willing to shave him, his beard would grow quite prodigiously. I gave him a present of a mirror and some razor blades; he would put the blades in the middle of a split piece of

288

bamboo and then fasten them tightly. In this way, he could shave more often. In gratitude he gave me the name of *apaio*, father. Chachubutawachugi had a basket because he was *pané*. But unlike Krembegi he was very strong, and though he had not used a bow for several years because of the *pané*, he continued to hunt coatis by hand and to stalk armadillos in their burrows. He would distribute his catch and receive presents from the other hunters in return. His shoulders, striped with thin black lines, attested to his efforts to overcome his bad luck with tattoos. But after repeated failures, he had given up and resigned himself to his fate. One of his brothers' wives had made a basket for him. He lived with them, more tolerated than welcomed. When his sister-in-law was in a bad mood, she wouldn't give him anything to eat. At those times, he would cook for himself. No woman would have agreed to become the wife of a *pané* man; he therefore had to take on feminine work himself. He had once been married, but his wife had died, leaving him alone. To judge by the evidence, Chachubutawachugi did not have the best of luck.

Krembegi, on the other hand, seemed comfortable with his situation. He did not say much, of course, but he looked serene. He lived with a family who accepted him completely. Cooking was not a question for him since he helped the wife in her daily household tasks. It was almost as if he was the co-wife of the man who lodged him. In the morning, he would go off with the *kuja* to look for larvae, fruits, and hearts of palm. His basket would be just as full as those of his companions when he came back. He would put it down, crouch on his heels, and diligently and efficiently begin to prepare the evening meal: husking berries, peeling roots, preparing *bruee*, a thick soup made of palm marrow mixed with larvae. He would fetch water and firewood.

When he had nothing to do, he would rest or make necklaces with the teeth of the animals killed by his host. They were very pretty, far more attractive than those made by the women. The women were content to pierce the teeth of all the different animals killed by their husbands and to string them through with a thin cord. It amounted to little more than a collection of teeth of different sizes placed in the order in which the animals had been killed. These necklaces were sometimes very long, six feet or more, containing hundreds of teeth from monkeys, agoutis, and especially pacas – those from pigs and roe bucks were not saved because they rattled against one another. When a woman is feeling happy, she puts on her necklaces in several layers, glad to wear the proof of her husband's prowess as a hunter. Then she puts them back in the bottom of her basket. Krembegi's necklaces showed more care. He would use only monkey canine teeth and only those that were more or less the same size. It is no little job to pierce all these tiny canines with nothing more than a paca tooth. But Krembegi had great patience.

No one in the camp paid particular attention to him, he was like everyone else. He did only woman's work, but this was known and taken for granted. Krembegi was no more or less anonymous than anyone else in the tribe, and he tranquilly filled the role destiny had given him. He lived with the women and did what they did; he did not cut his hair and carried a basket. He was at home in this role and could be himself. Why should he have been unhappy?

Chachubutawachugi was a different matter altogether. It was not at all assumed that he had found his niche or that he was content with his lot. And the proof was that no one took him seriously. Whatever he said or did was greeted by the Atchei with condescension. They did not openly make fun of him, because that was not done, but they found him rather ridiculous and smiled behind his back. The men were somewhat wary of him, and the women laughed into their hands when they saw him coming with his basket. The children, who were usually so respectful of their elders, forgot the rules of politeness and good conduct when they were with him. They ran wild, were insolent, and refused to obey him. Sometimes he would get angry and try to catch them, but they were always too fast; he would give up and sullenly take a walk in the woods or lie down somewhere off by himself. Everyone pretended to believe that he was stingy with what he brought back from the forest, while he was actually as generous as anyone else. For example, he had gone off in the morning one day saying that he was going to look for larvae. On his return he ran into a group of men. "Well?" "Nothing. No *guchu*." And he walked on. When he was out of earshot one of the men said: "Nothing? *U pa modo!* He ate everything up!" And they all burst out laughing. This was an unjust accusation.

Why were the Atchei so mean to poor Chachubutawachugi? It was true that they found him something of a clown, with his passion for adorning his neck and head with the most unexpected objects. If he saw a piece of metal, a cartridge case, or a bottle, he couldn't resist; he would pick it up, attach it to a string, and put it around his neck. He would walk around with his chest covered by a necklace made of a few dozen penicillin bottles, some sardine-can keys, and formless pieces of scrap iron. He would wear it for a while, then abandon it, and go find other things. The *kybuchu* were once given a rubber ball. After a short time they had ruined it. For him it was a godsend. He cut it in two and made one of the pieces into a superb skullcap that covered his whole head down to the eyes. He was very happy with his idea. The Atchei, however, looked at the elegant fellow with an air of pity. "Not at all surprising! That's his style, all right!" In other words, the victim of *pané* had found another way to call attention to himself through this rather awkward dandyism.

But there had to be another reason for the Atchei's ill will, for in the final analysis Chachubutawachugi's innocent faults were more than compensated for by his activity as a hunter of coatis and armadillos. This activity was of course somewhat limited, but it was by no means negligible. On the other hand, Krembegi, who never trapped animals, was not mistreated in the slightest way by the Atchei. This was why he was able to accept his fate with such placidity. What was the difference, then, between these two *pané* men? What was the difference that made people adopt different attitudes toward two *negatively* similar individuals — similar in that they were both excluded from the circle of hunters? As a rule, the Atchei would have had the same attitude toward both of them. But it was not at all the same. Therefore, the fact that both these men were *pané* did not make them identical. As it turned out, they were not.

Man = hunter = bow; woman = gatherer = basket: these two equations strictly determine the course of Atchei life. There is no third equation, no additional space to protect those who belong neither to the bow nor the basket. By ceasing to become a hunter, one loses one's very masculinity; metaphorically, one becomes a woman. This is what Krembegi understood and accepted: his radical renunciation of what he was incapable of becoming — a hunter — automatically put him on the side of the women; he was one of them, *he accepted himself as a woman*. He carried his basket in the same way they did, with a carrying strap around his forehead.

And Chachubutawachugi? It was simple: he hadn't understood a thing. For he, the innocent one, thought that he could remain in the masculine universe even after he had lost the right to do so, so blind was he in his desire to remain a man — he who was no longer a hunter, who was no longer considered a hunter. *Esse est percipi.* What did the others see when they saw him? Perhaps this is not the right question. Because from a certain point of view

Chachubutawachugi was *invisible*. Why? Because he did not live anywhere: neither among the men, because of the *pané*, nor among the women, for in spite of his basket, he refused to incorporate himself into their group, to inhabit their space. But the place he was obstinately trying to occupy, midway between the two, did not exist. And so he did not exist any more either; he was a pathetic inhabitant of an impossible place. This was what made him "invisible"; he was elsewhere, he was nowhere, he was everywhere. Chachubutawachugi's existence was unthinkable. He was walking in place. He could not dream of turning back, and he was afraid to go ahead.

And this was what annoyed the Atchei. What they reproached the *pané* man for without their even knowing it was his incomprehensible refusal to let himself be taken along by the logical movement of events, which should have put him in his new and real place, among the women. When you have a basket, it is because you are a *kuja*. But he did not want to be one, and this created disorder in the group and upset the ideas of the people — not to speak of the man himself. This was why he often seemed so nervous, so ill at ease. He had not chosen the most comfortable position for himself, and he had thrown things out of order.

You had only to see how Chachubutawachugi carried his basket. He did not do it as the women and Krembegi did, with the carrying strap around his forehead. In this position, the women walked with their heads lowered, somewhat bent, looking at the ground. But he carried his *naku* differently, with the strap in front and slung over his shoulders. Whenever he slipped, he would have to steady the basket with his hand, and often the strap would painfully squeeze his neck. But in this way he walked like a man.

As for Krembegi, his relations with the bow were the same as those of the women: he never touched a bow because this would attract bad luck to the owner of the weapon. Nothing set him apart from the *kuja*. That was why he had refused when I asked him to hold a bow for the photograph and had picked up his basket instead. But this was not all. Krembegi, who was separated from the bow and masculinity, had gone the full symbolic distance into the feminine world. This accounted for the Strangers' reticence and the hints made by the Atchei Gatu. What did the Atchei know about him? Why did the one group refuse to speak about him and the other group make only sarcastic remarks? It was because Krembegi was a *kyrypy-meno*, an anus-lovemaker, a homosexual.

The people of his tribe accepted it naturally, even though they were somewhat annoyed by it. But that was because the Atchei Gatu were very disapproving: "There are no *kyrypy-meno* among us! You have to be *Iroiangi* for that!" But everyone agreed that if Krembegi was what he was, it was because he was *pané*. The Atchei Gatu felt no contempt for him personally. For them, it was rather comic that a man would accept the compliments of another man by offering him his *kyrypy*. They laughed about it and saw in this yet another proof of their superiority over the Strangers. They could not recall any similar cases among their group. They only told the story of Bujamiarangi. It had happened a long time ago, when Paivagi was still a young man. An Atchei went out hunting and had the good fortune to fall upon a *kware*, who was caught unawares and did not have time to escape into the thickets. The man did not even have to use an arrow; he beat the animal with his bow and broke its spine. The vegetation in this spot was very dense, the underbrush a tangle of creepers and climbing plants. The hunter left behind his still dying prey and tried to open a hole in the vegetation by using his bow to knock down the plants and shrubs. He had progressed a few dozen yards when he came upon a more open space and then went back to get the anteater and put it on his back. He saw someone next to the animal. It was Bujamiarangi, a very young man, who had been following him. And what was he doing there? The hunter could not believe his eyes: Bujamiarangi was making *meno* with the dead anteater! He was so absorbed in taking his pleasure that he did not hear the man approach. The hunter did not hesitate for a second. Mad with rage over what the other man was doing with his game, he shot an arrow, and Bujamiarangi collapsed onto the cadaver of the *kware*. No one ever saw him again.

But as for *kyrypy-meno*, no, they didn't know anything about it. To be insensitive to the charms of women was something that surpassed the understanding of the Atchei Gatu. But then, to give in to the assaults of other men, that was too much! And all that because of *pané*. What did they say about Krembegi? First of all, of course, that he never "went" to women. But why? Because his penis was very small, like the penis of a coati. It was freely compared to the little barbs put on the tips of arrows: it was really not much of anything, he could not use it. It could well have been that this was simply malicious gossip. But who were Krembegi's partners? Were the Strangers also different from the Atchei Gatu in that their hunters all enjoyed *kyrypy-meno*? For obviously, Krembegi could not be a homosexual all by himself.

He did have partners. But not many and not those one would have thought. It would be logical to assume that, to the extent that a man like Krembegi represents a certain disorder in the ethico-sexual world of the Atchei, a subversion of all accepted and respected values, the field of his sexual activity would not be governed by any rules, that he could pursue his own pleasure at will: in other words, that any man of the tribe, if he so desired, could make love with Krembegi. But this was not at all the case; homosexual relations are not anarchic, they are governed by a very rigorous logic. Krembegi was the Atchei world upside down, but he was not a counterorder to the existing social order, he was not its negation; he was part of another order, another group of rules that were the image — even though reversed — of the "normal" order and rules.

The ultimate bases of Atchei social life are the alliances between family groups, relations that take form and are fulfilled in marriage exchanges, in the continual exchange of women. A woman exists in order to circulate, to become the wife of a man who is not her father, her brother, or her son. It is in this manner that one makes *picha*, allies. But can a man, even one who exists as a woman, "circulate"? How could the gift of Krembegi, for example, be paid back? This was not even imaginable, since he was not a woman but a homosexual. The chief law of all societies is the prohibition against incest. Because he was *kyrypy-meno*, Krembegi was outside this social order. In his case, the logic of the social system — or, what amounts to the same thing, the logic of its reversal — was worked out to its very end: *Krembegi's partners were his own brothers.* "*Picha kybai* (meaning *kyrypy-meno*) *menoia.* A *kyrypy-meno* man does not make love with his allies." This injunction is the exact opposite of the rules governing the relations between men and women. Homosexuality can only be "incestuous"; the brother sodomizes his brother, and in this metaphor of incest the certainty that there can never be any real incest (between a man and a woman) without destroying the social body is confirmed and reinforced.

That is why Krembegi's partners were so few in number. Of course, now and then a man without family ties would solicit his favors — the dissolute Bykygi for example. But these things rarely leave the family, so to speak. Such was Krembegi's fate: *pané*, homosexual, a complete inversion of the sexual and social order. But still and all, he was not too unhappy with his lot.

But now it was all over. He had run into his last bit of bad luck, and the vultures were in the process of devouring him. It would not have been a good idea to let them go on. Krembegi was going to be buried. One of the men went back to the camp to give the news. He would bring back several women so that they could do the death *chenga ruvara*. In the meantime, the others would prepare the grave. With a few quick blows of the machete, they cleared a small space in the woods at the center of which a hole was dug. It was a sort of well that was more or less cylindrical, just wide enough for a human body, and more than three feet deep. The thick humus that covered the ground of the forest was not hard to dig, and the machetes went into it easily. The vultures were still waiting, not at all scared off by our activities. They did not try to get closer to the corpse. A man went off a little ways under the trees to look for *chipo*, a fine creeper used as string.

The messenger came back, accompanied by three women. One was the wife of the chief, Karewachugi; she presided over all the tribe's rituals, she was always the first to intone the chants. The other two were Krembegi's sisters-in-law. They had brought two mats made of *pindo*. Crouching on their heels, they burst forth in the *chenga ruvara*. Their sobbing seemed even more lugubrious than it had the other times, because now it did not mingle with the quiet but constant noise of camp life. Silence, light, vultures. The men (among whom was a brother of the dead man) seemed indifferent. Krembegi's passing did not seem to affect them. Were the words they were speaking — so quickly that I could not understand them — an elegy to the dead man? I couldn't be sure, but I doubted it. When the farewell to Krembegi was finished, the men took over.

Working rapidly because of the stench, with almost brutal gestures they folded the legs high over the chest, having to force them a bit because rigor mortis had already set in. He was in the fetal position: as it is before birth, so it is after death. To keep the body in this position, it was tied tightly by the creepers that had been gathered a little while before. The same process was repeated with the arms: they were folded in to the torso against the ribs, the forearms bent up to the arms, the elbows against the body. The head was last. The men pushed on the neck to lower it against the chest. The hands were then pushed against the temples with the fingers slightly separated and closed, like the claws of a bird of prey. The head was put between the hands and a solid knot of creepers fixed it in this position. Krembegi's large body now resembled a kind of ball caught in a net. It was ready for burial.

A mat lined the bottom and the sides of the hole so that the body would not come into direct contact with the earth. Two men picked up the heavy bundle and lowered it into the grave, the face turned toward the west, toward the land of the dead. But the body was not put in straight, it was not resting on the heels. It was leaning forward, almost on the knees, the head lowered and leaning against the side of the hole. A piece of wood with holes in it supported the forearms, as if the dead man were leaning on a railing, meditating with his head between his hands. It also looked like an animal trying to leave its burrow. The body was then covered with a second mat, which was carefully arranged around the head and torso. The earth that filled the hole did not touch the body. They packed the earth down a little, but the well was not completely filled, only up to six or eight inches from the surface. All around the opening pieces of wood were stuck into the ground; this barrier would prevent the earth from falling down and hiding the location of the grave. It would also keep away animals. The last act of the burial was to put a straw roof over the grave, almost level with the ground, which made it look like a miniature shelter. And, in fact, it was a house that they were building: first of all to give protection from the rain, but also as a means of keeping the dead man in his grave. If this roof were not put on, he would get out and his ghost would harass the people. He was at home there, it was his *tapy*: the essential thing was that he stay there. A different method is used for young children; they are buried on their backs, wrapped up in two mats, and the grave is filled in completely so that all traces vanish quickly. There is no need to know where the grave is; no one will ever go back there. Children have no *Ianve*. They leave the living in peace. The proof is that they can even be buried under the *tapy*.

But Krembegi's grave had to be marked so that it could be found again. If he had died in the camp, the people would have buried him nearby and then immediately moved somewhere else, beyond the reach of *Ianve*. The Atchei always leave the area in which an adult is buried after destroying or burning his possessions: a woman's basket and mats, a hunter's bow and arrows. The bow is broken and thrown into the fire. The arrows are not burned but shot off at random in all directions. Aren't they *ove enda*, the dwelling place of the soul? After a person's death nothing must remain that belonged to him during his life. Those things are too dangerous. As soon as Krembegi's death was known, therefore, his basket was thrown into the fire. The smoke that rises into the air marks the path for the final departure of *Ove*. This time the Atchei did not move from their camp; the grave was too far away for *Ianve* to find it. On the other hand, the burial place had to be marked, for they would be coming back to complete and conclude the funeral ritual.

There is still more to do after a dead person has been put in the ground. After several weeks have gone by — the time necessary for putrefaction to have done its work, leaving a naked skeleton — the Atchei, who in the meantime have continued to wander through the forest, return to the grave site. No matter how far away they are or how long a time has elapsed, an irreversible sep-

299

aration must be made between the dead person and the living: they take leave of him, they get rid of him. The roof protecting the tomb is torn down, and the grave is opened. In the hole there is a skeleton held together by creepers. The remains are removed, special care being taken not to touch them. If they are touched, *baivwa* will be provoked, which is nearly always fatal for the person affected. A male relative of the dead person takes a piece of forked wood, puts the tips into the eye sockets, and separates the skull. Then he strikes it with his bow and breaks it apart. He then throws it into a fire that has been lit for the occasion, where it will burn up, the empty eyes turned upward so that *Ove* will know the direction by which it must depart. The rest of the bones are either burned or left where they are; the grave is not filled in again. Everything is abandoned, and the people go away. Whereas the burial itself is a rather solemn affair, the second phase of the ritual is performed hastily. What is the real purpose of this second phase? They have killed the dead person a second time by striking and burning his skull. Now that this has been accomplished, *Ianve* has been chased away, death has been abolished. But why not go to the trouble to repair the grave site? It wouldn't do any good; there are no more than a few bones left, and the animals and moisture will soon take care of them. The operation lasts only a few minutes, and yet the people sometimes come from very far away to participate in it: for it is the only way to keep the dead away from the living.

What is a *manove*, a dead person? It is something terrible, something that inspires fear, all the more so because the *manove* are aggressive and invisible. Worst of all, they are the absolute enemies of the Atchei: the dead are so perverse in their wickedness that they want to kill the living. A dead Atchei is no longer a person, it is something else. The dead want only Death to reign. There is a sort of kinship between the dead and the jaguar, the metaphor of all the mortal dangers hidden in the world that surrounds the Atchei. They do not say this in so many words, of course, but their actions indicate that they are well aware of it. When Krembegi's body was prepared, his hands were placed in that strange position against his face, his fingers like claws. "Why are the hands put this way?" "*Baipu pypo uwa.* So that the mark of the jaguar will be there."

Pypo is the track of a human foot or animal paw left in the ground or in the mud. Here, however, the word did not designate the imprint, but rather the thing that leaves the imprint: the jaguar's paw, which the hands of the dead man imitated with their spread and curled fingers. Why do the Strangers bury their dead in such an unusual position? Because, in so doing, they reveal the true nature of the *manove* and their new manner of existence: *the dead are jaguars.* Not only are they excluded from the community of the living, but they are even expelled from the social world of the culture by being transformed into jaguars and thrown back into nature. "We put the hands here; then he becomes a *baipu.* An Atchei ghost has a jaguar's head."

Furthermore, "souls" become jaguars. "*Ove ro baipu o. Ove* is transformed into *baipu.*" The Atchei rarely find themselves face-to-face with a real jaguar. The jaguars they see are almost always ghosts that have taken on this form to harm someone. Anyone, man or woman, young or old, can be transformed into a jaguar. But the only people one can be certain will become jaguars are the *yma chija,* the people with strong characters, such as Jyvukugi.

The *Ove* of the other Atchei become a Barendy, a "luminous being," a star in the sky. To reach the sky, *Ove* is carried by a coati who climbs along the creepers that hang from big trees, or else it travels upward on a beam of sunlight. The body of a Barendy is covered with hair. He does not speak but makes much noise with his anus when he appears at nightfall. The Atchei cover their ears

301

and stay silent: if they did not do this, Barendy would fall on them and burn their hair — just as they burn the hair of their game — and roast them. As soon as they hear him coming, they quickly cover their fires with dirt so as not to attract his attention. But he is not the master of fire. That is Dyvitata with the very white body: when he flies in the air, he spews forth a trail of fire from his anus: *kyrypy tata*, fire from the ass.

In any case, even if *Ove* becomes a Barendy, it will not necessarily remain fixed in this form; depending on the circumstances, it can become a jaguar or even a poisonous snake, or go up into a tree and make a snake fall down on the Atchei it wants to kill, or, finally, appear in the guise of some other animal, such as the otter that killed Terygi. Everyone knew that Krembegi was now going to live as a *jakucha* bird, which is the last form homosexuals take. The "souls" are omnipresent, come in many sizes and shapes, are sometimes called *Ove*, sometimes *Ianve*, and are kept at bay by the efforts of the Atchei. Are they the person after he is dead, or are they only his wicked double? Certain things follow from death: there is a splitting of *manove* into an enemy ghost and a neutral "spirit," which innocently goes to live where the sun sets, the resting place of the dead, which the Atchei describe as a great savanna or the Invisible Forest. When the Atchei Gatu and the Strangers compared their conceptions of the fate of the dead, they were shocked by the differences. The former contended that the Invisible Forest contains only *chingy* trees (*Ruprechtia laxiflora*), while for the others the only thing that grows there are *baikandy* (*ocotea*) with moss-covered trunks. That was why they buried their dead in the shade of these trees whenever possible. There, in the savanna or forest located above the terrestrial world, the "souls" lie curled up like fetuses in a womb, near the lord of those places, Chono, Thunder. Once up above, *Ove* cries, waiting for the *pichua*. Then the storm erupts with rain and rumblings in the sky.

One thing is sure, one point on which the Atchei Gatu and the *Iroiangi* agree: *Ove* decides when an Atchei shall die and prepares for his death. "*Ove* makes a pot of earth." Kybwyragi explained this with great solemnity, and the Strangers seated beside him agreed enthusiastically: "*Go! Go nonga!* That's it! That's it exactly!"

"The *Ianve* of the Atchei, the *Ove* of the Atchei puts the bones in the pot, in the pot that it has made. That is where it leaves the ashes, the ashes of the bones, the bones burned to ashes: in its own pot. With the bones it also puts the skull. The *Ove* of the Atchei makes its pot. It puts the bones that are beaten and then burned in the fire, in the pot, it carries its own skeleton burned to ashes. That is where it leaves them, its own bones, in the pot that it has made.

"Then, when the *Ove* of the person leaves, when it leaves to go into its own pot, when it strikes the pot that it has made, then death has already come, it is in the gaze of death that it places the ashes.

"The Atchei of old, the dead of long ago, made their own pots, but those of today do not make their own. One makes the pot when one is old.

"It puts the ashes there, the ashes of the skull, the ashes of the skeleton. All the bones are put in it and also the hair, all the shaved hair, all that is put in the pot.

"The Atchei* also lets out its excrement from its split belly; its own excrement is put there, the excrement of the dead, the contents of the entrails. Everything is put in the pot.

"In the heart of deepest darkness, *Ove* puts the excrement of the person into its pot, then the ashes, the ashes of the skeleton, and

---

* The speaker referred to the soul of the dead person (*Ove*) and the dead person himself (Atchei) interchangeably.

the hair and the skull completely burned by the fire, everything.

"When the Atchei is leaving, when the *Ove* of the Atchei strikes the pot that it has made, then it is going to die. It strikes, and the ashes of the skull enter the mouth: then death comes, then the mortal sickness comes.

"It strikes the bones of the one who is dying, it strikes the skull, it strikes the pot: then comes the mortal sickness, then comes death. In the heart of darkness, *Ove* strikes."

In this way, death is prepared in advance, *Ove* decides, and when it strikes and breaks the pot that contains imaginary bones, ashes, hair, and excrement — in anticipation of what will really happen later — the time has come, the soul leaves the body. At this moment *Ove* places the pot containing the ashes among the roots of a tree — where the Birds of *Ove* come, for the most part the Birds of Thunder. During the day they wait in the pot, crowded against one another. They leave it at night, companions of the "soul," which goes toward the Invisible Forest.

If the Machitara, the enemies and neighbors of the Atchei, had heard that, they would have been very surprised. For they used to put their dead in the ground and then gather up the skeleton — at least if the dead person had been a great chief or shaman — and enclose it in a large funeral urn that was placed in the grave. What was an actual ritual among the Guarani is found among the Atchei too, but only as a belief in the *ove moo kara*, the pot — which is nothing other than the mythical funeral urn. At the beginning of collective Atchei history, there was the great pot of Baio. Broken by a boy without a labret, the moon and the night escaped from it in a flood of ashes. This happened in the Invisible Forest, at a time when the jaguars did not yet exist. The fate of individuals was decided in this immaterial funeral urn. The ashes that slid out from a crack in the Baio urn were perhaps the prefiguration of the other ashes that the Atchei funeral rites had been reduced to and that *Ove* put in its small pot. In the myth of the great pot of Baio, we have not only the Atchei discourse on the origin of the cosmic order and the regular succession of day and night, but also — which is not very surprising — the first clear statement of the fact that death is the price paid by humankind for the order that makes the world habitable. When the sun began to move in the sky, the Atchei truly became the Atchei. But at the same time they took their place in the ineluctable order that makes men transitory beings. The myth of Baio together with the myth of the urn of *Ove*, forms the myth of the origin of Death, which is an integral part of all thinking about life.

This mythological discourse helps us to understand the Atchei's attitude toward ashes. If in Indian thought the ashes of the myths are a metaphor for death, the ashes of the campfires are the metonymy of the funeral ashes. To be covered or marked by ashes is to wear on one's body the truth of one's destiny, the sign of one's finitude. One therefore brushes them off quickly, for these are things one does not want to see. They are a sign of what will one day come to pass.

Krembegi had not been a hunter, and there would be no duel to honor his death. Besides, the Strangers did not like to engage in duels in front of white men. Several of the men had large scars on their heads from previous jousts, and they gloried in these marks. When a great *bretete* dies, his companions clear a space in the forest for their confrontation. These fights are a last farewell to the *manove* and are waged not for the purpose of killing one's opponent but rather to test his worth. A man crouches on his heels in the cleared space. He folds his arms across his knees and rests his head on them. The other man is supposed to hit him on the head. He offers no resistance, he does not try to avoid the blow. He must take it without crying out and without falling down. The striker faces him, standing firmly and holding his bow; he raises the wood and hits him just where the hair ends and the skin is naked. The blow is strong enough to cause a wound, but it is controlled so that there will be no danger of killing the man who receives it. Only one blow is struck, the skin breaks, and blood spurts onto the shoulders of the wounded man. He is brave; he does not fall down. Then, if he wants, it is his turn, and the other man takes his place. Once again a single blow is struck, and the duel is over. It is a tournament in which there is no enmity. Each knight is only helping the other to test his strength. There is no bitterness between them after these encounters. On the contrary, the scars are exhibited with joy as a sign of *kyrymba*, courage. *Pichua* will not be lacking for the one who bears them.

During Krembegi's burial, several Atchei Gatu, who had never seen a funeral ceremony conducted by the Strangers, asked them for explanations, which they gave generously. The Atchei Gatu asked these questions because they themselves dealt with the dead in a different way. I knew by then what they were. But it had not been easy to find out, for in the beginning they had lied to me horribly.

Chachubutawachugi.

Chachubutawachugi off to find honey in the forest.

Chachubutawachugi and his finery.

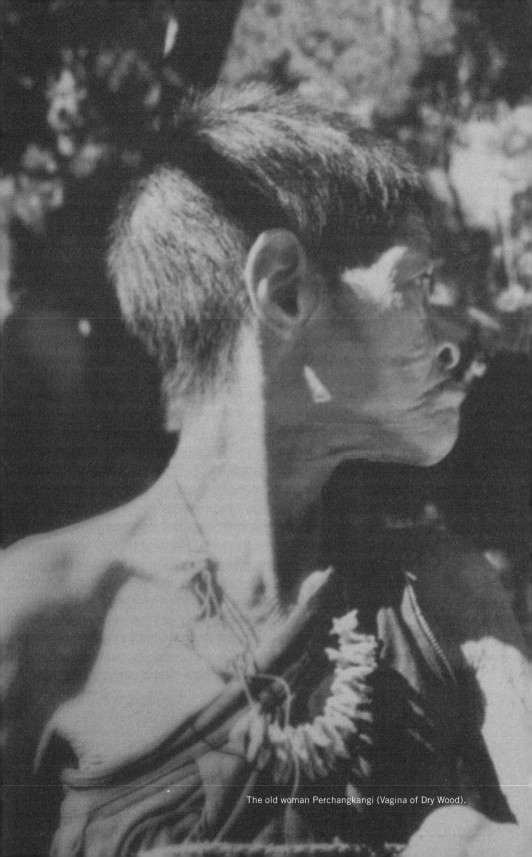

The old woman Perchangkangi (Vagina of Dry Wood).

CHAPTER EIGHT

Cannibals

For the *Iroiangi* there was no doubt about the matter: the Atchei who lived as nomads in the northeastern part of their territory were cannibals. The Atchei Gatu themselves made the same accusation against another tribe, which had once reigned over the forest that extended to the Paraná River. But they had not been heard of since the period when Terygi warred against them in order to steal their women. Furthermore, the Atchei Gatu added, the survivors had all been either captured or killed by the whites. These statements were not very credible, however, since they were made about enemies — that is, people they enjoyed slandering in every possible way: they are ugly, cowardly, stupid, do not know how to speak, and, above all, are eaters of men. *Atchei Kyravwa*: eaters of human fat. But how could one believe in these vehement statements, how could they be verified? The cannibal is always the Other! As far as the Atchei Gatu and the Strangers were concerned, the question was not asked. Nevertheless, when I arrived among the Guayaki, I was more or less convinced that all these Indians practiced cannibalism, for their reputation in this regard was long standing, dating back to the arrival of the first Jesuit missionaries in these regions. I had therefore been expecting — with delicious excitement — to be walking into the middle of a

311

tribe of cannibals. But I had been wrong. They were not cannibals.

Obviously, you can't walk right up to them and ask: are you cannibals? Besides, during the first part of my stay I did not know the term *kyravwa*. In my interviews with the people, especially the Atchei Gatu, concerning their methods of dealing with the dead, the answer always seemed to be quite definite: *ure juta*, we bury them. And they would go on to describe in great detail the grave, the position of the body at the bottom, and how the hole was filled in. "We gather up the earth, pack it down" — with a gesture of patting the earth and then moving their hands to show the shape of the grave — "and the dead person is buried." "And then?"

"Then nothing. We go away because of *Ianve*." This was surprising, to say the least. The Atchei Gatu funeral ritual had been reduced to its most simple expression: in other words, they did not have any. Still more bizarre was that the type of burial they described was exactly the same as the one practiced in the Western Christian world — a grave dug to the measure of the body, which is placed on its back — although South American Indians frequently bury their dead as the *Iroiangi* do, placing the body in a fetal position in a cylindrical hole. But in this case, nothing of the sort was described. One might have assumed that the similarity between Atchei Gatu and Western burial was simply a coincidence. I was tempted to attribute the lack of complexity of the ritual to a cultural loss, thinking that it was yet another illustration of the regression of Atchei history and that before they became nomads they had buried their dead with more elaborate ceremony. This was plausible, but not very convincing. Nevertheless, the Atchei Gatu were unanimous in their descriptions, and I felt obliged to accept what they said. I therefore had to assume that everything I had heard about the Guayakis from the Paraguayans, the Machitara-Guarani, and the chroniclers was merely fabrication.

Even so, Father Lozano was categorical when speaking of the Caaigua — "those of the forest" — who were none other than the Atchei: "Their fearlessness consists of attacking at night, through treachery, those who are sleeping; not so much for revenge or because they covet booty, but from their appetite for human flesh, for they are like tigers and gorge themselves with the corpses of the dead; they call these attacks war and have given themselves the name of warriors."

What are we to make of that? Either the Guayaki had once been cannibals and for unknown reasons had given up the practice, or the historian's information — which, under the circumstances, was merely a repetition of stories told by the Guarani, who were the sworn enemies of the Caaigua — was inexact and the accusation of cannibalism brought against this tribe was untrue. The second hypothesis seemed more plausible, for it would not have been the first time that the whites in South America had labeled a native population cannibals. When the first waves of Spanish conquistadores reached the islands, the shores of Venezuela, and the Guianas, they met up with powerful societies that were strongly addicted to warring against their neighbors. These were the Carib Indians, who were similar to the Tupi-Guarani in that they ceremoniously killed their prisoners of war and then devoured them at great feasts to which they invited their friends. Following this early contact between cannibals and Westerners, the latter were so horrified by what seemed to them the height of savagery that they used the name of the tribe to stand for all eaters of human flesh: *cannibal* is a Spanish deformation of *carib*.

As the whites moved farther and farther into the continent, they discovered more and more cannibalistic tribes, and South America no longer appeared as the earthly paradise Columbus thought it to be when he reached the delta of the Orinoco and confused its various tributaries with the seven rivers of Eden, but rather as a hell in which the inhabitants did nothing but eat one another. What was the truth of the matter? In the majority of cases there was no cannibalism — it was simply an invention. It was not the excusable invention of people arriving on the shores of a totally unknown world and exaggerating the risks they faced and the barbarity of the savages, who seemed to fall somewhere between men and beasts, but rather a cynical lie to cover up and justify the policies of the white colonialists. However, once the theologians, after long and patient debates, decided that the inhabitants of the New World were creatures of God and were possessed of immortal souls — once their humanity was recognized by the Christian world — it was impossible to proclaim the holy will to evangelize these spirits who had been prisoners of darkness and wickedness and at the same time reduce them to slavery. It was either one or the other. Naturally, the decisions of the courts of Madrid and Lisbon were of no great concern to the conquistadores, who were less eager than the Spanish and Portuguese clerics and functionaries to win souls for the Lord. Their chief ambition was to strike it rich in this world — and the sooner the better. But in order to do this, the Indians had to be exploited and enslaved. The problem was how to twist the new law, which was designed to "protect" this free workforce and was therefore against the interests of the new masters of America.

War against the tribes was illegal, except when it was considered justified: when the Indians were cannibals. Against them, it was permissible to wage brutal and pitiless war. The problem was thus resolved: it was enough to claim that a tribe practiced cannibalism to justify the expeditions against it. Slaves could be obtained, then, under the pious pretext that they were dangerous to their neighbors, that they wanted to kill them in order to eat them. The accusations were almost always false, but numerous tribes perished on the plantations and in the mines owned by the

Europeans, who were interested only in having a free hand to build their fiefdoms and increase their profits. In short, the Indians quickly acquired a reputation for being cannibals in the sixteenth and seventeenth centuries, and the list of cannibal peoples grew in proportion to the colonialists' need for slaves.

Was this perhaps the case with the Guayaki? I was inclined to think so. Perhaps the first Jesuits, following the example of the period, had automatically attributed to these Indians — who were so barbarous that they refused to listen to the words of peace — one of the two capital sins of the American natives. According to the Europeans, they spent their time committing cannibalism and *pecatus nefandus*, homosexuality.

In contemporary Brazil, Indians are often referred to by the name *Bugres* — *bougres* in French — which derives from "Bulgarians." At one time, this people was so notorious in the Western world for its taste for sexual inversion that "Bulgarian" became synonymous with sodomy. This word was commonly applied to the Indians. The Guayaki, then, like so many other tribes, were false cannibals, and Father Lozano had been wrong to take the old stories seriously. My work with the Atchei lost a certain attraction, but that was the way things were, and there was nothing to be done about it.

Two months had gone by since my arrival among the Guayaki. The weather continued to be very hot. The mosquitoes refused to let up in their attacks and this proved to be something of a hindrance to the advancement of science. Nevertheless, each day brought a copious supply of information, and even though the laziness of the tropical climate lessened my taste for work and my sense of duty, I had only to look around me at the daily life: even with a minimum of attention I could always discover something new.

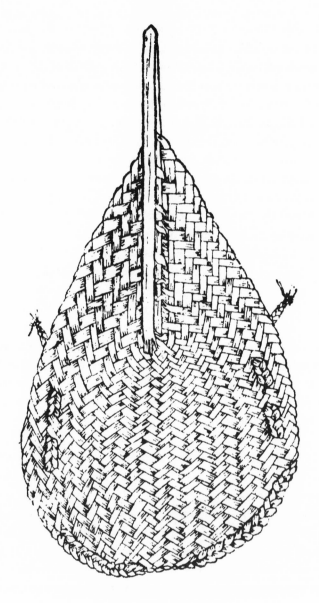

Peka, fan, used to revive a fire and chase away mosquitoes.

One day I found myself in the company of Jygi (Frog). When the jaguar ate Chachuwaimigi in January and Perechankangi (Vagina of Dry Wood) died a little later, probably of old age, Jygi became the oldest woman among the Indians. Small and withered, though still very alert, she did not balk at filling up her basket and going off into the forest with one of her sons. She paid little attention to what went on around her, and if some trifling task did not absorb her, she would play gently and tenderly with her *kimonogi*, her grandson. She felt little sympathy for the Strangers, whom she freely accused of being dirty and crude. When her unmarried son, Japegi, broke off his relationship with Kajawachugi's wife, Jygi was happy. She was not terribly enthusiastic about the idea of having an *Iroiangi* woman as a *katy*, daughter-in-law.

Going on the assumption — which was not always borne out — that the old people had known about things longer than anyone else and were therefore the best informants, and considering that Paivagi did not take me completely seriously — without saying it in so many words, he actually considered me a little *tawy*, idiotic — I asked Jygi if she would like to chat with me for a while. She accepted. Sitting on her knees in my hut, she examined each one of my *Beeru* possessions, all the while reaching into a nearby bag of sweets and extracting the candies from their paper wrappers with some difficulty. I wanted to question Jygi about the children she had had — there had been many of them, seven or eight — and about her different husbands. Almost all the Atchei women had had more than three children.

Why was the tribe's population declining so rapidly, when it should have been increasing or at least holding steady? First of all, because of the persecution of the whites, who had killed many Indians; then — though to a lesser degree — because of infanticide, both ritual, as in the case of "revenge," and for personal convenience, as when a woman already had an unweaned baby and had to do away with a newborn since she could not nurse two at once and live a nomadic life in the forest carrying two *kromi*. If all of Jygi's children had survived, they would have been middle-aged adults by now, since the youngest, Japegi, was a man of thirty. She told her story, and it was the same grim litany I had heard so often before that it no longer affected me: "*Beeru mata, Beeru juka.* The whites captured him, the whites killed him." Now and then Jygi would ask me: "You never met so-and-so, one of my children? The whites took him away from over there," and she would point to the place. "I haven't seen him, I haven't gone by that way yet." To tell the truth, I wasn't listening very carefully; we were both drowsing, at the edge of sleep, though she was a bit more lively than I was because she kept sucking away on the *kramero*. "And that one, who was it?" "A girl, this big." And she held up her hand, indicating a child of about three or four. "And she's dead?"

"Dead. The Atchei killed her."

"Why?"

"For revenge."

"Ah, I see. And then she was buried, *juta*." I did not even wait for her to say it, since this was what the Atchei always did. "And the other one?"

"*Juta-ia, kaimbre, duve ro u pa modo!*"

I only half heard what she had just said; my mind was filled with the torpor of the afternoon, the silence broken only by the strident chirping of insects that sounded something like our cicadas. It was more the tone of Jygi's voice that put me on the alert: she had spoken more loudly, and she sounded slightly upset.

"What did you say?"

She repeated emphatically: "*Cho memby juta-ia, ache ro u pa.*"

Silence. I looked at her, suddenly tense and startled; I had unexpectedly found out something I had spent so long looking for that I had given up. All of a sudden, I was no longer in the mood for taking a siesta; I was like a hunter tracking an unhoped-for prey. Jygi, who was dreamily sampling her candies, no longer paid any attention to me. But it was irrevocable, she had said it, and she could not take it back. I almost lost my breath. When I had spoken for her and said that the daughter who had been the victim of a ritual murder had been buried, she had adamantly corrected me: "Not buried! She was roasted; then they ate her!" Then she added: "My child was not buried. The Atchei ate her." Here it was: the Atchei Gatu were indeed cannibals, and I did not have the slightest doubt that this creased and wrinkled little old woman was telling me the truth. Quickly, so as not to let Jygi guess the value of the treasure she had laid in my lap — she might have become frightened — I asked her who had eaten her daughter, how she was cooked, and how she had been eaten. She answered everything willingly, slowed down only by her efforts to remember, since all this had taken place a long time ago. I took advantage of the opportunity and asked her about the more recent deaths: same thing. The Atchei Gatu had roasted and eaten the *manove*. What a day's work! It was useless to ask any more questions; Jygi was tired, and, besides, I wanted to savor my discovery by myself. I said good-bye to the delicious Frog and thanked her with a sincerity she could never have suspected. "You have spoken very well!" "*Go!* I speak very well!" she acknowledged without raising an eyebrow. She took away the bag of candy; she had earned it.

The next day, I began my detective work into the information given by Jygi. First, I wanted to confirm what she had said; second, I wanted to know why they had deceived me. Tokangi, Jakugi, and the other *kamevwa* were liars! I relished the thought of the confusion I would be creating for these sanctimonious characters and went straight into action. The first victim was my "father," Tokangi, who had been so loquacious in describing the long graves in which the dead were supposedly placed. He had even told how he had dug the grave of his godfather, Kyrypyragi, with his own hands. Kyrypyragi, who had succeeded Terygi as the head of the tribe, had fallen into a white ambush one day and had died of bullet wounds. The Atchei ran away but came back several days later to take care of the final duties. "I dug the grave of my godfather," Tokangi had told me. I recalled this interview to him; he had not forgotten it, and he even confirmed his statement: "Yes, I dug Kyrypyragi's grave." I had planned to catch him up on this very statement, for Jygi had gone into great detail about the posthumous fate of this man. I let my father swallow the bait, and then I said: "Well! Look at how things have turned out. Jygi told me everything." (I was obliged to reveal my source so that Tokangi could not contest what I was about to say.) And then I repeated what I had learned from the old woman. Tokangi was very attentive and even nodded his head several times, as if to say, "Yes, yes, that's the way it is." He did not seem surprised by my revelation, and if I had been expecting some easy triumph of this sort, I was wrong. He let out nothing more than a rather calm *Teeh!*, and then said, "*Nde kwa ma, ko!* So you finally found out!" He made not the slightest effort to contradict me and accepted what I said very tranquilly.

The case of Kyrypyragi was a good one because Tokangi and Jygi had been there when he died. Once they were sure the whites were no longer prowling around the area, the Atchei had returned to the spot. The corpse was already in the process of putrefying, so they could not proceed as normal. With their bamboo knives, the men cut off the pieces of edible flesh: shoulder muscles, legs, and arms. Jygi herself, who was then pregnant with the girl the Atchei later killed, was given a little meat from the arm. The penis had to be left: *ine pute*, it stank badly. Tokangi, however, did not eat, for one does not eat one's godfather. In fact, he buried the inedible remains, just as he said he had, but not in the long ditch; he simply dug a hole to protect the corpse from the animals. Later they would have come back to strike and burn the skull, if there had not been many whites in the area. My "father" had lied to me about the shape of the grave and had also committed a lie of omission by failing to tell me about the cannibalism. He willingly admitted this: *"Kamevwa provi!* I lied a little!" But why had he hidden it from me? If some kind of religious pressure had been put on the Atchei Gatu — either by Catholics or Protestants — they might have given up what had been presented to them as a terrible sin. But, thank God, there had been no evangelical effort among them; they had never seen any missionaries. Tokangi filled me in: their *Beeru* protector — who had been aware of the Guayaki practice for a long time and who found it utterly horrible — had formally forbidden them to talk about it with anyone. He had not given them any reason for this — and probably would have been incapable of doing so anyway. He could not have borne the shame of being considered the head of a tribe of cannibals. The Indians obeyed, although they were perplexed at having to remain silent about something that was merely a ritual in their religious life. Because of Jygi's age, no one had considered passing on this information to her, and she was therefore unaware of this new taboo. If it had not been for her, I might never have learned that Lozano was right in describing the Caaigua as passionate cannibals. Once the Atchei Gatu were sure that I knew, not one of them tried to hide it from me; they all agreed to discuss it openly. By common consent, however, in order to avoid useless complications for both sides, we decided not to discuss these questions in the presence of the Paraguayan. Nevertheless, he remained suspicious of many of our conversations until the very end.

Not that he was without justification. I spent so much time on this problem that the Atchei probably thought I was obsessed by cannibalism, even a practitioner of this rite myself. I had been stung by the Indians' attitude. For in spite of themselves, they had tried to hide something from me. And I considered myself worthy of their confidence, though one could very well ask why. At the same time, I was enthused by this opportunity to study what is most deeply alien to our culture: cannibalism. Being an ethnologist does not make one immune to the things that fascinate other Westerners, at least in the beginning.

"*Ure ro Ache vwa, Ache kyravwa.* We are eaters of men, eaters of human fat." The *kyravwa*, whom the Atchei Gatu placed in the east, were themselves. As soon as they no longer made a secret of it, it seemed that they were indeed passionate cannibals. It would be an understatement to say that they appreciated human flesh. They loved it. Why? "*Ee gatu,*" they explained, "it is very sweet, even better than the meat of wild pig." As far as taste goes, it is closest to the meat of the domestic pig of the whites. But beyond that, there is the fat. A man has more fat than any animal of the forest; between the skin and the muscles there is always a thick layer of *kyra*, and that is really good. "*Kyra gatu!*" "Good fat!" commented my joking informants as they pinched my biceps. "*Gaipara! Jypi pute!* It's thin! It's completely dry!" I answered, and everyone burst out laughing.

Cannibals are usually represented as perverse monsters who kill their neighbors in order to make a meal of them. This is indeed how Lozano portrayed them. It seems that in other parts of the world, Polynesia in particular, the nutritional value derived from cannibalism is essential, since there is a chronic scarcity of protein sources. Exceptional historical circumstances can also drive men who had seemed far removed from the possibility of such "horrors" to engage in cannibalism in order to survive.

322

Although no one likes to talk about it, this happened during the war in the Pacific, with both American and Japanese troops, and also, according to reports, in the Nazi concentration camps. None of this applied to the Atchei, however, since their diet was if anything too rich in proteins, meat being their basic food. They did not kill in order to eat, they simply ate their dead. The difference is considerable: this is what distinguishes exo- from endo-cannibalism. The Guayaki were endo-cannibals in that they used their stomachs as the final resting place of their companions. But no one was killed for this; the only Atchei who were eliminated by murder were impotent old women and very young girls for the ritual of *jepy*. But even exo-cannibalism, which consists of eating human beings outside the tribe — in other words, enemies — has little to do with the popular image of one tribe running after its hostile neighbors in order to feast on them. The Tupi-Guarani, who were strong and warring cannibals, according to the sixteenth-century French chroniclers, massacred and then ate their prisoners of war in solemn ceremonies, but they did not capture them in order to eat them. It was the destiny of a captive to be devoured by those who had captured him. But until the fatal day, the prisoner lived as a free man in the vicinity of his masters, sometimes even taking a wife and fathering children as he awaited the inevitable moment of his execution, which could take place several years after he had been captured. André Thevet and Jean de Léry were scandalized by this, but the Tupinamba were equally scandalized by the whites' practice of locking up prisoners and denying them their freedom, which they considered totally absurd and barbarous.

When Terygi and his men killed Atchei enemies in order to take their women, they would eat all the men they had killed. But they would not attack for this purpose. Rather, it was considered a good opportunity to partake of a meal of delicious human flesh because it was so rare — it was not every day that seven or eight *Iroiangi* were killed at once. Talking with Jvukugi one day, I asked him if he had ever eaten non-Atchei flesh, a Machitara, for example. Yes, he had once tasted the flesh of a Guarani who had been hunting alone in the forest and chanced to come upon a group of Atchei hunters. Before the unfortunate man could even make an attempt to flee, he was shot through with arrows; the tribe then had a feast, though the men who had done the killing, of course, did not participate. Here again, it was less a question of ritual than of taking advantage of a delicacy: why deprive oneself when an enemy has just been killed? "And have you ever eaten any *Beeru* flesh, Jvukugi?" "*U ia wyte.* I haven't eaten any yet," he answered, his eyes wrinkling with a joking smile. Was he telling the truth? In any case, it was not very important, and he would not say any more about it. In short, even though the Atchei Gatu had killed people outside their tribe and eaten them, they had not killed them for this purpose. I discovered only one exception to this, and it was a rather ambiguous case. A man was once shot with arrows because a woman had expressed the desire to eat human flesh. Bujamiarangi (a namesake of the man who copulated with the anteater) was an incestuous Atchei. One day, he forgot that the pretty *dare* who shared his hut was his own daughter; he could only see her as a desirable woman, and he possessed her.

These things rarely happened, and when they did, people would say harsh things and make fun of the guilty person but would feel no need to punish him: everyone knew that people like Bujamiarangi were transformed into roe bucks when they died. But he developed a taste for it and continued to make *meno* with his daughter instead of having his fun once and then forgetting about it. His obstinacy irritated the Atchei, and one woman beseeched her husband to kill Bujamiarangi: "Someone who makes love to his own daughter has no valor whatsoever. The Atchei don't want to see it. Go kill him!" And then she added, to give her husband more incentive to commit the murder: "I want to eat Atchei flesh. The one who must be killed, the possessor of his own daughter, is Bujamiarangi." The husband killed the incestuous father, and the Atchei ate him. What had been the stronger force in the irritated wife: the horror of incest or the desire for human flesh? Could the first have been nothing more than an excuse for the second? To describe Bujamiarangi's actions, the Atchei used the term, *meno* — to make love — much less often than its equivalent, which was far more brutal and savage even in the minds of the Indians: *uu*, or *tyku*, to eat. "Bujamiarangi eats his daughter, I want to eat Bujamiarangi." This in effect is what the woman was saying. Did she have an unconscious desire to copulate symbolically with the father while eating him in reality — in the same way that he himself symbolically ate his daughter while copulating with her in reality? Perhaps the semantic ambiguity of the words had aroused a need for flesh that secretly disguised a completely different kind of desire. Why should the Atchei be any less sensitive than we are to the erotic overtones of language?

I was given numerous descriptions of cannibalistic meals, for since their arrival at Arroyo Moroti a little more than three years earlier, the Atchei Gatu had eaten all their dead, except when it had been too risky for them to stay in the place where the death had occurred because of the whites. Eating human flesh is not like eating the meat of an animal: above and beyond the profane aspects of self-indulgence, it is a deeply sacred act in that it concerns the treatment of the dead by the living. The *Iroiangi* bury their dead, the Atchei Gatu eat them: in some sense, they are walking cemeteries. There are no exceptions to this rule. Regardless of age, sex, or the circumstances of death — violent or "nat-

325

ural" — all the dead are eaten. This applies to the children who
are victims of ritual murders (except, rarely, when they are said
to be *braa pute*, very black) as well as the old women who are
killed when they can no longer walk (although none of the
Atchei has any taste for these old women, who are so dried out
that there is no fat under the skin). There have to be insurmountable obstacles for the Atchei to give up these funeral banquets:
either they are sick and too discouraged, or else the whites are
too close, preventing them from spending the necessary time on
the ritual.

The first thing to be done when a group loses one of its members is to inform the rest of the tribe. If the others are nearby, one
or two days' walk away, a young man is sent to give them the
news and tell them to come: they arrive as soon as possible. But
sometimes the *cheygi* are too far away to let them know in time.
The preparations cannot be put off too long. When this happens,
the first group waits until everything is over and then goes off to
join the others and offer them a few pieces that have been saved
for them as a sign of friendship. "*Pire raa!* Take some skin!" they
are told. They are satisfied to see that they have not been forgotten, and this is good for the others. Not to take a bit of the flesh
of the departed companion to distant friends is considered an
inexcusable, unpardonable insult and can even become the cause
of hostilities — so that arrows become the only thing the two
groups exchange. It is just as serious to refuse a gift: one must
learn, of course, how to give, but also how to receive. Both in-
volve the same etiquette. The Atchei Gatu still tell of the great
anger of a man during the time of Terygi. He had killed some
howler monkeys and had given a portion to his brother, as is normal. But the brother, no doubt in a terrible mood, pretended not
to see the meat and did not touch it after it had been boiled. The
first brother was shocked: "You are not going to eat this *kraja*

326

meat?" "No, I'm not going to eat it," answered the other dryly. The hunter was outraged, and in one instant he became *by-ia*. He smashed his bow down on the head of the uncouth brother. The brother started to run away but was cut down by an arrow that killed him. The Atchei ate him. The murderer had to run away, leaving his wife, for his life was in danger. He asked a friendly group for asylum.

When all the *irondy* who have been invited are there, the feast begins. First, the grill, *byta*, is built. This task is given to young men who have recently been initiated. Four forked sticks about a foot and a half high are stuck in the ground to support four bars. This framework is completed by narrowly spaced crossbars that are fastened on with creepers. In this way, a flat surface about five feet long and three feet wide is made; a big fire is lit under it. All the Atchei are roasted on the *byta*, except very young children, who are boiled in earthen pots.

During this time, the corpse is attended to. A man — preferably the dead person's godfather, if he is still alive — cuts up the body with his bamboo knife. The head and limbs are separated from the trunk, the arms and legs are taken apart, and the organs and innards are removed. The head is carefully shaved, both beard and hair if it is a man, and usually it is the wife who does this; a mother usually shaves the head of her child. Unlike the muscles and organs — the meat properly speaking — the head and intestines are boiled in pots. Nothing is thrown out from the body of a man; the only thing removed from a woman is her *pere*, her sexual organs, which are not eaten, but buried. Sometimes the intestines are also put to the side, not because of a food taboo, but because they stink too much. In some cases, they are also buried. Everything else is put on the *byta*. There are many coals below, the flames do not reach the grill, and the meat cooks slowly. The fat, the Atchei's delicious *kyra*, crackles and drips in great aromatic globs along the slats. So as not to lose any of it, the Atchei catch the drippings with brushes that they then suck on noisily. When the meat is well done, when there are no more traces of blood, it is given out to those present.

Who participates in this meal? Who eats the dead person? All those present, young and old, men and women, everyone except the close relatives of the deceased. A father and mother do not eat their children, the children do not eat their parents and do not eat each other: this is the rule. But, like all rules, it is not always scrupulously obeyed, and some infractions are tolerated. Jakugi, for example, broke the rule when the Atchei ate his father, Wachugi, who had committed suicide. This was a strange end, for suicide is very uncommon among the Indians. "I was as big as that *kybuchu*," said Jakugi, pointing to a boy of about ten. Wachugi had gone through a period of unhappiness. His mother, who was very old, died. He was terribly affected by this and cried a great deal. He needed kindness and comfort, but at this very moment, his wife chose to get entangled in an affair with Tatuetepirangi, Armadillo with the Red Body. This was too much for Wachugi; he no longer wanted to live. What did he do? He did something that the Indians know is very dangerous, even fatal: he ate honey from the *iro* bee without mixing it with water. To eat pure honey is to lay oneself open to a pitiless disease, *baivwa*. And the inevitable results came to pass: Wachugi was successful, he became sick and died. Pure honey is extremely powerful. According to the ritual, the Atchei roasted him. "And you, Jakugi, did you eat your father?" (I asked this question almost aimlessly, since children do not eat their parents.)

"Yes, I ate some. Some meat from the leg," and he pointed to his calf.

"Oh! Jakugi! You ate your father, and yet *ja apa u ia*, one does not eat one's father!"

"Not very much! Only a little! This much!" And he held out his hands to indicate a piece as large as a good-sized steak. "I was little, I didn't know, they gave it to me, and I took it."

He was trying to make excuses because he knew he should not have taken it. But even so, this was not very serious; now and then this type of infraction is allowed. On the other hand, the more severe prohibitions are never broken: a brother never eats his sister, a father never eats his daughter, a mother never eats her son, and vice versa. Family members of the opposite sex do not eat each other. Why? Because to eat someone is in some sense to make love with him. If a father eats his daughter, he would metaphorically be guilty of incest, as was the case with Bujamiarangi. In short, the Atchei do not eat those with whom they are forbidden to make *meno*: the prohibition against incest and this eating taboo are part of a single unified system.

On the other hand, can anyone eat any part of the body? Yes, except for the head and the penis. The first, like the head of an animal, is reserved for the old people, men and women, and is forbidden to the young hunters for the same reason: they would become victims of *pané*. As for the penis — which, like the head, is boiled — it is always given to the women and to the pregnant women first. This guarantees that they will give birth to a boy. When the whites killed Kyrypyragi, Jygi was pregnant. Unfortunately, the penis could not be removed from the already rotting body, and Jygi, to whom it normally would have been given, had to pass it up. The result was that she gave birth to a girl, which would have been avoided if she had been able to eat the penis.

A vegetable is eaten with the human flesh: the marrow or bud of the *pindo* palm, which is boiled with the head and viscera, and then roasted on the grill with the meat. It is not a simple garnishing. The vegetable has a very precise function: to neutralize the excessive "hardness," the powerful "force," the *myrakwa* that makes human flesh a food different from all others and dangerous to those who eat it by itself. Like pure honey, human flesh that is not mixed with something else produces *baivwa*; water and *pindo* — neutral foods that never infringe on any taboo — nullify the harmful power of honey and flesh. Mixed with palmito, the flesh loses its "force" and can be eaten without fear like any other meat. And then one can comment tranquilly: *"Pire kyra wachu! Kyra gatu!* Such fat skin! Such good fat!" Not everything is eaten at this meal; there is too much. The leftovers are wrapped in palm leaves or ferns and are eaten cold over the next few days or taken to the *cheygi* who were too far away to come. The bones are broken so that the marrow can be extracted. The women, especially the old ones, are very fond of it.

The banquet is over. Now the young people who built the *byta* must undergo the ritual of purification. They are washed with water that has been dunked with shavings of the *kymata* creeper so that they will not be afflicted with *baivwa*. Then the skull is broken and burned, as is the case with the *Iroiangi*. Once that has been done, everyone leaves. The grill is left standing, at least if it has been used to roast an adult. The Indians give two reasons for this: if the *irondy* pass by, they will understand that an Atchei is dead and they will cry. But if the passersby are strangers, and therefore enemies, they will know that there are cannibals in the region and will become afraid and run away. If the *byta* has been used for a child, it is destroyed.

People rarely act without knowing why. We almost always have something to say about what we do — even if, as is usually the case, this explanation is inadequate and influenced more by ideology than the truth. This seemed to be the case with the Atchei Gatu. For even though they no longer made a secret of their cannibalism, they were curiously incapable of giving any reason for this ritual: they were cannibals without knowing why. "Why are you *kyravwa*?" The answers were always the same. "Because we do as our ancestors did." Or, with all the rigor of a tautology that explains nothing: "We eat the Atchei because we are cannibals." They would never say more than this. It was frustrating, but the goodwill of the Indians was nevertheless apparent: why, when talking with complete openness about their cannibalism, would they try to hide the meaning they attached to this practice? The clearest explanation I was given referred only to purely nutritional matters. Kybwyragi was telling me how he had eaten Prembegi, Tokangi's wife, ten or fifteen years before. The woman had died from *baivwa* caused by honey. Kybwyragi, who had recently been initiated, built the grill, and his brother, who was also young, cut up the body. Tokangi did not eat anything, because *ja ime u ia*, one does not eat one's spouse. "But I ate a lot," said the narrator.

"Why?"

"There was so much fat!"

"But why did you want to eat the fat?"

"I didn't want to go on being skinny."

This was obviously a sufficient reason for him, and I was wrong, it seemed to him, to go on looking for any nobler cause behind the Atchei's cannibalism than that of appetite.

The Strangers were not unaware of the fact that their new allies were *kyravwa*. In some way, they had known in advance, since for all Atchei groups the neighbors are considered to be cannibals. And when they arrived at Arroyo Moroti, they were very careful and reserved in their relations with the Atchei Gatu: for they felt that their neighbors were perfectly capable of killing them in a fit of hunger and devouring them. Nothing of the sort happened. When questioned on the cannibalism of the others, they also gave a nutritional explanation: "The Atchei Gatu are cannibals because they like human flesh."

331

"And why aren't you cannibals?"

"Because we do not like Atchei fat."

They did not show the slightest sympathy for this custom, which they disapproved of, though they did not say so publicly. You never knew what could happen. Both groups, however, seemed to have the same opinion: a cannibal is someone who likes human flesh. I was given no further insight into the matter until one day, while I was working with Kybwyragi, I asked him why the Strangers were not cannibals. He answered immediately and decisively: "*Manomba o*. Oh! But they are all going to die!"

"Yes? Why?"

"Because they do not eat their dead."

Finally! Things were at last beginning to clear up.

"*Ache pete bu ro, ove iko ruwy, ove tara iko, Atchei jachira vwa Beeru endape*. When the dead are buried, it is as if the *Ove* had come. There are many souls who want to take away the Atchei to the place of the ancestors. Then, *kyrymba ia*, we are very afraid. *U pa bu, ianve iko ia, ianve veve ma*: if we eat the people, then there is no *Ianve*. *Ianve* flies away." Cannibalism, then, was an additional method of fighting against the souls of the dead. To eliminate the soul, the body must be eaten; if it is not eaten, *Ove* and *Ianve* stay near the living, ready to act against them, to penetrate their bodies and bring about *baivwa*, which will kill them. That is why the Atchei Gatu had no doubts: the Strangers would die soon; they lived, literally, in the middle of a cloud of souls. "When you do not eat the dead, there is *baivwa*, you get very sick, you die." But why in heaven's name hadn't the Atchei Gatu said all this earlier! Strangely, in order for them to know the reasons for what they did, they had to be questioned about the *Iroiangi*, directed to the fact that the others were not cannibals, and made to think about this difference. When asked directly about themselves, they continued to speak in tautologies: we are cannibals because we are cannibals. But once they were torn away from this immediate and obvious certainty, they began to arrive at the truth by negation: not to be a cannibal is to be condemned to death.

Kybwyragi was surely the best informant among the Atchei. Subtle and patient, he immediately understood everything that was asked of him and seemed to take pleasure in explaining things about the tribe, while for the others, even Jyvukugi, the interviews soon became tiresome. Sometimes, when I lacked the vocabulary or when the questions were difficult to formulate, I began by saying: "Suppose I am an Atchei. What would I do in this case?" The Indian would be very surprised, look at me, and would always say: "*Teeh!* You are an Atchei? You?"

"No! Not at all! I'm pretending to be one!" And the man would burst out laughing, finding it too funny to contain himself. There was no end to it once this sort of thing started. With Kybwyragi this never happened; he would immediately anticipate the question I was trying to ask, and his answer would always be extremely clear. Unfortunately, of all the Atchei, he was the most collaborationist with the whites. He believed that this was the only realistic course for the future of the tribe. But he was wrong. Jyvukugi, by contrast, maintained a haughty refusal to compromise with the *Beeru*. He had been forced to live with them, but nothing more could be asked of him.

It was to Kybwyragi that I owed the explanation of the Atchei's cannibalism. It was based on the idea of *pakryra*. I had never heard this term before and did not understand it, but it was clearly and systematically analyzed for me. Kybwyragi began with the opposite of *pakryra*: "You are running very fast for a long time. Then, you must sit down to rest," and he pretended to be a panting runner, his chest heaving, striking his fist over his heart. "*Pakombo*, the beating heart," he said, "that is when you are in a state of non-*pakryra*." He went on: "You are very afraid, you have seen a

333

jaguar, or you have just been told of the death of a relative. You are completely without courage, you are almost dead." He fell down and leaned against a tree with an exhausted, lifeless look. "This is *pakombo* also, your heart is beating very fast. It is because you have lost *pakryra*." And little by little, through precise words and expressive gestures, Kybwyragi led me to discover what *pakryra* was — what the souls of the dead tear away from the living. It is the physical and mental condition of a normal man, unplagued by worry or self-doubt, with good health, and the heart and body in good balance. The opposite of this is *pakryra-ia*, anguish. It can take hold of you in various ways: a great fright at suddenly encountering a wild animal or learning a piece of bad news. But its most powerful form, which is almost insurmountable, is the anguish brought on by the invisible presence of the dead, which is the *anguish of death itself.* "When you do not eat the dead, you feel anguish. When you do eat them, you feel calm, your heart does not beat fast. Anguish is a deadly disease, tranquillity is health. When you are anguished, you have no strength."

A death causes a sociological disorder in the group, but one that is experienced personally by each individual. It is not an abstract disorder; it can be so deeply felt that it can produce unbearable worry and a terrible beating of the heart. The source of this anguish is easily identifiable: it is *Ove*, which wants to enter your body because it has lost its own. But its body is nevertheless still there, its last dwelling place in the world of the living. Since *Ove* cannot exist by itself, it tries to haunt places where it must not go. Both the Indians' thought and practice attest to this. They believe that death frees the soul from the body, which until then had kept it as a "prisoner" that could not do any harm; but it rejects its new freedom, it immediately tries to escape by finding another body, by invading the body of a living person. This always leads to death, because of *baivwa*. How can it be prevented? The Indians' practice supplies the answer: to put an end to all these efforts of the soul, the body it has just abandoned must be eaten. The joining of a living body and a dead soul can be blocked by creating a separation between the dead soul and its old body. When death sunders the living unity between body and soul, each of these two elements becomes independent from the other; from that point on, they are disconnected. They can no longer coexist: and isn't this precisely what the ritual of cannibalism is all about? The Atchei eat the bodies of their dead, and this prevents the souls from penetrating the bodies of the living. The barrier against *Ove* is the very body it inhabited while it was alive, the body that is now exactly where it wants to go — into the bodies of the living people who have ingested it. If *Ove* persisted in its efforts to enter a living body, what would it find there? Its former container, now broken up into pieces and eaten, the chewed debris of what it has been separated from: its material double, now scattered and destroyed. The joining through cannibalism of living and dead bodies is the disjoining of living beings and "dead souls"; by doing away with the body in the form of food, *Ove* is forced to recognize once and for all what it is: a ghost without substance that no longer has anything to do with the living. It is then carried away by the smoke that rises from the ashes of the skull that was turned to the west. It climbs into the sky to be lost in the upper world, the Invisible Forest, the great savanna, the land of the dead.

Because cannibalism is so repulsive to Westerners, we assume that someone who knows that he will one day be eaten by the people around him feels the same disgust and terror that we would. When an Atchei Gatu feels death approaching, what can he possibly think about except what he knows his relatives and friends are anticipating? He is certain of what will happen: in a little while, I will be cut up and roasted on the *byta*, my companions will feast on my body and break my bones to suck out the marrow. Can he face this certainty calmly, without horror? And if he can, must we think of the Atchei as creatures made of stone, as men even more indifferent than the most hardened stoics? Not at all.

To a dying man, the idea that he will soon become food for others is not in the least troubling. Quite the contrary, when he feels *Ove* about to leave him, it is he himself, in his last conversation with the others, who insists that he be eaten. He knows that in a very short while things will happen that he cannot control: *Ove* or *Ianve* will try to kill his friends. He is well aware of the process, and because of this he knows that he must be eaten. And he demands it, no doubt saddened by the thought of having to leave his near and dear ones, but above all anxious not to cause them any trouble. It is not that he is afraid of not being eaten; he can rest assured that he will be. The *irondy* gather around him, worried and insistent: "When you are dead, do not try to make us sick!" But there are perhaps other people, to whom he is tied by a deeper affection, that he especially wants to protect from *Ove*. So he reminds them that he must be eaten.

The same conversation always takes place between the Atchei and the dying person. I witnessed it with Kybwyragi's father, Prembegi, and many others. When Prembegi died, she had two husbands: the principal husband, Tokangi, and the secondary, Pyteragi (Hairy Back, for he had the nature of an anteater — an animal covered with thick, long hair). Of the two, she preferred the second; in fact, she loved him a great deal. When the Atchei realized that the honey disease was killing Prembegi, they asked her: "Are you going to give us *baivwa*?"

"No *baivwa*. Eat me completely!"

She then called for her husband Pyteragi, who was already in tears, and gave him her final advice: "I do not want the *baivwa* to make you sick and for you to die. Eat me! In this way, there will be no sickness, *Ianve* will not get in." He did this, and he did not become sick. This was the woman's final proof of love for her husband, the husband's final act of love for his wife.

The many conversations about cannibalism revealed other aspects of the Indians' religious life to me. "*Cho ro X ove*," they would sometimes say to me. "I am the soul of so-and-so." Was this a belief in reincarnation, was the person who claimed to be the *Ove* of a dead Atchei really that person's soul in a different guise? This was unlikely, for it seemed that *Ove* had no personal characteristics, that it was a purely neutral principle that had no influence on the new being that housed it. In fact, a man could be the soul of a woman, and a woman could be the soul of a man. But this did not affect them: a man carrying a feminine *Ove* was completely male, and a woman carrying a masculine *Ove* did not lose her femininity. "To be" the *Ove* of someone did not add anything to what you were, did not change you in any way. The person whose soul I carry does not live in me, I am in no way any different from those who are not the *Ove* of that person.

Not all the Atchei were the soul of someone else, and this belief in "reincarnation" was present only among the Atchei Gatu. The Strangers did not believe in it. And this was logical, since the way to "become" the *Ove* of a dead person was through cannibalism. "I am the *Ove* of Terygi," said Kimiragi, Jyvukugi's wife, not without a little pride. Why? Because when Terygi died, Dokogi was pregnant. The Atchei Gatu ate their chief and gave the penis to Dokogi so that she would give birth to a boy. However, it was a girl who came into the world, Kimiragi. In some sense, Kimiragi could say she was the *Ove* of Terygi. In the same way, Kybwyragi was the *Ove* of Brevipurangi, Kyrypyragi's son who was killed by a jaguar. Kybwyragi's mother, who was pregnant at the time, ate the young man's penis. Fulfilling everyone's

337

expectations, she gave birth to a boy: Kybwyragi was the *Ove* of Brevipurangi.

This transmigration of *Ove* was useful in that it provided approximate dates for certain events and helped to give something of a chronological order to the Atchei's recent past. Without any system for measuring time, marking off the annual seasonal cycle only by the coming of the cold, they dealt with the history of the tribe in terms of significant occurrences, saying, for example, "That was when Jakugi got his labret, when the whites killed Chimbegi, when we ate Chachugi," and so on. For Indians this was sufficiently accurate, and they referred to these events often. But what about for an outsider? One can get a fairly clear idea of dates from the practices of cannibalism. Kimiragi, for example, was a woman of about forty years old. And she was the soul of Terygi, whose mother ate his penis. Therefore, Terygi's death took place about forty years before, in the early 1920s. In the same way, Brevipurangi's death could be placed somewhere in the late 1920s since Kybwyragi, who carried his soul, was a man of about thirty-five. And since Brevipurangi's father — Kyrypyragi — survived him by several years, one can assume that Kyrypyragi, who succeeded Terygi as the head of the tribe, led the Atchei Gatu for about ten years. This proves that, in spite of the bad reputation he left behind, the Atchei were not too unhappy with him. If they had been, they would not have let him continue. This is scanty and fragile evidence. But there is nothing else to go on, and we should not be too proud to use whatever system we can — especially since this is the only means of satisfying our Western obsession with time.

In July I had to go away for several days. When I returned to Arroyo Moroti, I learned that the Strangers still had not returned from the distant place where they were celebrating the festival of honey. A few of their *kybuchu* had not gone along with the older people; among them was Wachugi, a brave little hunter of about twelve. He readily agreed to go with me to where Jyvukugi was camping, which was several hours' walk away. He trotted along in silence behind me: he could not have walked in front, and the Atchei travel only in single file. Now and then, when I did not know which turn to take, he would call out *"Govety!* That way!" and point me in the right direction. All of a sudden, as if unable to hold back an extraordinary piece of news, he blurted out: *"Ache ro Baipugi kromi u pa modo.* The Atchei have eaten Baipugi's child."

"Nde Kaury! Kamevwa! You're making it up! You're lying!"

"Kaury ia! U pa modo! I'm not making it up! They ate him!"

I knew very well that he was not lying, but I wanted to provoke him a little bit so that he would tell me more. But he was clearly just as interested as I was and went on to explain that the Atchei Gatu had wanted to eat human flesh and had boiled little Brikugi. He also gave me the names of the people who had participated in the meal. I could count myself lucky to have been told. Would the others have let me know? I couldn't be sure — especially as to who had been present. The baby's father, mother, and older sister later told me how it had happened.

In the first place, the circumstances were propitious for engaging in cannibalism again. They were alone, the *Iroiangi* and the whites were away; there was no one to disturb them. In addition, they were very depressed; an epidemic of the flu, aggravated by the cold weather of June and July, had killed about ten Atchei, including Krembegi and old Paivagi. The Atchei Gatu obviously had not considered eating them, since the *Beeru* had formally prohibited such practices. But this time, toward the end of July, there was no one present to watch them. I also feel that the incessant conversations about cannibalism had played a role and that from having talked about it so much the desire to begin again had grown in the Atchei Gatu, who probably felt that human flesh was the only remedy for the melancholy and apathy that had overwhelmed them.

That was exactly how Pikygi explained it: "I was sick, without courage. Baipugi's child was dead. Atchei meat is very good for not being sick. I wanted to get well." Little Brikugi was a baby of about eighteen months who had begun to walk shortly after our arrival among the Indians. He would totter about from his mother, Baipugi, to his father, Kandegi, letting out cries of joy and fear in the middle of a circle of beaming Atchei, who would encourage him with quiet voices. Everyone loved this child very much: of all the babies who had been born after the Indians' capitulation, he was the only one to survive, and this had somewhat restored the people's spirits. Pikygi, who was also the baby's father — he had made love with Baipugi while she was pregnant — showed no less love for the child than the principal father, Kandegi. The child fell sick and we all cared for him, the Atchei with their tenderness and the *Beeru* with their medicine. Around the middle of July, he seemed to be doing much better. But in our absence, brief as it was, the *kromi* who had delighted the eyes and hearts of the Atchei Gatu suddenly became much worse and died. What happened afterward was told to me almost indifferently. Only the mother, who had shaved off all her hair as a sign of mourning, cried as she spoke. I felt that it would have been better to leave her in peace.

"I wanted to eat him. Don't bury him! There is a lot of fat," said Pikygi, after letting out the *jeproro*, the savage cry of the Atchei hunters. He had let out this cry because his pain had been so terrible, but it was also intended to drive away *Ove*. "*U eme! Pete ro mi!* Don't eat him! Cover him with earth!" answered Baipugi. A short time before, in the woods, she had not said anything, but now her pain and sadness had changed things. However, she was not angry with Pikygi and understood his desire. Then Kandegi, the father, intervened: "If you are not going to bury him, then eat him." And Pikygi went on: "I am very sick, almost dead! I have a great desire to eat human flesh in order to get well. When you eat Atchei flesh, you get well quickly." But the mother's sad lament continued, as if in counterpoint: "Krei smothered my child during the night. And now I am going to die, too." Who was Krei? He was Airagi, the baby's paternal grandfather, who had been killed by the whites. Seeing that his son Kandegi was sick — almost all the Atchei were sick at that moment — he became irritated with Baipugi, his daughter-in-law. He held her responsible for his son's illness, and to punish her, he had killed her child, Brikugi. The father, who had died a long time ago, still watched over his son and had avenged him.

Baipugi had then shaved her baby's head and buried the hair "so that they could eat the skin." Pikygi cut up the little body, took out the innards, and buried them: "We do not eat the belly, it stinks too much." Then he divided up the pieces and put them in clay pots, where they were made into a kind of stew with *tangy*, hearts of young *pindo* palm. Then everything was put on to boil. The Atchei do not roast very young children for the simple reason that there would not be enough to go around. But when they are boiled in water with *tangy*, everyone can get a normal helping. When the meal was ready, everyone present ate, except the mother and the sister, Baipurangi, Jakugi's wife. The men and children dipped their brushes into the greasy liquid and exclaimed between each mouthful: "*Tapia gatu!* This fat is good!" They ate everything, not thinking it necessary to leave anything for the absent Atchei Gatu, as was the custom in the past. Jyvukugi and Kybwyragi had been out hunting for several days and did not get any when they returned, but they were not angry — things had changed.

Jakugi, who was very much in love with his wife, Baipurangi,

341

was suffering for two reasons: she was unfaithful to him and had not yet borne him any children. He wanted a son and was hoping to benefit from the opportunity offered by this meal. He held out the child's penis to her so that she would eat it. But she spitefully refused, saying that "one does not eat one's brother!" This was true. But her reason for refusing was less from a desire to respect the taboo than from wanting to hurt Jakugi. And when he then hit his wife, it was more out of anger than a desire to "avenge" little Brikugi. Pikygi was irritated: he was Baipurangi's father, since he had been Baipugi's first husband. He hit Jakugi a few times, and the younger man did not try to fight back. Then he told his daughter to sleep in his hut: "You should no longer want to be possessed by your husband!" She obeyed, and when evening came Jakugi took out his flute to sing of his unhappiness.

Several days later, the Strangers came back. They were told the news. They did not seem very surprised to learn that the others had eaten Baipugi's child. On the other hand, they were very intrigued — some of them were even very shocked — that their own *kybuchu* had participated in the cannibal meal. In fact, the Atchei Gatu had invited the boys because among the Atchei you do not let someone watch you eat. The *kybuchu Iroiangi* had thus become cannibals but were not very impressed by it, or less so than their parents were: "Was it good?"

"Very sweet, very good!"

"*Teeh!*" They could not believe their ears. They were not happy to learn that their sons had eaten human flesh. But they did not scold them, for they did not want to annoy the Atchei Gatu, who naturally would have taken it as a criticism. They merely shrugged and said that "they're children and don't know any better!" I talked with a young Stranger *betagi* whose lip had been pierced the year before: "We are not eaters of Atchei!" he said loudly.

342

"Why?"

He hesitated a second and then said: "*Oo iro pute!* It's very bitter meat!" Two or three of the *kybuchu* who had eaten Brikugi were standing nearby. I remarked to the *betagi* that this meat couldn't have been so bitter, because the boys had eaten it. My feigned objection took him aback. He turned to one of the *kybuchu* and asked: "*Iro ko?* Is it bitter?"

"Not at all bitter! I ate the liver!"

Then the young man shouted in triumph: "The liver isn't bitter! It's the skin that's very bitter!" His argument was indisputable, and he concluded: "We are the good Atchei! The others are cannibals!" His tone was absolutely contemptuous. He had successfully restored the hierarchy, and his own group was once again on top: the inferior ones are always the Others.

We visited the place where the meal had been held. The Atchei had preferred to conduct their ritual away from the camp. Baipugi fell to her knees and wept over the death of her child. Then she pointed to where the fire had been: "Those are the ashes, the ashes of the bones that were burned." The skull and the little skeleton had been broken and thrown into the fire. But not everything had burned up. The woman gently sifted through the dead ashes with the tips of her fingers and pointed to a fragment: "This is my child's shoulder blade. And here is a piece of his head and the bone from his leg." The tears were pouring down her cheeks, little by little washing away the black mourning paint. And it was this weary, confused, and empty face that told me the end of the Atchei had come.

343

Sick man covered in vulture down.

CHAPTER NINE

The End

Although I have been back to Paraguay several times, I have never seen the Guayaki Indians again. I have not had the heart to. What could I possibly find there? When I arrived at Arroyo Moroti, they had numbered about a hundred. When I left a year later, there were no more than seventy-five of them. The others had died, eaten away by illness and tuberculosis, killed by lack of proper care, by lack of everything. And the survivors? They were like unclaimed objects; hopelessly forced to leave their pre-history, they had been thrown into a history that had nothing to do with them except to destroy them.

And the truth of the matter is that all this was a very slight thing: just one more page of the monotonous census — with more and more precise dates, places, and figures — recording the disappearance of the last Indian tribes. What has become of the valiant Atchei hunters? At last word, obtained in 1968, there were no more than thirty of them. But what difference do numbers make when they and all the other tribes are condemned? The whole enterprise that began in the fifteenth century is now coming to an end; an entire continent will soon be rid of its first inhabitants, and this part of the globe will truly be able to proclaim itself a "New World." "So many cities razed, so many

345

nations exterminated, so many peoples cut down by the sword, and the richest and most beautiful part of the world overthrown for the sake of pearls and pepper! Mechanical victories." So Montaigne hailed the conquest of America by Western civilization.

And didn't the Atchei see that the loss of their freedom meant that they were not being allowed to survive? Of course. But they were resigned, they passively accepted their fate. On rare occasions, a man would let his anger burst forth, and he would shout that he wanted to kill the whites, but it never went farther than that. Where would revolt have led them? They knew that there were many *Beeru* and that the ones they killed would have been immediately replaced by others. They had no choice, there was nothing to be done. Because of this, they realized that there was death in their souls. Jyvukugi, who saw things more clearly than most of his companions, knew how to express what they were feeling. One day I asked him to sing the hunting *prera* so that I could record them. But he preferred to choose another theme. Each couplet, chanted in a tone of sadness and profound disgust, died in a moan that was then prolonged by the delicate melancholy of the flute. That day he sang of the end of the Atchei and his despair at seeing that everything was over.

"When the Atchei were the real Atchei, when the Atchei were the true Atchei, they used to kill animals with arrows, then the fat of the coati was good. And now, the Atchei are no longer the Atchei. Oooh!

"When the Atchei were the real Atchei, they would kill many coatis in the forest with arrows, and they all ate the skin and the thick fat. The Atchei are no longer the Atchei. Oooh!

"The Atchei, the Atchei in the forest would kill all the animals with arrows; to kill the smelly wild pigs they would gather all their arrows, there was much meat to eat. But the Atchei no longer kill animals with arrows in the forest. Oooh!

346

"The Atchei in the forest gathered their arrows to kill the wild pigs. They feasted on the meat that had very dry blood. Now the Atchei roll in ashes. They no longer kill animals with arrows in the forest. Oooh! And now when the animals cry in the forest, the Atchei no longer go after them with arrows. Oooh!

"The Atchei used to kill the *jaku* and would eat the good fat. Now they have become very thin, they stink beside their fires, all black with ashes, they stink very much. The Atchei no longer kill animals in the forest, they no longer shoot their arrows.

"The Atchei in the forest would gather their arrows to kill the great wild pigs. And when they had eaten the delicious meat, the Atchei were all very happy. They no longer attack animals in the forest. Oooh! When they used to hear the din of the great wild boars on the hunt, the noise of clashing jaws, then the Atchei would kill animals, and from their catch they would eat the good meat of the legs, they would suck it like children, they were all happy. The Atchei no longer kill animals! Oooh!"

Jyvukugi sang for a long time, mentioning nearly all the animals the Atchei hunted. He also mentioned the bird cries that announced the moment to go visit the *cheygi* for the festival of honey; and each time he mentioned something, it was to say that it was finished, that all these things had disappeared. No doubt he was exaggerating by saying that the Atchei had given up the life of the forest to roll in the ashes of their fires, for they still continued to hunt. But it was no longer the same. Jyvukugi's perceptions were accurate; he read the tribe's fate clearly, and he knew that it was already surrounded by the stench of death.

For myself, I most of all want to remember the Atchei's piety, the gravity of their presence in the world of things and the world of beings. To underscore their exemplary faithfulness to a very ancient knowledge that our own savage violence has squandered in a single instant. To keep alive, for example, the memory of the majestic greeting the Strangers gave to the white woman who was then unknown to them upon their return from the forest. When the men and women saw her, they immediately fell to their knees, hid their faces in their hands, and intoned a powerful *chenga ruvara* — not of mourning or sadness, but of pleasure and friendship, to show that she was welcome. Because they could not pronounce the sound of the letter *l*, which does not exist in the Atchei language, they changed her name slightly and she became known as Erenagi.

Is it absurd to shoot arrows over the new moon when it slides among the trees? Not for the Atchei: they knew that the moon was alive and that its appearance in the sky would make the *kuja* bleed menstrual blood, which was a possible source of bad luck for the hunters. They took revenge, for the world is not inert, and you must defend yourself. In this way, for many centuries the Atchei tenaciously maintained their furtive and timid life as nomads in the secret heart of the forest. But this shelter was violated, and it was like a sacrilege.

It was night. *Yva javu*, the storm was talking. There was thunder everywhere, the rain was whipping the palm huts, the wind twisted the high branches of the old giants of the forest. When *Chono* left a brief respite of silence, you could hear the dry noise of wood cracking in the gale. The violent whiteness of the lightning tore the silent camp out of darkness, and the flashes were so brilliant that you could no longer see the light of the fires bending in the wind. These were the *pichua* of an *Iroiangi* woman who had died the night before and whom the Atchei had just buried. Her son-in-law, Kajawachugi, sat pensively by his fire, idly stirring the flames. They were truly big *pichua*; *Ove* had joined *Chono*, the lord from above. It was going on too long, and Kajawachugi decided to calm his mother-in-law. After each clap of thunder, he cried out in a sharp voice, his face turned to the sky: "*Nde pichu-are, baky emeeee!* You who are making all these *pichua*, please, no more raaaiiin!" He went on for two hours, during which time the old woman was not at all appeased. At long last, she consented to hear the man's supplication. The wind fell, the rain stopped, and *Chono* went off toward the north. The Atchei did not wake up; Kajawachugi had protected their sleep. Beyond the lively crackling of the fire, you could hear nothing but the water splattering down on the leaves. Long after the stars came out in the clear sky, the rain continued to drip slowly from the high branches.

Designed by Bruce Mau with Barr Gilmore

Typeset by Archetype

Printed and casebound by Maple-Vail on Sebago acid-free paper